Given

in loving memory

of

Raymond F. Heinold

December 10th, 1985

to the

Apostolic Christian Church

of

Valparaiso, Indiana

Zion's Harp

A Collection of

Hymns and Songs

For the
Apostolic Christian Church
of America

Translated from the German.

1958

Illinois Valley Printing, Inc.
Peoria, Illinois

1. PRAISE YE THE LORD

2, 3, 4.

1. O hal - le - lu - jah, sing God's praise! Your
2. Praise Him, the heav - en's might - y host; Earth,
3. O Zi - on's chil - dren, lift your voice In
4. Hal - le - lu - jah! Thy Spir - it, Lord, Re -

harps and voic - es to Him raise, His ho - ly name ex -
air, and sea His love shall boast, All who this earth in -
glo - ry and in grace re - joice, Praise Him in con - gre -
veals it - self in Thy good Word; The morn - ing star has

alt - - ing! Draw near un - to His ho - li - ness
hab - - it! Sun, moon, and stars, yea, ev - 'ry soul
ga - - tion! Let your thanks-giv-ing songs a - bound;
ris - - en, In bright - est splen - dor now it shines;

His might and pow - er to con - fess, Sing
The glo - ry of the Lord ex - tol, Whose
Pro - claim His Word with trump - et sound In
And Sa - tan's base and dark de - signs Shall

praises with-out halt - - ing! Love Him, praise
throne is high in heav - - en! He loves; He
high - est ex - ul - ta - - tion! His Word goes
soon be cast in pris - - on. God's Light shines

Him all ye na - tions, Con - gre - ga - tions, hon - or
gives all cre - a - tion An - i - ma - tion. Light and
forth in its glo - ry; Gos - pel's sto - ry, truth will
bright in our spir- it; We in - her - it grace and

bring - - ing, Joy - ful - ly the new song sing - ing.
glad - - ness Come from Him, the Sun of great - ness.
flour - - ish; And the lies of Sa - tan per - ish.
glo - - ry In His sac-red sanc - tu - ar - y.

5. And now the Spirit of the Lord
   Strikes in our hearts the sweetest chord,
   Makes music all-enchanting;
   We're happy as we live and love;
   The Spirit, given from above,
   To us His grace is granting.
   Wondrous, glorious,
   Sweet and cheering to our hearing
   Is the singing.
   Brethren, rise; your praise be bringing!

3.

2. A CHRISTIAN'S JOY AND HOPE

1, 3, 4.

1. O hal-le-lu-jah to our King! Ye Zi-on's children,
   O mag-ni-fy His wondrous might! The Lamb, which for our
2. His glo-rious king-dom shall en-dure. What e-quals it? What
   The mes-son-gers of His great fame In re-gions far and

come and bring Praise, wor-ship and sub-mis-sion!
sins has died, De-serves our ex-al-ta-tion
is so sure On earth, or yet in heav-en?
near pro-claim: "Sal-va-tion shall be giv-en!"

Thank Him! Praise Him! Bring al-le-giance And o-be-dience
Hear them call-ing, "Cease from sin-ning; Child-hood win-ning,

ev-'ry ho-ur For His mar-v'lous strength and pow-er.
Seek His fa-vor; Walk the path-way of the Sav-iour!"

3. O Lamb of God, to Thee we sing,
   Our gratitude and honor bring
   To Thee, our Lord forever.
   To all the people be it known
   That unto Jesus Christ alone
   Our heart and soul is given.
   Grant we pray Thee, understanding,
   Knowledge giving, of salvation
   And Thy graceful dispensation.

4. What joy we shall in heaven see
   When we united are with Thee,
   Before Thy throne adore Thee,
   When perfect Thy great work shall be,
   When after night Thy light we see,
   And gathered are before Thee.
   Envy shall be far removèd,
   Well Belovèd, all who own Thee
   Will as Bridegroom then acclaim Thee!

3. THE GOSPEL OF TRUTH
1, 2, 4.

1. The heav-ens with God's praise re-sound; It reach-es earth's re-mot-est bound, Wher-e'er our gaze is wend-ed.

Blest is the coun-try, blest the clime, To which the Word of Life sub-lime Of light and truth is send-ed. Truth-ful, joy-ful, heart re-new-ing, Sin sub-du-ing, Com-fort spend-ing, To the soul its glo-ry lend-ing.

2. Though all this world should pass a-way, The truth-ful Word of God will stay. It gives us bread from heav-en,

Il-lum-in-ates our earth-ly course, Of strength and cour-age is the source. The hum-ble now are giv-en Know-ledge, wis-dom; Earth re-lent-eth; Faith as-cend-eth pure, im-mor-tal, Out of death to heav-en's por-tal.

3. All honor to our Saviour's name!
His everlasting gospel's fame
Throughout the earth resoundeth.
On angel's wings it swiftly flies,
With voice and accent sweetly cries,
"Redemption now aboundeth."
Amen! Amen! Invitations
To all nations God has given.
Through Him earth be turned to heaven.

5.

4. OPEN WIDE THE GATES
1. 2, 3.

1. Let ev-'ry gate be o-pened wide, The King of glo-ry to in-vite With grace and truth a-bound-ing! He that from sin has turned his face A-woke from death-ly

2. A-round Him sings the might-y throng Which suf-fered in their fet-ters long, In free-dom now re-joic-ing. Once they were bound, but now are free; Once they were blind, but

3. All who to Christ's es-tate be-long Come now with glad and joy-ful song, His cov-e-nant es-tab-lish! Let us His hand-i-work be-hold, His king-dom help to

4. O Thou who did our sor-row bear, When shall there be e-nough-of prayer And praise in this world sound-ing? When shall the na-tions, Thee, Lord, know, And to Thy ho-ly

5. Lord, here do we a-wait Thine hour, The time so full of love and pow'r When all shall reach fru-i-tion; The des-ert blooms as par-a-dise. In bit-ter springs sweet

sleep by grace In light is now a - bid - ing.
now they see; Once they were dead, now liv - ing.
build and mould; His Word will stand for - ev - er.
tem - ple go, With grace and love a - bound - ing?
wa - ters rise When Thy Word fills its mis - sion.

Hear Him, See Him, Fight - ing glo - rious
Gra - cious, pre - cious, to the faint - ing
Go ye! Strive ye, to in - spi - re
To Thee hum - bly All may en - ter;
Lord, Thou say'st now: "Storm, be go - ing!

And vic - to - rious; Night is lift - ed,
He is grant - ing Free sal - va - tion
And to hi - re Heirs of heav - en!
In Thee cen - ter Hope for - ev - er;
Light, be glow - ing! Flee, dark sad - ness!

All with light and glad - ness gift - ed.
With - out bound or lim - i - ta - tion.
Heart and soul to Christ be giv - en.
May we leave Thy serv - ice nev - er!
Zi - on, grow thou strong in glad - ness!"

7.

5. THE PRAISE OF GOD

6.

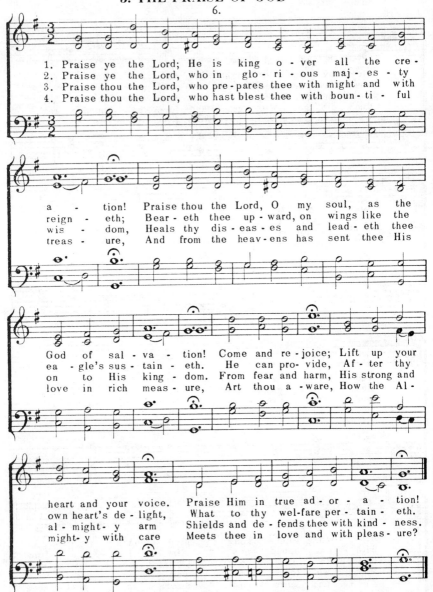

1. Praise ye the Lord; He is king o - ver all the cre -
2. Praise ye the Lord, who in glo - ri - ous maj - es - ty
3. Praise thou the Lord, who pre - pares thee with might and with
4. Praise thou the Lord, who hast blest thee with boun - ti - ful

a - tion! Praise thou the Lord, O my soul, as the
reign - eth; Bear - eth thee up - ward, on wings like the
wis - dom, Heals thy dis - eas - es and lead - eth thee
treas - ure, And from the heav - ens has sent thee His

God of sal - va - tion! Come and re - joice; Lift up your
ea - gle's sus - tain - eth. He can pro - vide, Af - ter thy
on to His king - dom. From fear and harm, His strong and
love in rich meas - ure, Art thou a - ware, How the Al -

heart and your voice. Praise Him in true ad - or - a - tion!
own heart's de - light, What to thy wel - fare per - tain - eth.
al - might - y arm Shields and de - fends thee with kind - ness.
might - y with care Meets thee in love and with pleas - ure?

5. Praise to the Lord; Oh, let all that is in me adore Him!
   All that have breath sing with Abraham's children before Him!
   He is our light, Fountain of glory and might,
   Peace to my spirit restoring.

8.

6. APPEAL TO THE SAVIOUR

5.

1. Christ, Thou my life and my hope, Thou my faith and sal-va-tion. Wor-thy to take from me hom-age, and true con-se-cra-tion. Lead Thou my mind, Sav-iour so true and so kind, Un-to de-vout ad-o-ra-tion.

2. Joy of my heart, my be-lov'd, I ex-alt Thee for-ev-er, Whol-ly I sac-ri-fice bod-y and soul to Thee ev-er. Great is my gain, If I with Thee shall re-main. May naught my soul from Thee sev-er!

3. One thing, O Lord, a-bove all will I cov-et and cher-ish, Rest for my soul and may all oth-er vain ob-jects per-ish. My on-ly joy! All oth-er pleas-ures des-troy, In me Christ on-ly shall flour-ish.

4. Rul-er of Life! O now rule in my heart and en-deav-or, That all my life may be ho-ly and God-pleasing ev-er; Thy Spir-it give, that to Thy glo-ry I live Here and in heav-en for-ev-er!

7. CHRISTMAS CAROL
199.

1. Our song of praise to God as - cend, And there with
2. From heav-en, in the dark of night, He came and
3. And in the Fa-ther's im - age pure He came earth's
4. He, who in glo - ry there doth reign, Did dwell on

an - gels' voic - es blend. The day of
brought e - ter - nal light. Be - hold now
tri - als to en - dure. He leads us
earth as hum - ble man; That through His

glad - ness now is here; Sing hal - le -
how this light di - vine Through-out this
with a gen - tle hand To that long
no - ble sac - ri - fice, We find the

lu - jah with good cheer. Hal - le - lu - jah!
pil - grim's dale doth shine. Hal - le - lu - jah!
cher - ished, hap - py land. Hal - le - lu - jah!
path to par - a - dise. Hal - le - lu - jah!

5. And when our days here are complete,
As brethren, we our Lord shall meet,
And be transformed before His sight
To glory and celestial light. Hallelujah!

10.

8. THE RESURRECTION FROM BAPTISM

7.

1. A - rise, my song to Christ the King, From whom the
2. Earth trem-bled with His won-drous might; From heav-en
3. And clothed in glo - ry, bright and fair, Which He e–
4. The might - y foe still seeks in vain Us in His

fount of life did spring When from the grave He did a - rise
came an an-gel bright. The stone was moved from its re - pose
ter - nal-ly did wear, He leads be-neath His Shepherd's rod
pow - er to re - tain. The blood of Je -sus makes us free,

To sev - er death's de-ceiv-ing ties! Hal - le - lu - jah!
When Je -sus Christ from death a - rose. Hal - le - lu - jah!
Freed pris'ners to the House of God. Hal - le - lu - jah!
And jus - ti - fied by faith are we. Hal - le - lu - jah!

5. The victory He has achieved
For all who have in Christ believed.
Flesh, Satan, death have lost their sting.
Oh, come and choose this heav'nly King! Hallelujah!

6. We know that Satan's yoke is shame,
And strive to work in Jesus' name;
Reborn by faith, we go our way,
And sin we never shall obey. Hallelujah!

7. As Jesus died for all our sin,
So all His own new life begin;
Through baptism we renewed shall be,
And clothed in immortality. Hallelujah!

8. Thus by this Spirit-birth may we,
Lord Jesus, have a part in Thee
And show ourselves obedient, Lord,
In love and faith unto Thy Word. Hallelujah!

9. GLORY TO GOD IN THE HIGHEST

1. Glo - ry to God in the High - est! In re - mote - ness
2. Peace and good will to all na - tions! Ye, the heirs of
3. Joy - ous - ly sound ye His prais - es! Men, whom to His

and near by us Rul - eth He with might and grace. Let us
His sal - va - tion, Far and near, O sons of men, Praise the
choice He rais - es, Tri - umph To a high es - tate! We are

bring our thanks and praise! Let us bring our thanks and
Lord with glad re - frain! Praise the Lord with glad re -
bought by love so great! We are bought by love so

praise! Hal - le - lu - jah! Hal - le - lu - jah!
frain! Hal - le - lu - jah! Hal - le - lu - jah!
great! Hal - le - lu - jah! Hal - le - lu - jah!

10. BEFORE BAPTISM

11.

1. Oh, my God, my heart de-sir-eth great-ly To in-
her-it Thy sweet rest.

In Thy cov-e-nant wilt Thou re-ceive me, Num-ber
me a-mong the blest. As Thy twelve dis-ci-ples in their

2. To pro-claim to those like me in man-ner, Lord, Thy
gos-pel's mess-age true.

And to warn the un-re-pent-ing sin-ner Of the
wrath that God will shew. That by un-der-go-ing this im-

tri-al, So I pledge my-self in self-de-ni-al To en-
dure re-proach, dis-may, And Thy good Word to o-bey.

mer-sion, Be-ing dead to sin through my con-ver-sion, I enjoy the Sav-iour's grace, Heav-en-ward di-rect my face.

3. A new being by regeneration,
   I do pledge myself to bear
   With my Master cross and tribulation,
   Likewise with His body share.
   But, my Lord, to suffer and to labor
   Give me strength, and grace, and godly favor
   That I follow Thee alone,
   Till I stand before Thy throne.

13.

11. THE UNION IN JESUS' DEATH

10.

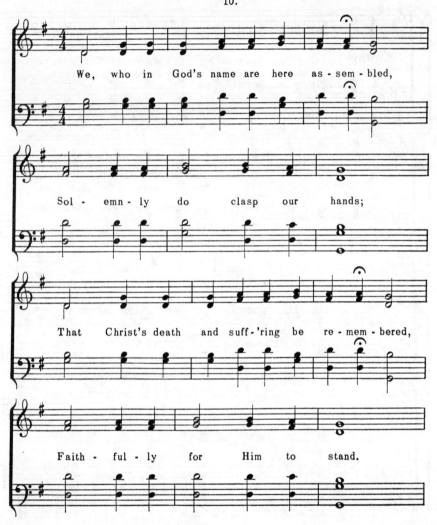

We, who in God's name are here as-sem-bled,

Sol - emn - ly do clasp our hands;

That Christ's death and suff-'ring be re-mem-bered,

Faith - ful - ly for Him to stand.

Thus in un - i - son our hearts have spok - en.

Lord, to show Thy fav - or give the tok - en;

Speak Thy bless - ing. ev - er true; "A - -

rit.

men," Peace be un - to you.

12. LORD JESUS, THOU ART KING
13, 42, 45, 79.

1. Lord Je - sus, Thou art King; At God's right hand Thou reign - est. Thy praise the an - gels sing; Thy serv - ants Thou sus - tain - est. The world's re - lease didst Thou Up - on the
2. Thy gos - pel free and pure Send forth to ev - 'ry na - tion. Let all per - ceive Thy light, And wel - come Thy sal - va - tion. Raise up Thy peo - ple true; Let ev - 'ry
3. Let ev - 'ry heart and knee In rev - 'rence bow be - fore Thee, And in the ver - y dust In hum - ble - ness a - dore Thee. Let ev - 'ry tongue con - fess That God His
4. Come, joy - ful day, oh come! The prom - ised word ful - fill - ing. The long - ings of our heart, The soul's de - si - res still - ing. The King - dom and the might, All glo - ry

16.

cross	a -	chieve.	Look	down	in	pit -	y
tongue	and	clime	Sound	forth	Thy	glo -	rious
Son	did	raise	To	be	a	Sav -	iour,
and	all	pow'r	Be	giv -	en	now	of

now,	Its	wretch - ed - ness	re -	lieve.
praise,	Ex -	alt Thy	name	sub -	lime.
King,	Un -	to His	Fa -	ther's	praise.
God	To	Christ the	Lord	this	hour.

5. His glorious rule shall be
   Unending and unbroken.
   The sceptre of His might,
   Of peace shall be the token.
   Ye nations, shout for joy;
   His praise let all proclaim.
   The whole round world tell forth
   The honor due His name.

6. The angel host on high
   Doth sing His praise in cadence,
   With cherub's mighty power,
   With seraph's purest radiance.
   The choir with golden harps
   Beside the crystal sea
   Doth raise the glad new song:
   "The Lamb's high praise sing we."

7. Four beings 'round the throne,
   The elders there before them,
   Exalt God and the Lamb,
   His glory spreading o'er them,
   Before Him cast their crowns,
   Fall down and Him adore,
   Who saith: "I was, I am,
   And shall be evermore."

8. Glory to God on high,
   To Father, Son and Spirit,
   Whose faithful children all
   The Kingdom shall inherit.
   The host of Thine elect,
   The heavens broad and free,
   Praise Thee, great Trinity,
   Through all eternity.

13. PRAISE AND THANKS FOR GOD'S BLESSINGS
12, 42, 45, 79.

1. Lord God, we hon - or Thee And praise Thy
2. So now a - gain Thou hast To us a
3. Thy liv - ing Word is sent Our souls to
4. We sing our heart - felt thanks, Thy truth and

mild com - pas - sion, That Thou so grace - ful -
bless - ing giv - en. Our hand - i - work is
feed and nour - ish. Thou wilt that in our
love a - dor - ing. For guid - ance and for

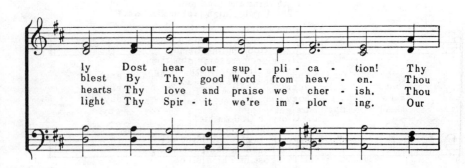

ly Dost hear our sup - pli - ca - tion! Thy
blest By Thy good Word from heav - en. Thou
hearts Thy love and praise we cher - ish. Thou
light Thy Spir - it we're im - plor - ing. Our

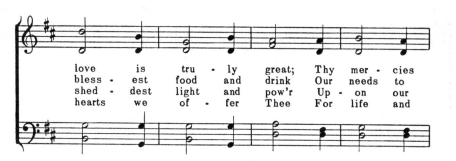

love	is	tru - ly	great;	Thy	mer - cies
bless - est	food	and	drink	Our	needs to
shed - dest	light	and	pow'r	Up - on	our
hearts	we	of - fer	Thee	For	life and

are	un - told;	Thou	giv - est	food	and
sat - is - fy.	There - fore,	we	give	Thee
pil - grim	way,	And	lead'st	us	by	Thy
ev - 'ry	day,	That	with	Thy	grace	we

drink	for	Spir - it,	flesh	and	soul.
thanks;	Our	song	shall	rise	on	high.
hand	To	heav - en	day	by	day.
tread	The	straight	and	nar - row	way.

14. THE SHEPHERD AND HIS FLOCK

1. Lord Je-sus, hon-or, thanks and praise Be to Thy good-ness
2. In lov-ing care stay by our side, For none ex-cept Thee
3. The rag-ing wolves, Lord, from us keep; A li-on's cour-age

all our days. Thy peo-ple in Thy grace re-joice, In
can pro-vide. Con-vert all who know not Thy name, All
give Thy sheep. All those who for-eign ways have learned Be

com-fort they lift up their voice: "Thou shalt re-main in
ev-il work-ers put to shame! And let the tempt-ed
speed-i-ly to Thee re-turned. So draw and bind us

all e-ter-ni-ty!" Thus we re-pose in blest se-cur-i-ty.
feel Thy won-drous might, That in the darkness they may see the light.
close-ly un-to Thee, Till in one flock we all u-nit-ed be.

15. THE FAITHFUL SHEPHERD
33, 36, 51.

1 Don't you see on heav'nly pas - tures Our good, pa - tient,
2. See, a lamb a - way has wan - dered And the Shep - herd
3. Fol - low this good Shep-herd sole - ly, Earth- ly pil - grims
4. Would you on this earth- ly jour - ney Feel such care and

Shep - herd pass, And by blood - y foot - marks trac- ing
runs in haste, Leaves the rest to seek the stray-ing
one and all! Let Him then di - rect you whol- ly,
kind re - gard? Come to Christ, the lov - ing Shep-herd;

Sheep and lambs in sore dis - tress? Do you know His
Till He finds and holds it fast. In His arms He
Fol - low glad - ly at His call! Let Him to the
Con - se - crate to Him your heart! Lead me to Thy

flock so pre - cious? Do you know His Shep-herd's staff, Which new
bears it gent- ly, Soothes its sor - row and its pain, Caus-es
flock then take you. Trust ye in His pow'r to save! Glad His
pleas- ant past-ures, To Thy liv - ing fount, O Lord; And through

life and light so gra- cious Un-to earth and heav - en gave?
all its fears to van-ish, Brings it to the fold a - gain.
ways for-e'er will make you Blessed who his heart Him gave!
joy and sor-row bring me To that great and blest re - ward!

16. A LAMB OF JESUS
184.

1. What glo-rious state, to be a lamb of Je - sus, To
   In all the earth there is no high - er stand-ing Than
2. In pas-tures green the sheep will find its pleas-ure; To
   No hu - man eye the grace can ev - er meas-ure Which

feel the faith - ful Shep - herd's lov - ing grace.
this -- to fol - low in the Sav - iour's ways.
quench its thirst the pur - est foun-tains flow.
He in rich - est full - ness does be - stow.

What all the world could nev - er give, A
A peace - ful life the sheep will spend In

lamb of Je - sus from its Shep - herd will re - ceive.
ev - er - last -ing pleas - ures that will nev - er end.

3. The lamb abides in this good Shepherd's keeping;
   Though all the depths of hell in anger roar,
   No raving wolf shall pluck it from His bosom;
   It trusts in Jesus' might forevermore.
   It rests in blest security,
   And in the vale of death, the Lord its shield will be.

4. All who would live and spend their days in comfort
   Should come and draw unto this Shepherd nigh;
   With heav'nly bread He'll satisfy their hunger,
   Which worldly husks can never satisfy.
   No lack of blessings there shall be,
   Since to God's treasures He, the Shepherd, has the key.

5. Yet this is but the foretaste of the fullness
   Of the joys to follow in eternity.
   The Lamb's elect shall feed on heav'nly pastures,
   With waters from life's stream supplied shall be.
   Then shall be fully manifest,
   How happy is a lamb of Jesus and how blest.

17. JOY IN THE SAVIOUR

1. I'm a lamb of Je - sus' flock;
2. Safe be - neath His staff, I go
3. Shall I not then hap - py be?

Un - told bless - ings
On my jour - ney,
Je - sus loves me

are my lot; For my Shep - herd gives pro - tec - tion;
to and fro, In - to pas - tures sweet and ver - dant,
ten - der - ly. When my earth - ly days are end - ing,

Show - ers on me His af - fec - tion; And with peace and
Find - ing joys and food a - bun - dant; And my thirst to
With the an - gel host as - cend - ing, In my Sav - iour's

gen - tle love, Calls to me from heav'n a - bove.
quench, He knows Where the sweetest foun - tain flows.
arms I'll be Blest in all e - ter - ni - ty!

18. JESUS, THE TRUEST FRIEND

47, 49, 72.

1. Who is He that cares and watch - es
2. Ere Thy light shone in with bright - ness,
3. Mor - tals love their friends sin - cere - ly;
4. We can feel Thy grace and com - fort,

O'er our life and soul's es - tate?
Did'st Thou see us in our woe.
Hu - man love is thus con - fined.
Light and strength, the Spir - it's seal;

Who is He that thus has drawn us?
Thou did'st die to give sal - va - tion
In His death, He loved us dear - ly,
All the blight of sin and sor - row,

Christ a - lone, His love is great.
To the lost ones here be - low.
Friends and en - e - mies com - bined.
None but Thee our wounds can heal.

5. Heav'nly blessings for the pilgrim
   Here on earth are kept in store.
   After sorrows, we Thy children
   Shall rejoice forevermore.

6. Saviour! Since Thy blood is healing,
   There is rest for heart and mind.
   Let us now, Thy peace enjoying,
   Grace, sufficient, in Thee find.

7. Teach us all Thy true obedience;
   Teach us, Lord, to do Thy will.
   Lead us in Thy holy presence;
   Through this world do guide us still.

8. Though Thou lead us thru the darkness,
   Thou art evermore our light.
   When death comes in awful stillness,
   We behold Thy face so bright.

9. Thus we love Thee, and adore Thee,
   Thou art worthy of our love.
   When in death and pain and sorrows,
   Let us trust in Thee above.

10. Though the world our souls is calling
    From the Lord, who loves us best,
    May our love to Him be constant
    Till we meet there with the blest.

19. THE INCOMPARABLE

1. Who is Lord, like Thee, Sweet re-pose for
2. Bridegroom of the soul, Lamb of God, my
3. Life which tast-ed death, That from all dis-
4. With Thy gen-tle mind, With Thy meek-ness

me? For us sin-ners Thou wert tak-en,
All! I will praise Thy lov-ing kind-ness,
tress I, Thy child, might be de-liv-ered,
kind, Clothe me, heart and mind re-new-ing,

Life to bring to the for-sak-en.
Which from dark-ness, sin, and blind-ness,
And the chains of death be sev-ered,
Pride and an-ger still sub-du-ing.

Thou our light shalt be, Sweet re-pose for me.
Drew me, Lord, to Thee, Nailed up-on the tree.
Raised sin's heav-y load, Lead-ing me to God.
For naught can en-dure But Thy im-age pure.

5. Make my soul to feel
   All Thy Spirit's zeal.
   May I watch in pray'r and pleading,
   Joyfully Thy face beholding,
   Pure and unfeigned love
   May my spirit move.

6. Courage strong give me,
   Willing to give Thee
   Life and blood and ill possessions,
   Hating sin and all transgressions.
   Courage brave and true,
   Give each day anew.

7. Here through scorn and strife,
   There the crown of life;
   Here the hoping and believing,
   There the seeing and receiving;
   Here we bear disdain,
   There the crown we gain.

8. Jesus grant to me
   That I valiantly
   Overcome the world's temptations.
   For Thy victory and patience
   Show how valiantly
   Thou hast fought for me.

9. Thou, O Light sublime,
   Chosen ere all time
   To bestow on us God's favor,
   Wast made flesh to be our Saviour,
   In the full of time,
   O Thou Light Sublime.

10. Thou art Victor, Lord,
    Over Satan's horde;
    All the power of the devil
    Is destroyed, and all the evil,
    Through that ransom high
    For which Thou didst die!

11. Majesty most high,
    King and Prophet, Thy
    Scepter here we kiss, believing,
    At Thy feet the Truth receiving;
    As in Bethany,
    Mary learned from Thee.

12. Draw us close to Thee,
    Lord, eternally;
    Serving Thee in love unceasing,
    Praising Thee with joy increasing;
    For eternally,
    We abide in Thee.

13. Wake us, Lord, we pray,
    That to Thee our way
    We pursue with firm endeavor,
    Seeing naught and halting never
    In this earthly day --
    Further Thou our way!

20. LABOR ON
21, 22.

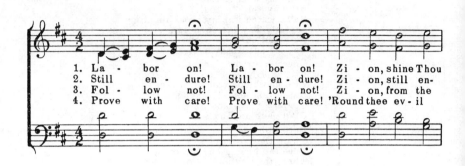

1. La - bor on! La - bor on! Zi - on, shine Thou
2. Still en - dure! Still en - dure! Zi - on, still en -
3. Fol - low not! Fol - low not! Zi - on, from the
4. Prove with care! Prove with care! 'Round thee ev - il

forth in light! As a ci - ty on a moun-tain, In thy first love
dure all pain, All contempt, re-proach, af-flic-tion. Faithful un - to
world ab-stain, Not in world-ly greatness ris-ing. Seek not aft-er-
spir-its stand, Which on ev-'ry side are calling, But o-bey not

still a-bide, Seek-ing for the liv-ing foun-tain. Zi-on, pass-ing
death re-main; Make the crown of life thy por-tion. Zi-on, if thou
earth-ly gain, And the Dragon's throne despis-ing. Zi-on, tho' much
their command. Let God's hand keep thee from fall-ing. Whether straight or

thru the nar - row gate, Do not wait; Do not wait.
feel the ser-pent's lure, Still en - dure, Still en - dure.
joy could be thy lot, Fol - low not! Fol - low not!
crook-ed, shun the snare, Prove with care; Prove with care.

5. Press thou on! Press thou on!
   Zion, press thou on to God!
   With His strength thy spirit glowing,
   Be not like a withered rod,
   But a vine in vigor growing.
   Zion, let hypocrisy be gone;
   Press thou on! Press thou on!

6. O break forth! O break forth!
   Zion, O break forth in might!
   Brother-love in thee be burning,
   Show thyself as His by right,
   Who as Bridegroom is returning,
   Zion, through thine open door on earth;
   O break forth! O break forth!

7. Hold thou fast! Hold thou fast!
   Persevere now as of old;
   Lukewarm let not Jesus find thee;
   On, behold the crown of gold;
   On, forget what is behind thee.
   Zion, in thy struggle to the last,
   Hold thou fast! Hold thou fast!

21. TO THOSE IN CONFLICT

20, 22.

1. Up and strive; Up and strive; Breth-ren, for the
2. Put it on; Put it on! Put God's might-y
3. There-fore strive; Therefore strive 'Gainst the cun-ning
4. For 'tis true; For 'tis true That the conflict

true faith strive. For - ti - fy your-selves in Je - sus; Bat - tle
arm - or on, Whereby you may bring un-do-ing To the
and the might, Of the hordes of ev - il spirits Who in
on life's path Is not on - ly with the hu-man; But a -

for the crown of life. Strive to win the Mas-ter's praises; Gird
ad - ver - sar - y's plan, Who de-signs your ov - er - throwing, Seek-
dark-ness and in night Wage a-gainst the Christ their conflict. For
gainst the dev-il's wrath Is our con-flict-- He our foeman; There-

your-selves with might and pow'r each day, On your way, On your way.
ing you up-on your pil-grim way To de-lay, To de-lay.
the prince of dark-ness fears the light And the right, And the right.
fore, with your Head u - nit - ed stay, Watch and pray, Watch and pray.

30.

5. Steadfast be, Steadfast be,
   Brethren, stand ye fast and fight;
   Gird your loins with courage duly,
   Gird your minds with truth and right;
   Ye shall be victorious truly.
   Righteousness shall be your breastplate strong.
   Fight the wrong! Fight the wrong!

6. Battle on, Battle on,
   Let your faith be your best shield,
   By the Lord Himself erected;
   In its shelter hold the field,
   'Gainst the enemy protected;
   For he would with fiery, deadly darts
   Pierce your hearts, pierce your hearts.

7. Be supplied, Be supplied
   With the helmet naught can pierce;
   Hold the hope of your salvation,
   Though the foe wage battle fierce
   With his powers of temptation;
   Turn the light your hope doth now accord
   To the Lord, To the Lord.

8. Firmly seize, Firmly seize,
   Brethren, take the Spirit's sword,
   Which is God's own Word of power.
   If you keep it close at hand,
   Satan will before you cower,
   For he, when God's mighty sword he sees,
   Turns and flees, Turns and flees.

9. O beware, O beware,
   Brethren, walk as in the light,
   And abide in love forever;
   Turn not to the left or right
   From the way of your dear Saviour.
   Pray ye to the Lord in every need,
   He will heed, He will heed.

10. Carry on, Carry on,
    Carry on the work of God,
    And the souls of men be winning;
    With the Gospel's peace be shod.
    Waken those still dead in sinning;
    Bring them, through the gracious Gospel-Word,
    To the Lord, To the Lord.

22. THE INCARNATION OF CHRIST

20, 21.

1. Ho - ly One, Ho - ly One, Ho - ly God of Sa - ba-
2. Praise and thanks, Praise and thanks Bring we ev- er un - to
3. Day and night, Day and night Shall our song of praise re-
4. Son of man, Son of man, Let Thy gold-en lamp shine

oth! Earth and heav- en hom-age ren-der Thee of all cre-
Thee That for us Thy Son was giv- en, That we should Thy
sound In the church which is His bod- y, Which in Him Sal-
bright; Grant that Zi - on tru - ly know Thee; Scat-ter Thou the

a - tion, God. And of all who have sur - ren - dered, And are
peo-ple be. He e - ter-nal life in heav- en And re-
va -tion found. Death reigned in our sin - ful bod- y; Christ, to
shades of night. Help us bring the praise we owe Thee, And to-

sanc-ti - fied thru Je - sus' blood, Cleansing flood, cleansing flood.
demp-tion from our sin and grief, Did a - chieve, did a - chieve.
give us life be-came a man, Glo-rious plan, glo-rious plan.
geth-er bless be-fore the throne, Christ the Son, Christ the Son.

5. Holy Lord, Holy Lord, Holy and almighty Lord,
   Let the light of Christ shine o'er us,
   Brightly all our journey through;
   May His grace and truth most glorious,
   Still illume our path, till also we
   Dwell with Thee! Dwell with Thee!

23. BURIED WITH CHRIST
21, 22.

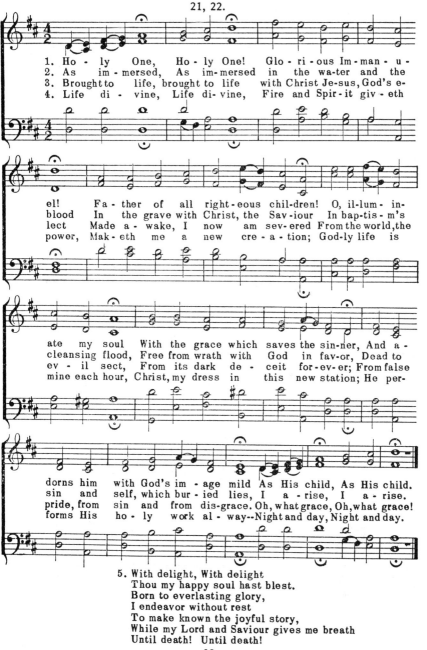

1. Ho - ly One, Ho - ly One! Glo - ri - ous Im - man - u -
2. As im - mersed, As im - mersed in the wa-ter and the
3. Brought to life, brought to life with Christ Je-sus, God's e -
4. Life di - vine, Life di - vine, Fire and Spir - it giv - eth

el! Fa - ther of all right - eous chil-dren! O, il-lum - in-
blood In the grave with Christ, the Sav-iour In bap-tis - m's
lect Made a - wake, I now am sev-ered From the world, the
power, Mak - eth me a new cre - a - tion; God-ly life is

ate my soul With the grace which saves the sin-ner, And a -
cleansing flood, Free from wrath with God in fav-or, Dead to
ev - il sect, From its dark de - ceit for-ev-er; From false
mine each hour, Christ, my dress in this new station; He per-

dorns him with God's im - age mild As His child, As His child.
sin and self, which bur - ied lies, I a - rise, I a - rise.
pride, from sin and from dis-grace. Oh, what grace, Oh, what grace!
forms His ho - ly work al - way--Night and day, Night and day.

5. With delight, With delight
Thou my happy soul hast blest.
Born to everlasting glory,
I endeavor without rest
To make known the joyful story,
While my Lord and Saviour gives me breath
Until death! Until death!

33.

24. COMMUNION HYMN
20, 21.

1. Come with - in, come with - in, Of Thy
2. Sanc - ti - fy, sanc - ti - fy! Sanc - ti
3. Prince of life, Prince of life! Show - ers
4. Be it so, be it so. Do you

church the Head to be! Speak to us the peace - ful
fy this liv - ing bread To our in - ward an - i -
from Thy bless - ed flood Bring, and quench our souls so
feel His bless - ed tread Draw - ing near to our as -

mess - age Of Thy love. We wait for
ma - tion, As Thy bod - y un - to
thirst - y. As Thy sac - ri - fi - cial
sem - bly, Heav 'nly gifts for us to

Thee,   Of our   cov - e - nant the   au - thor,
death   Thou didst   give   in   con - se - cra - tion.
blood   For us   flowed   in   great com - pas - sion,
spread,   Liv - ing   bread   and   drink to   ren - der?

Come,   to   hold   with   us   this   feast   of   love,
Let   our   spir - it,   free   from world - ly   mind,
Give   us   strength   in   all   e - ter - ni - ty
Streams   of   bless - ing   from   His   hand   par - take,

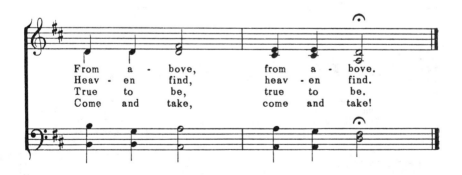

From   a -   bove,   from   a -   bove.
Heav - en   find,   heav - en   find.
True   to   be,   true   to   be.
Come   and   take,   come   and   take!

25. THE LORD'S SUPPER
41, 145, 220, 221.

1. We wor - ship Thee with tears of glad - ness,
2. To break Thy bread we now have gath - ered,
3. Thine is the pow'r and will to strength - en,
4. Yet clos - er un - to Thee u - nite me,

Lord Je - sus Christ, for Thy great love!
In cov - e - nant to drink Thy wine;
Thou lov - 'dst me un - to the death!
As Thou with God u - nit - ed art.

To re - con - cile us with the Fa - ther,
As breth - ren we u - nite to - geth - er,
In Thee I find life and sal - va - tion;
In truth Thine own and not pre - tend - ing,

To die, Thou cam - est from a - bove.
That un - to death we might be Thine.
Thou'lt com - fort me in my last breath.
A Chris - tian true, in mind and heart;

How great has been Thy sac - ri - fice!
This prom - ise we, with heart and will;
O pre - cious Je - sus, dear - est Lord,
This will I seek, this is my aim,

To Thee our thanks and praise shall rise.
Give grace our prom - ise to ful - fill.
All gifts to us Thou dost ac - cord.
My heart, Lord, as Thy dwell - ing claim!

5 And ye, the Church's members, truly
Are folded in my heart's embrace!
In Christ ye are my brethren duly;
We share salvation through His grace.
We drink one cup; we break one bread;
One Saviour suffered in our stead.

6. As here, in Jesus' name invited,
His people meet to share His love,
So shall the ransomed be united,
A mighty throng, in heaven above,
To praise Him there before the throne,
Our Lord and Saviour, Christ the Son.

7. Nor shall the scorn of those who hate me,
Nor joy nor earthly vanity,
From Thy dear love e'er separate me;
In death it shall my stronghold be;
Thou art and ever wilt be mine,
And I forever, Saviour, Thine!

37.

26. COMMUNION HYMN

Reverently

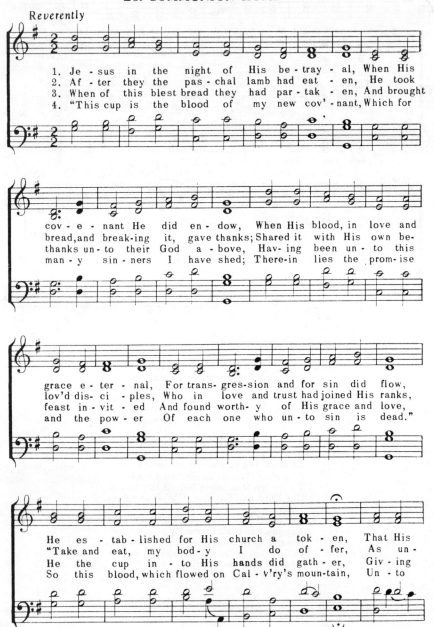

1. Je - sus in the night of His be - tray - al, When His
2. Af - ter they the pas - chal lamb had eat - en, He took
3. When of this blest bread they had par - tak - en, And brought
4. "This cup is the blood of my new cov' - nant, Which for

cov - e - nant He did en - dow, When His blood, in love and
bread, and break-ing it, gave thanks; Shared it with His own be-
thanks un - to their God a - bove, Hav - ing been un - to this
man - y sin - ners I have shed; There-in lies the prom- ise

grace e - ter - nal, For trans- gres-sion and for sin did flow,
lov'd dis - ci - ples, Who in love and trust had joined His ranks,
feast in - vit - ed And found worth- y of His grace and love,
and the pow- er Of each one who un - to sin is dead."

He es - tab - lished for His church a tok - en, That His
"Take and eat, my bod- y I do of - fer, As un-
He the cup in - to His hands did gath - er, Giv - ing
So this blood, which flowed on Cal - v'ry's moun-tain, Un - to

38.

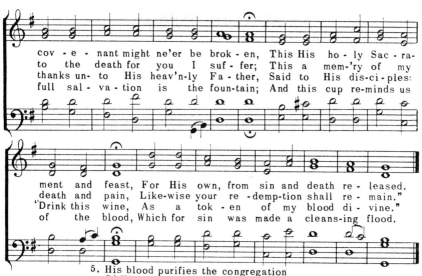

cov - e - nant might ne'er be brok - en, This His ho - ly Sac - ra-
to the death for you I suf - fer; This a mem-'ry of my
thanks un - to His heav'n-ly Fa - ther, Said to His dis-ci-ples:
full sal - va - tion is the foun-tain; And this cup re-minds us

ment and feast, For His own, from sin and death re - leased.
death and pain, Like-wise your re -demp-tion shall re - main."
"Drink this wine, As a tok - en of my blood di - vine."
of the blood, Which for sin was made a cleans-ing flood.

5. His blood purifies the congregation
   Of His children, whom He did atone,
   Whom He loved sincerely ere creation.
   He to them says: "Ye are Mine alone!"
   Constantly His Church He is adorning,
   And His faithfulness is new each morning.
   His good Spirit giveth He as seal,
   As His sacred promises reveal.

6. Come then to the feast of His New Covenant,
   Members of His Church, your faith renew;
   Thank the Founder of this precious Covenant
   Through the chalice He pours out for you.
   Here your hands in faithfulness uniting
   And the fire of brother-love new lighting,
   Let your common prayers rise to His throne.
   Thank and praise Him who hath made you one!

7. By their love His members are united
   In a union godly and devout;
   All who love their holy vows have plighted;
   All who do not love belong without.
   In their love this blessed meal is taken,
   In their love they shall abide unshaken;
   Many members are as one arrayed,
   As from many grains one bread is made.

8. Therefore, when ye to your Master's glory,
   Come to keep this holy feast of love,
   Ye must truly hear salvation's story,
   Joining those whose homeland is above!
   Then true love will heart to heart bind ever,
   And no discord will this union sever;
   One in Jesus Christ they all shall be,
   He the Head of His community!

9. There is life and there is peace and gladness,
   There contentment, grace, and mercy flow;
   There the light of Jesus scatters sadness,
   Shining with a soft and blessed glow.
   O, who would not joy in this salvation,
   Yearn to dwell within that habitation
   Where the Light of life shines full and free,
   Giving men new life and liberty!

39.

27. ON TO THE COMBAT
159.

1. Rise, O Christian gen-er-a-tion, Cling-ing to your
2. Fol-low then the Sav-iour's ban-ner; Trust in His al-
3. On His word then take the ven-ture, Clad with pray'r and
4. For His pow-er hath been test-ed By the saints who

Lord al-way! Up, a-rise in con-se-cra-tion,
might-y arm; Though your foe in dread-ful man-ner
watch-ful-ness. This a-lone will make you fear-less,
stead-fast stood; Know-ing that in ov-er-com-ing

Lest your soul be led a-stray! For your foe
O'er the bat-tle-field doth swarm, Je-sus' host
Strength and cour-age to pos-sess, War to wage,
They had con-quered by His blood. Shall not we

dar-eth you, Un-to com-bat dar-eth you!
con-quers most, If near Him it takes its post.
and en-gage Through Christ's blood the en-emy's rage.
stead-fast be, Fight for Je-sus val-iant-ly?

5. Those who love sin's baleful bondage
    Are to conflict disinclined;
    None who yield themselves her servants
    Can their soul's salvation find;
    Sinful night, Satan's might
    Has deprived them of their sight.

6. But the one whom wisdom teacheth
    Freedom is the Christians' part,
    He whose mind to God inclineth
    As the hope of his whole heart,
    Seeks to be from guile free,
    Christ's own servant faithfully.

7. O how wretched is existence
    Without Christ and liberty!
    Those who offer God resistance
    Shall have woe and misery.
    Comforts new, blessings true
    Come to those who sin subdue.

8. Through the Word and blood of Jesus
    Let us then our foes defeat;
    He'll deliver us from danger,
    He will be our safe retreat.
    We shall see victory;
    From the world He'll make us free.

9. May our life be ever hidden
    Here in God with Christ our Lord;
    Then shall we upon that morning
    Stand illumined by His Word;
    All the care we now share
    Will be changed to glory there.

10. On that day God's faithful servants
    Shall receive their faith's reward;
    In the tents of all the righteous
    Shall their vict'ry's song be heard.
    There God's band e'er shall stand
    In that bright and happy land.

28. JESUS, OUR HEAD

29, 93, 186, 217.

1. Je - sus, bo - som friend so gen - tle, Son of
2. Come, in - vig - or - ate each mem - ber, Thou, Thy
3. Let our heart and our whole be - ing Turn to
4. Let the eyes of ev - 'ry teach - er Look to

truth and right - eous - ness, Dwell - ing in Thy ho - ly
bod - y's ho - ly Chief! Cast - ing out all op - po -
Thee, e - ter - nal light! What Thy gra - cious kind - ness
Thee, O Christ, our Lord! Give each hear - er un - der -

church - es Who their faith in Thee con - fess.
si - tion, From temp - ta - tions grant re - lief!
of - fers May we choose both day and night.
stand - ing Of Thy pres - ence in Thy word.

En - ter in as we as - sem - ble; Pour up -
Come, un - fold to us in clear - ness Grace and
May Thy light and life be flow - ing, Bless - ings
May its sound each heart then en - ter; May it

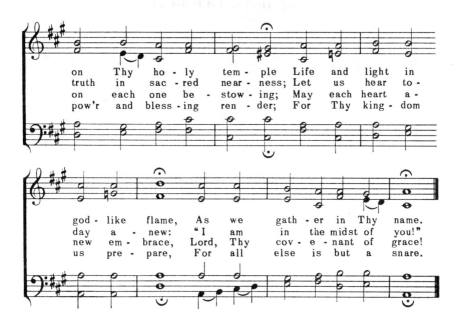

on Thy ho - ly tem - ple Life and light in
truth in sac - red near - ness; Let us hear to -
on each one be - stow - ing; May each heart a -
pow'r and bless - ing ren - der; For Thy king - dom

god - like flame, As we gath - er in Thy name.
day a - new: "I am in the midst of you!"
new em - brace, Lord, Thy cov - e - nant of grace!
us pre - pare, For all else is but a snare.

5. Make each soul Thy habitation;
   Come, O Lord, and dwell within!
   May each one make preparation
   In Thy ranks e'er to remain!
   Thy good gifts we all desire,
   And Thy majesty admire;
   Make Thy truth and holiness
   In Thy children manifest.

6. What has flowed from Thy clear fountain
   Heart and spirit shall assure!
   May what hungry souls have tasted
   Make us righteous, meek and pure!
   Come, O Jesus, do Thou bless us,
   Meet us in Thy love so gracious;
   That in love and truth with Thee
   Each one may united be!

43.

29. THE MEDIATOR

28, 93, 186, 217.

Moderato

1. Great and priest-ly Me - di - at - or, Sit - ting on Thy Fa - ther's right, Hosts of serv - ants now de - fend - ing In the realm of grace and might, Whom with- in His sanc - tu - ar - y, In the roy - al crown of glo - ry,

2. Thy great work of our re - demp - tion And a - tone -ment is a - chieved; All that was to be ac - complished Thou in wis - dom hadst con - ceived. For us, Lord,Thou didst ex - pi - re, Grace and fav - or to ac - qui - re;

3. This is now Thy oc - cu - pa - tion In that ho - ly sac - red place; Words and pow - ers of sal - va -tion By the gos - pel of Thy grace, Give to all those to be shar -ing Who are to Thy throne re - pair- ing;

4. And the names of all the god - ly Thou dost bear up- on Thy breast; All who come to Thee be - liev- ing In de - light shall be ca - ressed. All the faith-ful Thou dost cher - ish, That not one of them might per-ish;

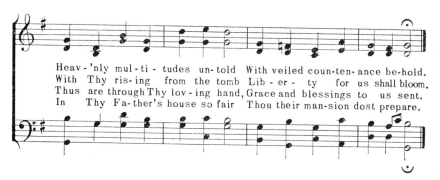

Heav-'nly mul-ti-tudes un-told With veiled coun-ten-ance be-hold.
With Thy ris-ing from the tomb Lib-er-ty for us shall bloom.
Thus are through Thy lov-ing hand, Grace and blessings to us sent.
In Thy Fa-ther's house so fair Thou their man-sion dost prepare.

5. Thou dost not forget the wretched,
   Who still serve the world of sin;
   Yea, Thy heart doth break in pity
   For the bondage they are in;
   That Thy Father may yet spare them,
   In His mercy still forebear them,
   That their hearts He yet might turn,
   Ah, for this Thou, Lord, dost yearn!

6. When Thou here in flesh didst sojourn
   And our sins upon Thee lay,
   Thou didst turn unto Thy Father;
   For the sinners Thou didst pray,
   Both with weeping and with sighing,
   For the sinners' pardon crying,
   Oh, in what humility
   Then arose Thy fervent plea!

7. Now Thy eloquent petitions
   Are supported by Thy might,
   As Thou in Thy heavenly glory
   Sittest at Thy Father's right;
   Now, though Satan may accuse us,
   Pardon Thou wilt not refuse us;
   For Thy blood for us was spilt,
   And this blood removed our guilt.

8. Precious Saviour, we commend Thee,
   That in this, Thy sacred place
   Thou hast shown such untold mercy;
   We bring honor, thanks and praise.
   Do Thou still make intercession
   When we offer our petition;
   Lead us by Thy faithful hand
   Till we reach our Fatherland!

30. THE SEVEN CHURCHES
28, 29, 32, 186.

Moderato

1. Hark! and earn-est-ly be heed-ing What the Spir-it thee doth
2. He, who sev-en stars is hold-ing In His right hand thus does
3. "Blest is he who ov-er-com-eth, And the first true love main-
4. Thus speaks Je-sus, the Be-gin-ning, And the Last, the A and

teach; How the Word, its truth re-veal-ing All the church-es
speak: "Clearly all things I'm be-hold-ing, And my serv-ants'
tains, Who in truth builds firm foun-da-tion, And false teach-ing
O, Who from death, as Prince is reign-ing, Did a-rise; He

doth be-seech. Hark! for God to Him is speak-ing Who for
deeds I seek, What they do, their works com-par-ing, And where
doth dis-dain. Him with fruit I'll ev-er nour-ish From the
speaketh so: "I know all your trib-u-la-tions; Pov-er-

know-ledge pure is seek-ing. He dis-cerns each hid-den
al-so they are err-ing; I judge all things here a-
tree which there doth flour-ish, Which a-bove in par-a-
ty, strength, works, temp-ta-tions. Thou art rich; in pa-tience

thing And to light our thoughts doth bring.
right, Bring-ing them in-to the light!
dise Is pre-pared by God all-wise."
bear All re-proach; do not de-spair.

46.

5. "Blest is he who overcometh,
Fleeing not when pain besets;
When in fear and tribulations,
Doth this comfort ne'er forget,
That I will the true and grateful
Give the crown of life, who faithful
Did remain in trials severe;
Second death he need not fear."

6. He from whom is now proceeding
The two-edged, sharp piercing sword
Speaks: "I know all things, perceiving
Your strong faith kept in accord.
Satan's throne is where thou dwellest;
Therefore see that thou repellest
All who vex my children sore,
And whose teachings I abhor.

7. "Blest is he who overcometh,
Whose brave heart naught can deceive,
Who in time of grace repenteth,
Worldly splendor ne'er receives.
Him with manna I'll be feeding,
And the faithful one providing
With a new white stone of fame,
Where is written his new name."

8. God's own Son to thee is speaking,
Whose bright eyes as fire do blaze;
"Deeds of heart and hands I'm seeking,
Blest ye battlers rich in grace!"
Thou, thy faith and love retaining,
Art in patience e'er enduring;
For thy love doth burn with zeal,
And thy deeds much fruit do yield.

9. "But thou hast to my displeasure
Jezebel who doth mislead,
Who appears as having treasure
Of the true and righteous creed;
But she sadly is deceiving
All my servants who receiving
Aught from her of doctrines vile
Of the world, which doth defile.

10. "Blest is he who overcometh
And doth teach the statutes pure,
Who resists the fascination
Of the world, which doth allure.
They shall rule in close relation
Then with me o'er all the nations;
Who in deeds now faithful are,
Shall receive the morning star."

11. Thus says He, Who seven spirits
Has of God and seven stars,
"Where now is thy zeal of merit?
From the goal thou hast gone far.
Thou art dead, without faith living,
Who should others strength be giving.
Rise, awake, lose not the strife!
Seek new vigor and new life!

12. "Blest are they who trials enduring
Who do daily here await
For the day in preparation,
Keep their raiment pure in faith,
Who in little proving grateful,
E'er with me, remaining faithful.
Their new names which they attain
In life's book shall e'er remain."

13. So doth speak the true and holy,
Who the key of David has
Who retains the power solely
O'er the door of life and grace,
"See, before thee I have given
Now an open door to heaven,
For thou hast thy strength preserved,
Which though small, and kept my word.

14. "See! to thee I will surrender
Satan's seemingly true band,
Who appear as truth's defender,
But in faith they do not stand;
They shall yet in grave depression
Then acknowledge with confession
That I love and hold thee dear,
Who in faith doth persevere.

15. "Blest is he who overcometh
And his crown doth hold secure,
Who the truth have as their armor
And reproach with joy endure;
They, as pillars, in my mansion
There above of great expansion,
Shall then bear my name so true,
In Jerusalem the new."

16. And the Faithful, Amen, saith,
Refuge and the Witness true,
"Oh, thy works to me are hateful;
From my mouth I will thee spue;
Neither cold nor hot, thus living
Art thou me now sadly grieving;
As lukewarm thou dost not burn
In the love for which I yearn."

17. "O that thou wouldst now consider,
And in sorrow realize
Thy lamentable condition,
And the blindness of thine eyes;
Yea, thy naked situation
And thy poverty's vexation.
Purchase gold, my treasure bright,
And eyesalve and raiment white."

18. Blest is he who overcometh,
And the Lord's rebuke so meek
Doth receive in true submission,
When he knocks and entrance seeks.
For our heart He is desiring
To unite with Him. Inspiring
Us, He shows where He doth reign;
Great reward the victor's gain.

31. JESUS, OUR PRIEST AND KING

28, 32, 94, 186.

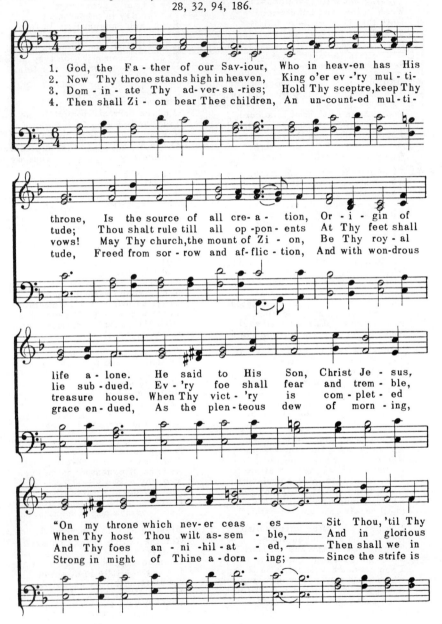

1. God, the Fa - ther of our Sav-iour, Who in heav-en has His
2. Now Thy throne stands high in heaven, King o'er ev -'ry mul - ti-
3. Dom - in - ate Thy ad - ver-sa -ries; Hold Thy sceptre, keep Thy
4. Then shall Zi - on bear Thee children, An un-count-ed mul-ti-

throne, Is the source of all cre-a - tion, Or - i - gin of
tude; Thou shalt rule till all op -pon - ents At Thy feet shall
vows! May Thy church,the mount of Zi - on, Be Thy roy - al
tude, Freed from sor - row and af-flic - tion, And with won-drous

life a - lone. He said to His Son, Christ Je - sus,
lie sub - dued. Ev - 'ry foe shall fear and trem - ble,
treasure house. When Thy vict - 'ry is com - plet - ed
grace en - dued, As the plen-teous dew of morn - ing,

"On my throne which nev-er ceas - es ———— Sit Thou, 'til Thy
When Thy host Thou wilt as-sem - ble, ———— And in glorious
And Thy foes an - ni -hil-at - ed, ———— Then shall we in
Strong in might of Thine a-dorn - ing; ———— Since the strife is

48.

foes shall be ———— Made a foot-stool un - to Thee." ————
vic - to - ry ———— Shalt put on Thy maj-es - ty. ————
ho - li - ness ———— Wor-ship Thee with joy and praise. ————
o'er, they sing ———— Joy-ful in e - ter- nal spring. ————

5. Verily our God hath spoken,
   And His promise He will hold.
   Lord, Thou art a Priest forever,
   As Melchizedek of old.
   Thou shalt be a High Priest ever,
   Prince of Peace, the only Saviour;
   Yea, Thou shalt in majesty
   King and Priest and Prophet be.

6. Thy work is to bless Thy people
   From the Holy Place above,
   Granting grace to all believers,
   Who are praising God in love.
   Since Thy lifeblood Thou hast given,
   Opening the way to heaven,
   He who now repents shall live,
   If he truly doth believe.

7. When the Lord brings all to judgment
   And avenges every wrong,
   When He humbles all the haughty,
   Breaking Satan's power strong,
   Then will Jesus' crowns be gleaming
   Far beyond man's fondest dreaming,
   And His people's joy will be
   Him to serve eternally!

32. WHO SHALL ABIDE?

28, 29, 31, 93.

1. Lord, who liv - eth in Thy dwell - ing? Who stays on Thy
2. Lord, who liv - eth in Thy dwell - ing? Who stays on Thy
3. Lord, who liv - eth in Thy dwell - ing? Who stays on Thy
4. Lord, who liv - eth in Thy dwell - ing? Who stays on Thy

moun - tain high? He who in the truth a - bid - eth,
ho - ly hill? He who keeps his tongue from sin - ning,
ho - ly hill? He who does not heed the god - less,
ho - ly hill? He whose hands are clean and spot - less,

Stays a - far from ev - ery lie; And with all his heart is
Helps his neigh- bor, cheer - ful still. He who noth-ing harmful
Shun - neth false-hood with a will, Doth not practice fraud nor
And whose heart is free from ill, Keeps his conscience pure and

striv - ing,	Seek-ing truth, all	good re - viv - ing;	He will in the
preach- es,	On - ly what God	fear-ing teach-es;	He will in the
swear- ing,	Right and in - no -cence	up-hold-ing:	He will in the
ho - ly,	Trusts in God, is	meek and low - ly:	He will in the

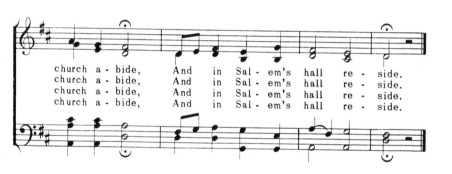

church a - bide,	And in	Sal - em's hall	re - side.
church a - bide,	And in	Sal - em's hall	re - side.
church a - bide,	And in	Sal - em's hall	re - side.
church a - bide,	And in	Sal - em's hall	re - side.

5. He who stayeth in Thy dwelling
And upon Thy holy hill
Shall from God receive the blessing,
Mercy, comfort and good will.
He who truth and love attaineth
And in holiness remaineth;
He will in the church abide
And in Salem's hall reside.

33. THE FELLOWSHIP OF THE SAINTS

35, 36, 51, 52.

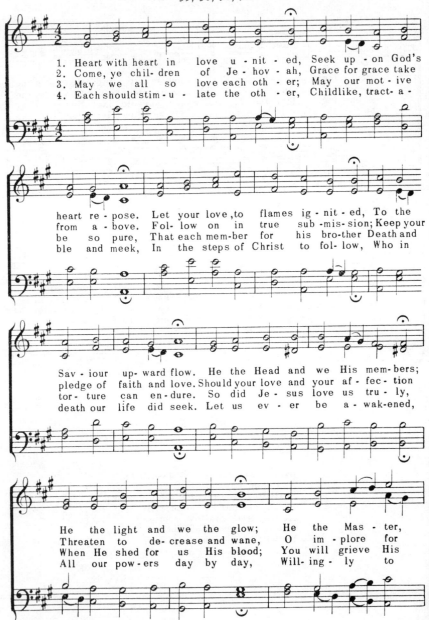

1. Heart with heart in love u - nit - ed, Seek up - on God's
2. Come, ye chil- dren of Je - hov - ah, Grace for grace take
3. May we all so love each oth - er; May our mot - ive
4. Each should stim - u - late the oth - er, Childlike, tract- a -

heart re - pose. Let your love, to flames ig - nit - ed, To the
from a - bove. Fol- low on in true sub -mis- sion; Keep your
be so pure, That each mem-ber for his bro-ther Death and
ble and meek, In the steps of Christ to fol- low, Who in

Sav - iour up- ward flow. He the Head and we His mem-bers;
pledge of faith and love. Should your love and your af - fec - tion
tor - ture can en - dure. So did Je - sus love us tru - ly,
death our life did seek. Let us ev - er be a - wak-ened,

He the light and we the glow; He the Mas - ter,
Threaten to de- crease and wane, O im - plore for
When He shed for us His blood; You will grieve His
All our pow -ers day by day, Will- ing - ly to

we	His	breth - ren,	In true fel - low - ship	we	grow.
God's	cor - rec - tion	Till its strength it	may	re - gain.
heart	un - du - ly	If you seek your	self- ish	good.
give	in serv - ice	And His kind- ness	to	re - pay.

5. Hallelujah! Oh, what glory!
Oh, what depth of love we trace,
When we see the heart of Jesus,
Who redeemed our guilty race;
Now He, King of all the spirits,
Is our Father, dear to us
Though invisible, our Master
Yet is truly near to us.

6. O Thou gracious friend, unite us
As Thy consecrated band;
And, as was Thy last instruction,
May in fervent love we stand!
Do Thou join in sacred nearness
With Thyself and with Thy fold
All who see Thy light and clearness
And Thy glory do behold.

7. Thus Thy pray'r to God the Father
Its fulfillment shall behold,
When all those whom Thou hast chosen
In His love He would enfold.
As Thou art with them united
They also as One should be
In true love should serve each other,
Finding joy in unity.

8. Prince of peace! O let Thy concord
Find in us a welcome warm!
Love, O let us ne'er grow weary
Thy blest service to perform.
Naught can ease our earthly burden
And our weariness remove
In our warfare 'gainst the evil,
As the power of Thy love.

9. Love, since thou hast then commanded
That in love we should be rife,
O revive each drooping spirit,
Bring the dying back to life!
Light the flames of love undying
That each one may plainly see:
We, as of one tribe and family
To one Lord devoted be.

10. Let us then be so united
As Thou with the Father art,
That not one of Thy weak members
Here on earth shall stand apart.
From the flames of Thy own burning
May our light partake its glow;
And that we are Thy disciples
All the world may surely know.

34. THE NEW BIRTH FROM ABOVE

33, 15, 36, 51.

1. Glo - ry be to God in heav - en, Praise to
2. This new be - ing now a - ris - es, Hav - ing
3. Out of wa - ter and of Spir - it Thou, O
4. So sin - cere is our af - fec - tion, Be - ing

Christ, our Sav - iour great! By the pow - er
died with Christ be - fore; What in Ad - am's
child, art born to - day; You've es - caped the
but one bod - y here, And our hopes are

of Thy Spir - it A new man Thou didst cre - ate.
fall had per - ished Christ the Sav - iour did re-store.
old op - pres - sor, In God's cov - e - nant you'll stay.
so u - nit - ed That all en - vies dis - ap-pear.

An - gels see in joy - ous rap - ture God's own
Dear - est child, we bid thee wel - come In our
Of one vine we all are branch- es; Of Christ's
All is com - mon to the breth - ren, Yet each

Word in deed ful - filled; And a - mid our
bless - ed broth - er - hood; From the wild tree
bod - y mem - bers we; And for Sa - tan's
one of us is free; Un - con -strained we

glad em-brac - es Is this child of God re - vealed.
thou art graft - ed On this ho - ly tree and root.
gall so bit - ter, Streams of life our drink shall be.
all do off - er Love, with-out hy - poc - ri - sy.

5. Gladly we relieve thy suff'ring;
   At thy welfare we rejoice;
   And, while for the Lord we battle,
   We are joined in heart and voice.
   This our unity exceedeth
   All the bounds of time and space,
   And what here has been provided
   Shall eternity embrace.

55.

35. THE SPIRITUAL CONFLICT

33, 15, 36, 51.

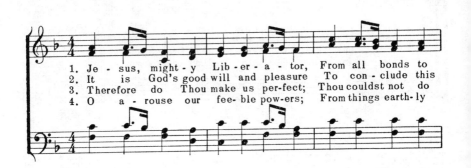

1. Je - sus, might - y Lib - er - a - tor, From all bonds to
2. It is God's good will and pleasure To con - clude this
3. Therefore do Thou make us per-fect; Thou couldst not do
4. O a - rouse our fee-ble pow-ers; From things earth-ly

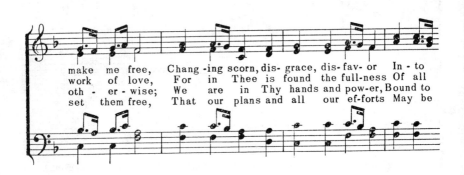

make me free, Chang -ing scorn, dis- grace, dis- fav- or In - to
work of love, For in Thee is found the full-ness Of all
oth - er - wise; We are in Thy hands and pow-er, Bound to
set them free, That our plans and all our ef-forts May be

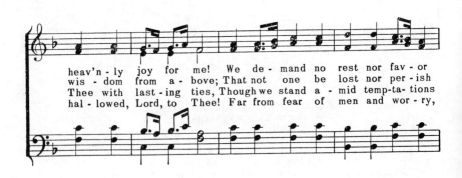

heav'n - ly joy for me! We de - mand no rest nor fav - or
wis - dom from a - bove; That not one be lost nor per - ish
Thee with last - ing ties, Though we stand a - mid temp-ta - tions
hal - lowed, Lord, to Thee! Far from fear of men and wor - ry,

56.

For our flesh in earth - ly clime; Deal with us as
Who be - gan this heav - 'nly race, But be led from
Press-ing us on ev - 'ry side, And our cross and
Far a - bove mere rea - son's scope, Past all dread of

seem - eth need - ful Here be - fore our part - ing time!
earth - ly tu - mult To that joy - ful rest - ing place.
trib - u - la - tions Soul and bod - y e'er be - tide.
scorn and suff - 'ring Lift us by our bless - ed hope!

5. Let those who were dearly purchased
   Not become the slaves of man,
   For since Thou hast died to save us,
   Keep us pure, as is Thy plan.
   Clean and spotless, true and perfect,
   After Thy resemblance fair,
   There is grace for all partakers
   Of Thy fulness sweet and rare.

6. Lord, into Thy death include us
   Let with Thee be crucified
   All that meets Thy disapproval;
   Lead us into Paradise!
   Come then, Lord, and do not tarry;
   Let us never slothful be!
   We shall sing with great rejoicing
   When we gain our liberty.

36. SOWING AND HARVEST

15, 33, 35, 52.

1. Tear - ful sow - ing brings glad har - vest Where our
2. Days of suff - 'ring ben - e - fi - cial For the
3. Pass - ing are the flesh's af - flic - tions, Tran - sient
4. Man - y strong temp - ta - tions meet us Who u -

Mas - ter's will is done, When for Him, the Lord of
Mas - ter's breth - ren here; As these bod - i - ly af -
are the spir - it's needs. Pass - ing are all vain af -
nit - ed are with Christ. Sa - tan bold - ly would de -

har - vest, Through His Spir - it fruits are grown.
flic - tions Chast - en those who God do fear.
fec - tions, Not the ev - er - last - ing deeds.
lude us That with him we should u - nite;

Love, hu - mil - i - ty and meek - ness, Faith and
As the gold by fire is bright- ened, Al - so
Pain and tor - ture soon are end - ed In those
He would have us seek the pleas - ures Which at

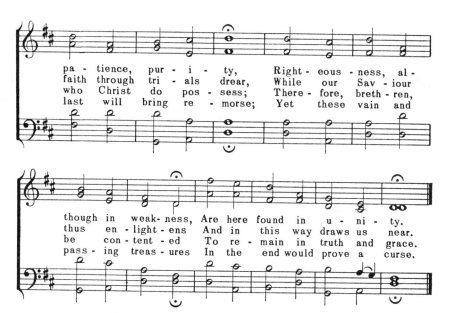

```
pa -  tience,    pur - i - ty,     Right - eous - ness,  al -
faith  through   tri - als  drear,  While    our      Sav - iour
who    Christ    do   pos - sess;   There - fore,    breth - ren,
last   will      bring re - morse;  Yet      these   vain  and

though in   weak- ness, Are  here  found in  u - ni - ty.
thus   en - light - ens And  in    this  way draws us   near.
be     con - tent - ed  To   re - main in  truth and  grace.
pass - ing  treas - ures In  the   end would prove a    curse.
```

5. Satan's host through seeming gladness
   Shall go unto endless pain,
   But the saints by way of sadness
   Shall the marriage-supper gain.
   Then, my soul, let nothing move thee
   From the straight and narrow way,
   Even though the body weaken,
   Ere you reach your burial-day.

6. Since our Lord once bore the anger,
   When He wrought our peace with God,
   Love is now the only purpose
   Of the Father's chastening rod.
   Then, O Pilgrim, think not lightly
   Of the Father's chastening;
   Seek that it may bring you onward,
   While you're heavenward hastening.

7. With correction, God remindeth
   Every child that it must be;
   And the more of fruit he findeth
   On Christ's branches, fair to see.
   All the more the shoots that hinder,
   He doth prune with watchful eye,
   That more fruit each branch may render
   For His kingdom there on high.

8. As the sultry days of summer
   Swiftly ripen earthly grain,
   So in days of dire affliction
   Shall our faith its growth attain.
   And beneath this heat and burden
   Shall the Christian be prepared
   For his happy home in heaven,
   Where God's bliss and joy is shared.

9. Soon, perhaps, you too may enter
   Where the golden harps resound;
   Where the saints the palms are bearing
   And the faithful ones are crowned;
   Therefore, cling to Christ your Savior;
   Daily wrestle, hope, and fight;
   With Him pierce through all the darkness
   Into His eternal light.

10. If He all your heart is filling,
    Is the Hope of all your dreams,
    From your body will be welling
    Of His grace the brightest beams.
    All the light of morning breaking
    Ushers in a joyous day,
    So your lips with fervor speaking,
    Will declare: Christ is the Way!

37. LOVE

15, 33, 36, 52.

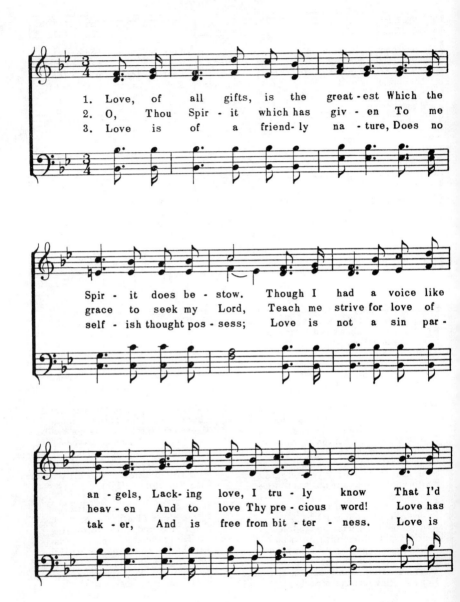

1. Love, of all gifts, is the great-est Which the
2. O, Thou Spir - it which has giv - en To me
3. Love is of a friend- ly na - ture, Does no

Spir - it does be - stow. Though I had a voice like
grace to seek my Lord, Teach me strive for love of
self - ish thought pos - sess; Love is not a sin par -

an - gels, Lack- ing love, I tru - ly know That I'd
heav - en And to love Thy pre - cious word! Love has
tak - er, And is free from bit - ter - ness. Love is

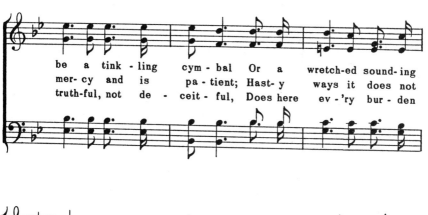

be a tink - ling cym - bal Or a wretch-ed sound-ing
mer- cy and is pa - tient; Hast- y ways it does not
truth-ful, not de - ceit - ful, Does here ev - 'ry bur - den

brass; For al - though the sound were
own; Hum - ble - ness of mind is
bear; And, en - dur - ing, is so

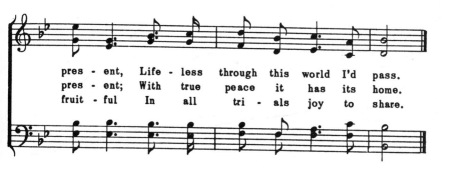

pres - ent, Life - less through this world I'd pass.
pres - ent; With true peace it has its home.
fruit - ful In all tri - als joy to share.

61.

38. COMFORT IN DISTRESS
166, 197

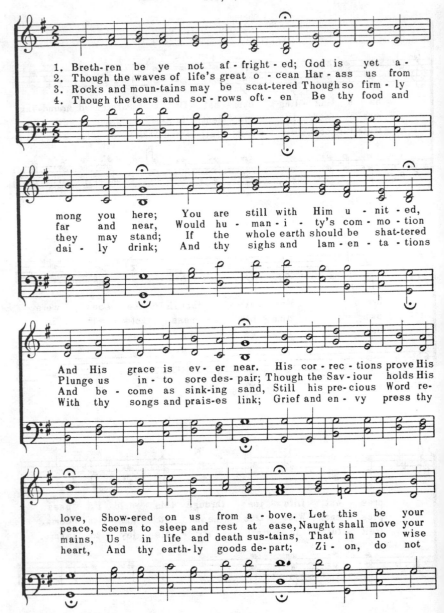

1. Breth-ren be ye not af-fright-ed; God is yet a-
2. Though the waves of life's great o-cean Har-ass us from
3. Rocks and moun-tains may be scat-tered Though so firm-ly
4. Though the tears and sor-rows oft-en Be thy food and

mong you here; You are still with Him u-nit-ed,
far and near, Would hu-man-i-ty's com-mo-tion
they may stand; If the whole earth should be shat-tered
dai-ly drink; And thy sighs and lam-en-ta-tions

And His grace is ev-er near. His cor-rec-tions prove His
Plunge us in-to sore des-pair; Though the Sav-iour holds His
And be-come as sink-ing sand, Still his pre-cious Word re-
With thy songs and prais-es link; Grief and en-vy press thy

love, Show-ered on us from a-bove. Let this be your
peace, Seems to sleep and rest at ease, Naught shall move your
mains, Us in life and death sus-tains, That in no wise
heart, And thy earth-ly goods de-part; Zi-on, do not

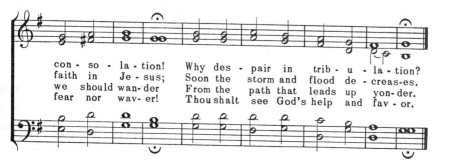

con - so - la - tion! Why des - pair in trib - u - la - tion?
faith in Je - sus; Soon the storm and flood de - creas-es.
we should wan- der From the path that leads up yon- der.
fear nor wav- er! Thou shalt see God's help and fav - or.

5. If with anguish thou art shaken,
If men bind and torture thee,
Thou wilt never be forsaken --
Think upon eternity!
Stand in faith and do not fear,
For thy Lord is ever near.
Zion, let His hand direct thee;
He will strengthen and protect thee!

6. Then rejoice! The end is coming
And the evening draweth nigh;
Yield to God in true submission;
He will free you from on high.
For your sorrow, grief, and strife,
He'll bestow the crown of life;
God, thy shield, will watch and cherish;
But the world in shame will perish.

7. Hallelujah! Bliss and rapture
Now with glorious might appear!
For the sun of grace and splendor,
Jesus Christ, the King, draws near,
Greets thee with thy soul's release
And bestows the kiss of peace;
Zion, all thy tears and sadness
Vanish now in joy and gladness.

39. THE PENITENT'S CONFLICT
40, 189.

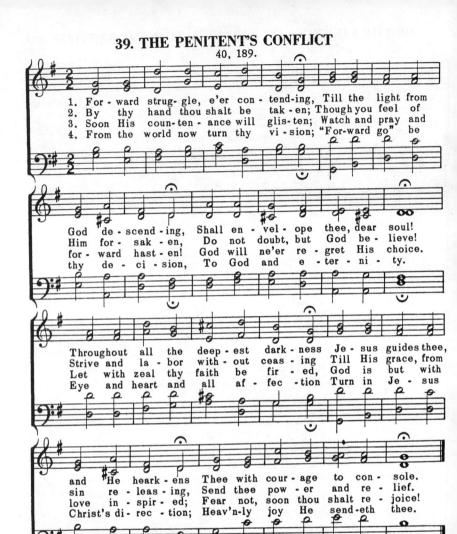

1. For - ward strug- gle, e'er con - tend-ing, Till the light from
2. By thy hand thou shalt be tak - en; Though you feel of
3. Soon His coun-ten - ance will glis-ten; Watch and pray and
4. From the world now turn thy vi - sion; "For-ward go" be

God de - scend -ing, Shall en - vel - ope thee, dear soul!
Him for - sak - en, Do not doubt, but God be - lieve!
for - ward hast - en! God will ne'er re - gret His choice.
thy de - ci - sion, To God and e - ter - ni - ty.

Throughout all the deep - est dark - ness Je - sus guides thee,
Strive and la - bor with - out ceas - ing Till His grace, from
Let with zeal thy faith be fir - ed, God is but with
Eye and heart and all af - fec -tion Turn in Je - sus

and "He heark - ens Thee with cour - age to con - sole.
sin re - leas - ing, Send thee pow - er and re - lief.
love in - spir - ed; Fear not, soon thou shalt re - joice!
Christ's di - rec - tion; Heav'n-ly joy He send -eth thee.

5. Oft' He's saved thee from destruction,
From the wild waves of affliction
With His strong and mighty hand.
If our love is pure and fervent,
There is not a single servant
Whom He will not refuge grant.

6. Locked within thy chamber's stillness
Pour into His heart the fulness
Of thy sorrow and thy grief.
Though thou canst not feel His nearness
Canst not pray nor speak with clearness
Groans and sighs will bring relief.

7. Though in silence, God will hear thee,
As a Saviour will be near thee;
Have no doubt; He hears you pray!
Just believe Christ intercedeth;
Just believe that all He pleadeth
God will grant without delay!

40. THE LIKENESS OF THE CREATION TO BAPTISM

39, 189

1. When God did cre - ate the plan - ets Through His Word's al-
2. As a poor and help-less in - fant Lay the earth in
3. When He had all things cre - at - ed, This great plan- et
4. But, a - las! man soon transgress - ed And thus lost his

might-y ten - ets, Out of dark and sil - ent night, All the
ev - 'ry in- stant Un- til light His Word did give. God's true
had com -plet - ed, Last-ly He cre - at - ed man In the
Ed - en bless-ed; He be -lieved not God's true Word; Stub-born -

earth was void and cheer- less, Till God's Word with might and
Spir - it on the wa - ters Brought a - bout im - port - ant
like - ness of His Mak - er, That he should be a par -
ly re - fused to hear it, Spurned the lead - ing of the

clear - ness Filled it with His glo - rious light.
mat - ters So that man on earth could live.
tak - er Of the good gifts in His plan.
Spir - it, And would not o - bey the Lord.

God pronounced on man the sentence,
For his sin and disobedience
And his scorn of grace and faith!
Then to cleanse the earth of sinning
And to make a new beginning
He decreed a healing faith.
All bold sinners, helpless, crying,
In the deluge dread were dying,
Buried in one watery grave.
Death, begotten of transgression,
Comes to them without compassion,
And no one is found to save.

7. One alone did heed the warning,
One just man true wisdom learning
From the teaching of God's Word.
Noah, by God's hand delivered,
With his wife and children entered
In the cov'nant with the Lord.

8. This creation is reflected
Unto Christ and his elected
Who in this blest union stand;
Who by grace escape destruction,
Live no more to see corruption.
In baptismal grace they stand.

65.

41. THE BAPTISMAL COVENANT

25, 75, 145, 220.

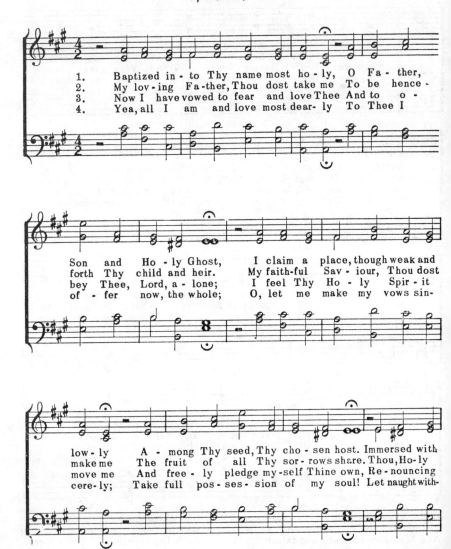

1. Baptized in-to Thy name most ho-ly, O Fa-ther,
2. My lov-ing Fa-ther, Thou dost take me To be hence-
3. Now I have vowed to fear and love Thee And to o-
4. Yea, all I am and love most dear-ly To Thee I

Son and Ho-ly Ghost, I claim a place, though weak and
forth Thy child and heir. My faith-ful Sav-iour, Thou dost
bey Thee, Lord, a-lone; I feel Thy Ho-ly Spir-it
of-fer now, the whole; O, let me make my vows sin-

low-ly A-mong Thy seed, Thy cho-sen host. Immersed with
make me The fruit of all Thy sor-rows share. Thou, Ho-ly
move me And free-ly pledge my-self Thine own, Re-nouncing
cere-ly; Take full pos-ses-sion of my soul! Let naught with-

Christ, I'm dead to sin; Thy Spir-it now shall live with-in.
Ghost, wilt comfort me When dark-est clouds a-round I see.
sin to keep the faith And war with e-vil un-to death.
in me, naught I own Serve an-y will but Thine a-lone.

5. Depart, depart, Thou prince of darkness!
No more by thee I'll be enticed!
Mine is indeed a chastened conscience
And sprinkled with the blood of Christ.
Away, vain world! O sin, away!
Lo, I renounce you all this day.

6. And never let my purpose falter,
O Father, Son and Holy Ghost!
But keep me faithful to Thine altar
Till Thou shalt call me from my post.
So unto Thee I'll live and die,
And praise Thee evermore on high.

42. BETHESDA, THE HOUSE OF GRACE
12, 43, 45.

1. With-in that won-drous pool Whose waves were ag-i-
2. In those five porch-es there Great mul-ti-tudes were
3. Like-wise, ye sin-ners, come; Be healed of your trans-
4. But has-ten; tar-ry not Lest you should be for-

tat - ed When-e'er the an - gel's pow'r Un-
gath - ered; Blind, lame, deaf, rheu - mat - ic, With
gres - sion! O come both great and small, Here
sak - en! If you would find the cure, From

seen its depth per - vad - ed; There ev - 'ry
pal - sy struck and with - ered, Con - sump-tive
you will find re - mis - sion, Sal - va - tion
sin - ful sleep a - wak - en! The Lord has

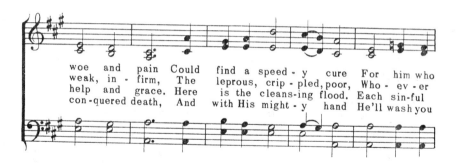

woe and pain Could find a speed - y cure For him who
weak, in - firm, The leprous, crip - pled, poor, Who - ev - er
help and grace. Here is the cleans-ing flood. Each sin-ful
con-quered death, And with His might - y hand He'll wash you

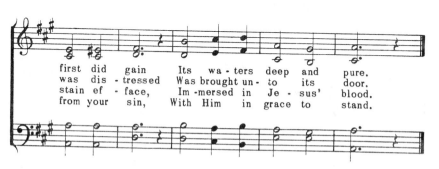

first did gain Its wa - ters deep and pure.
was dis - tressed Was brought un - to its door.
stain ef - face, Im -mersed in Je - sus' blood.
from your sin, With Him in grace to stand.

5. As man before his fall
   Are we restored through Jesus;
   Though many members called,
   By One God's grace increases.
   True faith will make you whole
   If you His Word embrace,
   Pure, holy, without sin,
   Endowed with Jesus' grace.

6. As witness of God's love
   The Spirit then descendeth;
   As unction hallows all
   Whom Christ as His commandeth.
   But they who have this grace
   And then to sin revert
   Shall double stripes receive,
   To their eternal hurt.

7. We bring our prayer to Thee;
   O Lord, in mercy hear it!
   And now impart to them
   Rich measure of Thy Spirit
   Who now have entered in
   The household of Thy grace;
   Keep them from Satan's yoke,
   Grant them in heaven a place.

69.

43. BAPTISMAL HYMN

12, 42, 79, 45.

1. A Chris-tian, now bap-tized, To me much grace is giv - en. Why was this grant - ed me? That I with Christ am ris - en! This is the ho - ly

2. I'm bap-tized in Christ's name And in His death I'm bur - ied; How should I fur - ther bear The load so long I car - ried? Thou, Lord, art He who

3. Bap-tized, I feel His grace My sin - ful mind sub - du - ing; And look in all dis-tress To God, my faith re - new - ing. Thou art the cen - tral

4. O grant me now Thy grace That I, with true de - vo - tion, May ev - er by Thee stand, Though storm - y be life's o - cean. And with Thy bless- ing,

aim;	He	who	does	this	neg - lect	Can - not	truth-
died	And	who	a - rose	a - gain;	There- fore	in
force,	Help	me	to	man - i - fest	What	true	bap-
Lord,	May	I	in	faith	re - main,	And	to	that

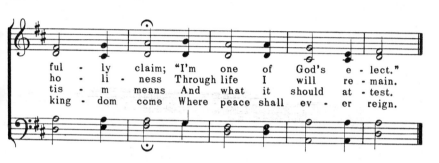

ful - ly	claim;	"I'm	one	of	God's	e - lect."
ho - li - ness	Through	life	I	will	re - main.
tis - m	means	And	what	it	should	at - test.
king - dom	come	Where	peace	shall	ev - er	reign.

5. Baptized am I; now may
   This truth the whole world ponder.
   I live no more as they
   Who in deep darkness wander;
   Baptism urges me
   That I by constant prayer
   Resist the enemy
   With power, everywhere.

6. Baptized am I; now shall
   No wayward thought of erring
   Cast o'er my heart a spell,
   My soul to evil snaring.
   For what may tempt my heart,
   And every sinful pride,
   Upon Thy cross, O Lord,
   Shall hence be crucified.

7. Now grant to me Thy power
   So that I may not waver,
   And bless me every hour,
   O my beloved Saviour!
   Thus shall I safely fare
   Upon this blessed way,
   And reach the city where
   Thy peace shall reach for aye.

44. ONE FOR ALL
12, 43, 45, 79.

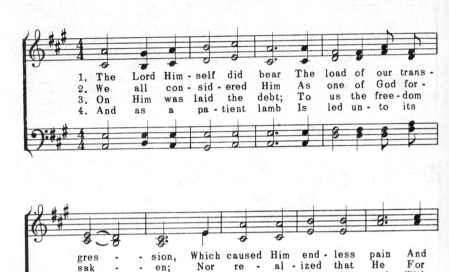

1. The Lord Him-self did bear The load of our trans-
2. We all con-sid-ered Him As one of God for-
3. On Him was laid the debt; To us the free-dom
4. And as a pa-tient lamb Is led un-to its

gres - - sion, Which caused Him end-less pain And
sak - - en; Nor re-al-ized that He For
giv - - en. He sat-is-fies the soul With
slaugh - - ter From past-ures fresh and green And

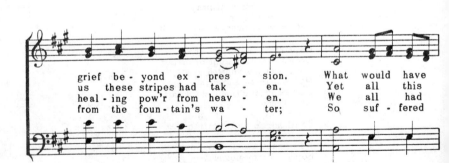

grief be-yond ex-pres - sion. What would have
us these stripes had tak - en. Yet all this
heal-ing pow'r from heav - en. We all had
from the foun-tain's wa - ter; So suf-fered

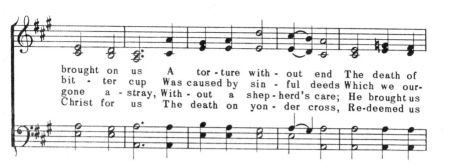

brought on us A tor-ture with-out end The death of
bit - ter cup Was caused by sin - ful deeds Which we our-
gone a - stray, With-out a shep-herd's care; He brought us
Christ for us The death on yon - der cross, Re-deemed us

Je - sus Christ In mer - cy did for - fend.
selves had done, As we must now con - cede.
to His fold When He our sins did bear.
with His blood From sin, dis - tress and loss.

5. Thy conflict is our peace.
   Thy death is our salvation,
   Thy bonds, our liberty,
   Thy pains, our consolation.
   Thy cross doth comfort give,
   Thy wounds, a balm that heals.
   Thy blood a ransom is,
   Thy Word a hope reveals.

6. Lord, help and make us brave
   To bear our cross and burden,
   That we may not grow faint
   Nor yet give up the battle.
   Yea, from Thy crown of thorns
   Let us our courage take,
   That through reproach and shame
   We ne'er Thy ways forsake.

45. REPENTANCE

12, 42, 43.

1. Oh, Je - sus look up - on My help - less sit - u - a - tion;
2. I've been mis - led in sin, In chains of death I lan - guish;
3. My soul doth yearn for rest; I seek, but fail to find it;
4. Thou, Je - sus, canst a - lone De - liv - er me from sor - row;

My heart feels dead - ly fear, My spir - it, con - dem -
I may turn where I will, Noth - ing re - lieves my
Naught can my heart re - lease, Or from sin's chain un -
The strength to ov - er - come From Thy strong hands I

na - tion. With - in me is the wish, But not the power to
an - guish. I stood ex - alt - ed here, Must now lie in the
bind it. The law to me re - veals The vol - ume of my
bor - row. The long - ings of my heart Will bring me naught but

do, Be - cause my wear - y soul Is full of grief and woe.
dust, The fame I would have shared Has now been turned to rust.
sin, But fails to give me power A new life to be - gin.
pain, Un - less the grace to live A - new from Thee I gain.

74.

5. Have mercy then, O Lord!
   Before Thy feet I'm bowing;
   Let into my weak heart
   The stream of grace be flowing.
   I pray I'll leave Thee not
   Until Thy blessing's pow'r
   Can conquer death in me,
   And bring life's blessed shower.

6. Thy promise standeth sure,
   That Thou wouldst truly cheer me,
   If my perverted mind
   Will learn but to revere Thee,
   If it will lay aside
   All earthly vanity,
   So that Thy love and grace
   May hold its sway in me.

7. So take my pledge, O Lord,
   Too long in sin I've bided;
   I'd live henceforth for Thee,
   By Thee, my Saviour, guided!
   O do Thou hold me fast;
   From sin, O make me free,
   So that henceforth my heart
   Thy temple pure may be!

46. THE BEST REFUGE

1. In sor-row and pain Thy trust do re-tain In Je-sus the mer-ci-ful Sav-iour.
2. When bur-dened with care, When thou wouldst de-spair, Then call on thy lov-ing Re-deem-er.
3. He'll light-en the load, And lev-el the road And bear thee on hands of com-pas-sion.
4. He's gen-tle and kind, Rich bless-ings thou'lt find; His Word gives thee peace ev-er-last-ing.

5. He'll shield and defend His child to the end;
   No suff'ring or death shall appall thee.

6. Keep Him for your gain, Earth's pleasures are vain;
   Sweet rest is found only in heaven.

7. In patience then bear All trial and care;
   Above streams of bliss will refresh thee.

47. STRIVE ARIGHT
18, 48, 72.

1. Strive a-right when God in mer-cy His com-
2. Strive to en-ter at the port-al, Walk the
3. Strive with zeal and pas-sion glow-ing In the
4. Bat-tle 'gainst the pow'r of Sa-tan! Grow not

pas-sion turns to you, That your soul so long o'er-
nar-row path of life; Here we wan-der in the
strength of your first love; Break the bonds of earth that
wea-ry in the fight, Strug-gle for-ward to the

bur-dened, Freed from sin might live a-new.
val-ley; Death a-bounds with toil and strife.
keep you From your bright a-bode a-bove.
king-dom Of your God in end-less light!

5. Trembling, keep your soul from falling;
Prize your ransom more and more;
Daily round your mortal body
Countless dangers hover o'er.

6. Grasp the crown of glory firmly;
God's own precious gift retain.
Perseverance brings the vict'ry;
Sinful fall brings inward pain.

7. Until death the true and faithful
Constantly shall fight with sin.
Faith unwavered is their weapon;
Every victory they'll win.

8. Faith so true adores the Saviour,
Loves His care and all His ways;
Does not cherish worldly pleasure,
Gives to God alone its praise.

9. Faithfulness will never venture;
Of this world it is aware.
If your treasure is in heaven,
Then your heart is also there.

10. Ye, who fight, do this consider;
Strive aright, and trembling stand!
Daily let your feet move onward
Till you reach the heav'nly land.

48. MORNING HYMN
47, 49, 72.

1. Once a - gain a night has van - ished, And the ris - ing sun so bright, Through its rad - iance fair has ban - ished Gloom and dark - ness of the night.

2. We, Thy chil - dren, come as - cend - ing, Lov - ing Fa - ther, to Thy throne, Thanks and praise to bring be - fore Thee, Thee the Fa - ther, Thee the Son.

3. In this night of dread and dark - ness Thou hast cared with watch - ful eye; Thou hast giv - en joy - ful vi - sion Of the light that draw - eth nigh.

4. God, for Thy great love and mer - cy Thy re - deemed Thy prais - es bring; Whom through - out the night just end - ed Hast pro - tect - ed with Thy wing.

5. May we find this day as ever,
Lord, Thy kind and loving face.
Vice and sin, Oh may they never
Mar the joy of Thy rich grace!

6. Comfort, peace and joy be given
Through Thy Holy Spirit, Lord;
May our hearts by it be driven
In Thy ways with one accord.

7. When we seek Thee, let us find Thee;
May our pleading voice be blest;
In our midst Thy light be kindled;
May our souls find peaceful rest.

8. Let Thy word in life and Spirit
To our eyes and hearts be shown;
Light and truth give all who hear it
Who with joy Thy ways have gone.

9. Thy supporting spirit send us;
Thy sweet peace and love bestow;
Sanctify our heart and spirit,
And Thy Spirit's impulse show.

10. Let Thy love our hearts inspire
That we love Thee fervently;
Let Thy cov'nant bind us nigher;
Lead our conflict valiantly.

11. Ev'ry day, O Lord, we pray Thee,
Let Thy blessing on us flow;
May our hearts with peace and gladness
Ever by Thy radiance glow.

77.

49. EVENING HYMN
18, 47, 72, 246.

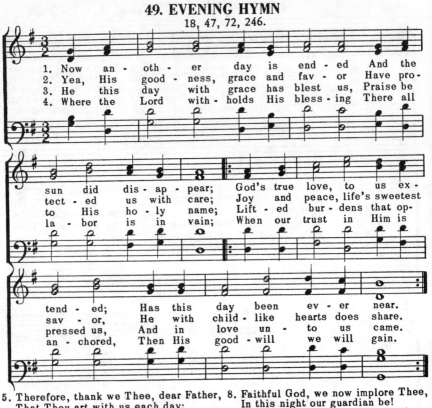

1. Now an-oth-er day is end-ed And the sun did dis-ap-pear; God's true love, to us ex-tend-ed; Has this day been ev-er near.

2. Yea, His good-ness, grace and fav-or Have pro-tect-ed us with care; Joy and peace, life's sweetest sav-or, He with child-like hearts does share.

3. He this day with grace has blest us, Praise be to His ho-ly name; Lift-ed bur-dens that op-pressed us, And in love un-to us came.

4. Where the Lord with-holds His bless-ing There all la-bor is in vain; When our trust in Him is an-chored, Then His good-will we will gain.

5. Therefore, thank we Thee, dear Father,
   That Thou art with us each day;
   For Thy good and blessed counsel,
   And Thy help upon our way.

6. Also in this evening hour
   Come we, Father, nigh to Thee,
   Praise with heart and tongue Thy power;
   Hearken to our childlike plea!

7. May Thy word in heart and spirit
   Give us joy and comfort sweet;
   May the torch of heav'nly wisdom
   Be a light unto our feet.

8. Faithful God, we now implore Thee,
   In this night our guardian be!
   If Thou shouldst refuse protection,
   Then our watch in vain would be.

9. Thou art still our shield and Saviour,
   Our good sentinel at night;
   In our prayers we seek Thy favor,
   Trusting only in Thy might.

10. Unto Thee we draw in chorus,
    Praying that we may be blest;
    Guard us on our pilgrim journey;
    Grant us joy and peace and rest!

50. BE PREPARED
83, 154, 178.

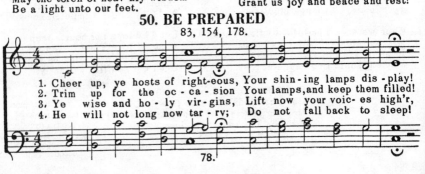

1. Cheer up, ye hosts of right-eous, Your shin-ing lamps dis-play!

2. Trim up for the oc-ca-sion Your lamps, and keep them filled!

3. Ye wise and ho-ly vir-gins, Lift now your voic-es high'r,

4. He will not long now tar-ry; Do not fall back to sleep!

78.

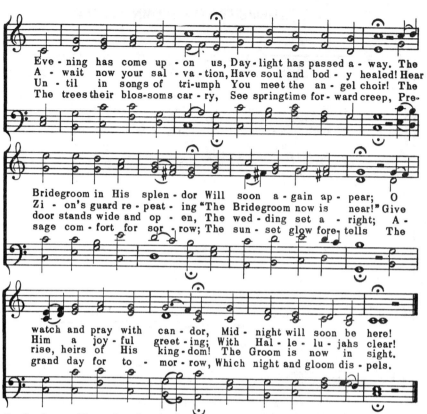

Eve - ning has come up - on us, Day - light has passed a - way. The
A - wait now your sal - va - tion, Have soul and bod - y healed! Hear
Un - til in songs of tri - umph You meet the an - gel choir! The
The trees their blos - soms car - ry, See springtime for - ward creep, Pre -

Bridegroom in His splen - dor Will soon a - gain ap - pear; O
Zi - on's guard re - peat - ing "The Bridegroom now is near!" Give
door stands wide and op - en, The wed - ding set a - right; A -
sage com - fort for sor - row; The sun - set glow fore - tells The

watch and pray with can - dor, Mid - night will soon be here!
Him a joy - ful greet - ing; With Hal - le - lu - jahs clear!
rise, heirs of His king - dom! The Groom is now in sight.
grand day for to - mor - row, Which night and gloom dis - pels.

5. O who would now be sleeping?
   The wise will keep awake.
   God's wrath will soon be sweeping,
   And vengeance He will take
   On all who are not watchful,
   And homage did award
   Unto the beast and idol,
   Instead of Thee, O Lord.

6. Advance now for the meeting,
   All who love Zion here,
   With joyful, happy greeting;
   Thy griefs now disappear.
   The hour of joyful tiding
   Now for the bride will sound,
   Who, long in faith abiding,
   In glory shall be crowned.

7. Ye saints, who here in patience
   Your cross and suffering bore,
   Shall live and reign forever
   The Lamb's bright throne before;
   With joy ye shall in glory
   The Lamb Himself behold;
   In triumph cast before Him
   Your diadems of gold.

8. There is the vict'ry's emblem;
   There is the snow-white dress;
   We'll sing the joyful anthem,
   And heaven's peace possess.
   Instead of tears and sadness,
   The hour of joy will chime,
   And after winter's bleakness,
   Eternal spring sublime.

9. O joyful city yonder,
   Jerusalem the New,
   Where the redeemed shall tarry;
   O were the time soon due
   When we with Thee united,
   Our brethren one and all,
   Whom Thou, Lord, hast invited,
   Enter the wedding hall!

10. O Jesus Christ, our pleasure,
    Come soon and reappear!
    O Jesus Christ, our treasure,
    Advance Thy progress here!
    We pray for termination
    Of all combat and strife,
    And hope our full salvation
    May speedily arrive.

51. ENCOURAGEMENT TO FAITH'S BATTLE

15, 33, 35, 52.

1. Lit - tle flock, in haste as - sem - ble And to Zi - on's mount re - pair! Lo, the prince of world and dark - ness For the con - flict does pre - pare. See, the judg - ment day is com - ing, As a

2. Do not hes - i - tate, my breth-ren, For your life - time on - ward rolls; Ded - i - cate your hearts and mem - bers To the bridegroom of your souls. Though with-out the camp ye suf - fer In - sult,

3. Though our tears oft flow with sad -ness And in sor - row oft we sigh, They shall change to songs of glad - ness, Bit - ter cup to wine of joy. Though we oft - en see them gleam - ing, Sa - tan's

4. Here in - deed the tear - ful sow - ing Is our watch-word and our fate; Toil and strife be - fall the Chris-tian Till he en - ters heav-en's gate. O, then let our tears be giv - en To the

80.

thief in dark - est night; Then a - wake and
scorn and vile re - tort, Sigh- ing "O, be -
ar - rows, sword and spear, Yet we need not
Lamb who came in tears, Till we sing our

watch, ye right-eous; Walk as chil-dren of the light!
hold my lean-ness!" From the Lord comes your re - ward.
lose our cour- age, Heav-en's host is draw-ing near.
praise in heav- en In those hap- py, end-less years.

5. Spirits of the just made perfect
   Bid us to be strong and brave,
   Saying, "Brethren, in His service
   Be ye faithful to the grave.
   Hallelujah! Stand in union
   To the end of earthly strife,
   Till you sing the song of triumph
   With us in eternal life!"

6. Who, then, would not from this Babel,
   From this world's confusion flee?
   There to rest in Zion's pastures,
   Its glad citizen to be?
   There we shall be out of danger,
   'Neath the Father's safe retreat;
   And we'll find on that blest morning
   Heaven's bliss for strife and heat.

7. Cheer up, then, and strive, ye ransomed,
   In this toilsome, trying time;
   God will comfort and reward us
   With eternal rest sublime!
   Only he who is victorious
   Shall the crown of life receive;
   Then prevail in prayerful watching,
   Love, endure, hope and believe!

52. REPENT YE!
15, 33, 36, 161.

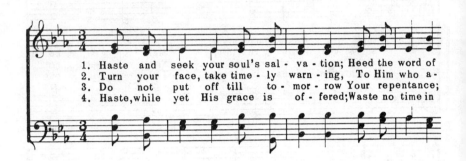

1. Haste and seek your soul's sal - va - tion; Heed the word of
2. Turn your face, take time - ly warn - ing, To Him who a -
3. Do not put off till to - mor - row Your repentance;
4. Haste, while yet His grace is of - fered; Waste no time in

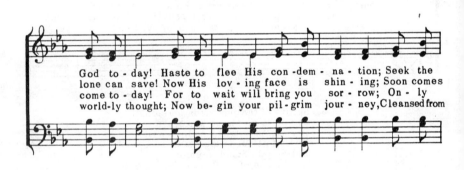

God to - day! Haste to flee His con - dem - na - tion; Seek the
lone can save! Now His lov - ing face is shin - ing; Soon comes
come to - day! For to wait will bring you sor - row; On - ly
world - ly thought; Now be - gin your pil - grim jour - ney, Cleansed from

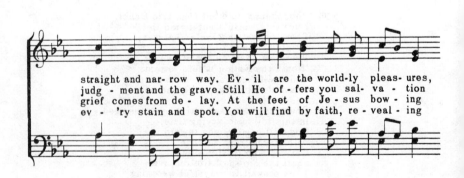

straight and nar - row way. Ev - il are the world-ly pleas- ures,
judg - ment and the grave. Still He of - fers you sal - va - tion
grief comes from de - lay. At the feet of Je - sus bow - ing
ev - 'ry stain and spot. You will find by faith, re - veal - ing

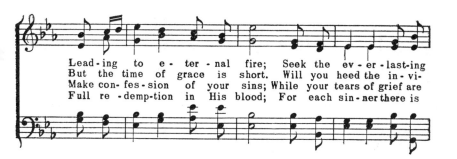

Lead-ing to e-ter-nal fire; Seek the ev-er-last-ing
But the time of grace is short. Will you heed the in-vi-
Make con-fes-sion of your sins; While your tears of grief are
Full re-demp-tion in His blood; For each sin-ner there is

treas-ure, Ere the day of grace ex-pire.
ta-tion? Come, and hard-en not your heart.
flow-ing, Let the lov-ing Sav-iour in.
heal-ing, Bap-tized in this cleans-ing flood.

5. Having clothed yourself with Jesus
And your faith has made you whole,
Do not fear the tribulations
That assail and try your soul:
For the enemy oppresses
All who would the world forsake,
Seeking that he might compel them
On themselves his yoke to take.

6. Heavenward, then take your journey;
Let your course in faith be trod;
Face the crafty adversary
Boldly as a man of God.
Go with courage to the conflict
As the sanctified to be;
And retaining still your treasure,
Win a crown of victory.

53. PASSIONATE LONGING
80, 81, 82, 183.

1. Oh Je - ru - sa - lem, the gold - en, Where God's prais-es
2. In this pil - grim hab - i - ta - tion, In the heat of
3. Ah, how much I long to meet Thee, Je - sus, my soul's
4. Come and lead us full of glad - ness, Gen - tle Shep-herd,

ev - er ring; Heav'n - ly choirs to Thee be - hold - en,
trials se - vere, Ere our suf - f'ring finds ces - sa - tion,
bos - om - friend, There on Sal - em's peace-ful pas-tures,
by Thy hand, Aft - er all this pain and sad-ness,

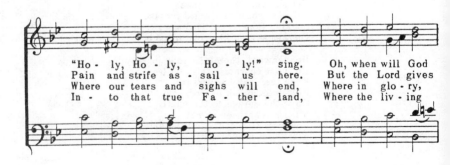

"Ho - ly, Ho - ly, Ho - ly!" sing. Oh, when will God
Pain and strife as - sail us here. But the Lord gives
Where our tears and sighs will end, Where in glo - ry,
In - to that true Fa - ther - land, Where the liv - ing

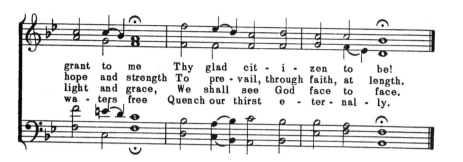

grant   to   me   Thy glad cit - i - zen to   be!
hope   and strength To   pre - vail, through faith, at length.
light   and grace,   We   shall see God face to face.
wa - ters free   Quench our thirst e - ter - nal - ly.

5. O that chosen, holy dwelling,
   Full of bliss and fair delight!
   O that I, on soaring pinions,
   Might arise from this world's night,
   That new city there to see,
   Where my Lord the sun shall be!

6. But if I must longer tarry
   On this wild, tempestuous sea,
   Where on frail bark I am sailing,
   Storms and waves are tossing me,
   Though the cross and death I see,
   Still let hope my anchor be!

7. Then I'll have no fear of sinking,
   Be the ocean e'er so wild;
   I shall see Thy beacon beaming
   From the landing, clear and mild.
   Thou, by its consoling ray,
   Into port wilt show the way.

54. THE SERMON ON THE MOUNT

53, 81, 183, 249.

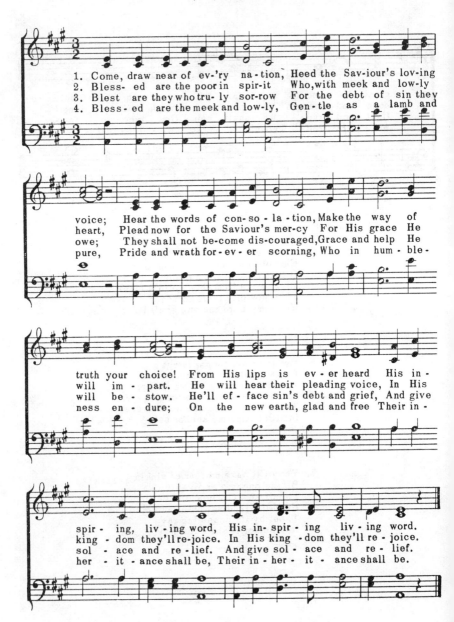

1. Come, draw near of ev-'ry na-tion, Heed the Sav-iour's lov-ing
2. Bless-ed are the poor in spir-it Who, with meek and low-ly
3. Blest are they who tru-ly sor-row For the debt of sin they
4. Bless-ed are the meek and low-ly, Gen-tle as a lamb and

voice; Hear the words of con-so-la-tion, Make the way of
heart, Plead now for the Saviour's mer-cy For His grace He
owe; They shall not be-come dis-couraged, Grace and help He
pure, Pride and wrath for-ev-er scorning, Who in hum-ble-

truth your choice! From His lips is ev-er heard His in-
will im-part. He will hear their pleading voice, In His
will be-stow. He'll ef-face sin's debt and grief, And give
ness en-dure; On the new earth, glad and free Their in-

spir-ing, liv-ing word, His in-spir-ing liv-ing word.
king-dom they'll re-joice. In His king-dom they'll re-joice.
sol-ace and re-lief. And give sol-ace and re-lief.
her-it-ance shall be, Their in-her-it-ance shall be.

5. Blest are they who thirst and hunger
   After truth and righteousness;
   For, such real, essential virtues
   God will give them to possess.
   All whose soul doth long for grace
   :: Shall these precious gifts embrace. ::

6. Blest are they, who, showing mercy
   Without favor, without fear,
   All mankind in love embracing,
   To the needy ones draw near.
   They who merciful remain
   :: Mercy also shall obtain. ::

7. Blessed are the pure and spotless,
   Who in chastity abide;
   In whose heart the Saviour's likeness
   Shall be truly glorified.
   They shall in yon heav'nly light
   :: See God's countenance so bright. ::

8. Blessed are the peaceful children
   Who in peace live day by day,
   And, unlike the godless sinner,
   Evil works with good repay.
   He who peace and love has taught
   :: Shall be called a child of God. ::

9. Blessed are those who must suffer
   For the sake of righteousness;
   Through such trials God prepares them
   For that home of joy and bliss.
   Those who die in Christ the Lord
   :: Find in heaven their reward. ::

10. Blest are you, when people chide you,
    Hate you, slander scoffingly;
    Lie about you, and deride you: -
    "Yours the Kingdom yet shall be."
    You shall, in your gracious Lord,
    :: Share the prophets' rich reward. ::

11. Blest are all who here reproaches,
    Without blame, and scorn must bear,
    Patient till the end approaches,
    God will then reward them there:
    Crowns of righteousness will there
    :: All the patient sufferers wear. ::

12. But woe to the rich whose fulness
    Is their God and their reward;
    Hence they shall go empty-handed;
    Tears and hunger is their part.
    Woe to those who laugh and scorn;
    :: They shall surely weep and mourn. ::

55. THE HIGH PRIEST

106, 109, 153, 177.

1. Lord Je - sus, praise to Thee as - cend, Thou
2. Through Thy as - cen - sion to the skies We
3. Thy wounds en - a - bled Thee to pass In -
4. Since Christ, our Head, in heav'n doth reign, Then

strong help and foun - da - tion! Thy priest- hood
see the heav - ens op - ened; The way to
to Thy sanc - tu - ar - y; Thou hast at -
shall each of His mem - bers By faith - ful -

great will nev - er end, Nor cease Thy blest sal -
God, the great and wise, Thou hast re - vealed and
tained a life of bliss That shall not change nor
ness ad - mis - sion gain; Each one He will re -

va - tion. Lord, Thou art He who an - swers
spok - en. True faith the con - fid - ence sup -
var - y. Through Thy own might Thou dost pos -
mem - ber. They shall with Him u - nit - ed

pray'r, Re - lieves our fears and ev - 'ry
plies That Thou for us in Par - a -
sess And bring to us the right - eous -
be And in e - ter - nal glo - ry

care, If we in faith draw near Thee.
dise A man - sion hast pre - pared us.
ness That shall en - dure for - ev - er.
see Their glo - ri - fied Re - deem - er.

5. Draw us to Thee, O Lord, we plead!
   May we a heav'nly nature
   In word, in thought, in ev'ry deed
   Adopt as newborn creatures.
   Draw heavenward each longing heart,
   And in Thy kingdom be our part,
   Repose and conversation.

6. What is above, in future we
   Shall seek it unabating;
   All vanity, Lord, teach us flee,
   All sin and evil hating!
   Away, O world, all thy pretense
   Is truly wretched, an offense
   To all those heaven-minded.

7. O treasure, bright with heav'nly ray,
   My heart holds Thy impression!
   O pearl, whose price no world can pay;
   Thou shalt be my possession!
   O gratifying heritage,
   O haven of my pilgrimage,
   Be mine through Jesus' favor!

56. THE COMING OF CHRIST

55, 106, 109, 177.

1. The Lord will come, and He is near To meet His own with glad - ness. O that His vi - sion would ap - pear; Great joy would ban - ish sad - ness. If
2. O, that be - fore Him now the earth And heav - en would be flee - ing, And we the tok - en of the Son, High in the clouds were see - ing, In
3. O Je - sus, come; we wait for Thee With all the true and faith - ful! Do not de - lay, but let us see Thy re - ap - pear - ance grace - ful! We
4. Yes, A - men, come! Thy bride doth call In spir - it and with long - ing, Un til Thy face she may be - hold, And rest up - on Thy bos - om. Yea,

now	to -	day	in	maj -	es -	ty,	We'd
god -	like	maj -	es -	ty	a -	bound!	O,
shall	re -	joice	to	hear	Thee	say;	"Come,
earth	and	heav -	en	doth	re -	sound	With

see	Him	come,	then	sure -	ly	we	Would
that	we'd	hear	the	trump -	et	sound	Of
bless -	ed	Ones"	and	when	we	may	Thus
ech -	o	sweet,	in	true	hearts	found,	A

weep	for	joy	and	glad -		ness!
an -	gels	com -	ing	near -		er!
un -	to	Thee	be	car -		ried.
thous -	and -	fold,	fond	wel -		come.

57. CHRIST, OUR PREDECESSOR
116.

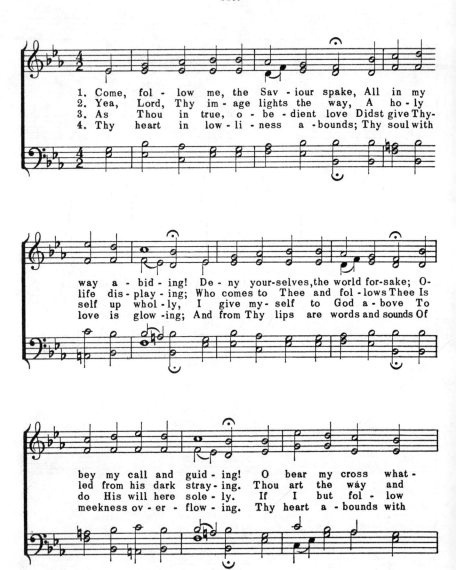

1. Come, fol - low me, the Sav - iour spake, All in my
2. Yea, Lord, Thy im - age lights the way, A ho - ly
3. As Thou in true, o - be - dient love Didst give Thy-
4. Thy heart in low - li - ness a - bounds; Thy soul with

way a - bid - ing! De - ny your-selves, the world for-sake; O-
life dis - play - ing; Who comes to Thee and fol - lows Thee Is
self up whol - ly, I give my - self to God a - bove To
love is glow - ing; And from Thy lips are words and sounds Of

bey my call and guid - ing! O bear my cross what-
led from his dark stray - ing. Thou art the way and
do His will here sole - ly. If I but fol - low
meekness ov - er - flow - ing. Thy heart a - bounds with

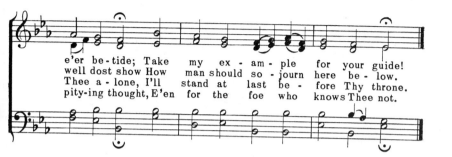

e'er be-tide; Take my ex - am - ple for your guide!
well dost show How man should so - journ here be - low.
Thee a - lone, I'll stand at last be - fore Thy throne.
pity-ing thought, E'en for the foe who knows Thee not.

5. Thou teachest us to shun and flee
What harms our soul's salvation,
Our heart to purify and free
From sin's abomination.
Our Shepherd true Thou art always,
Who seeks what in the desert strays.

6. And if too hot we find the fray,
Thou at our side art ready,
Defending us, to lead the way
At all times firm and steady.
A coward he, who then can pause,
When our brave captain leads the cause.

7. Who loves his life here more than Thee,
Without Thee he shall lose it;
Who consecrates it all to Thee,
In God will introduce it.
Who bears no cross, nor follows hard,
Deserves not Thee nor Thy reward.

8. Then let us follow our dear Lord,
Bearing the cross appointed,
And bravely clinging to His Word,
In suff'ring be undaunted.
He who shall bear the battle's strain,
The crown of life shall there obtain.

58. THE INNER LIFE OF A CHRISTIAN

1. The in-ner-most life of the true Chris-tian
2. In out-ward ap-pear-ance they have no at-
3. Though out-ward-ly they all in Ad-am are
4. In spir-it their birth is of god-ly de-

shin-eth Though out-ward-ly dark-ened by tri-als at
trac-tion, A sight for the an-gels, des-pised by the
broth-ers, Who car-ry his like-ness by na-ture in-
scen-sion, For God by His might-y Word brought them to

hand; What they have re-ceived of the king-dom of heav-en
world; But in their hearts dwelleth a love-ly col-lec-tion
deed; They suf-fer the ill-ness of flesh as all oth-ers;
life; A spark of the flame from the heav-en-ly man-sion

No-one but them-selves can in truth un-der-stand. What
Of treas-ures to garn-ish the crown of the Lord. The
They eat and they drink, as they dai-ly have need; In
Is nour-ished and in their hearts e'er kept a-live. And

no   one per - ceiv - eth, what no   one re - ceiv - eth Hath
won - der of   ag - es, their true heart en - gag - es To
each un - der - tak - ing, in sleep- ing and wak - ing, They
when they are voic - ing their songs of re - joic - ing It

filled and en - light - ened their mind and their spir - it, And
love and a - dore their great King in His bright-ness And
do   as all oth- ers, and noth- ing neg - lect - ing Save
pen - e -trates where the bright an - gels are sing -ing, And

led   them to heav - en - ly hon - or and mer - it.
greet Him at last in their gar - ments of white - ness.
that the world's fol - ly they all are re - ject - ing.
joins with their praise, in e - ter - ni - ty ring - ing.

5. They walk on the earth, but their life is in heaven.
   They are without power, and yet shield the world;
   'Mid turmoil of earth they have peace and are given,
   Though poor and rejected, what they may desire.
   They stand in affliction, yet full of affection;
   Are dead to all outward enjoyment and pleasure,
   They're tasting the fruits of their faith in rich measure.

6. When Jesus, their life, is at last manifested;
   When He shall appear with His banner unfurled;
   Then they will as angels and saints, unmolested,
   Appear as a miracle unto the world.
   They never shall perish, but govern and flourish;
   In crowns and in garments of heavenly merit
   The new earth and heaven forever inherit.

95.

59. ANTICIPATION

60, 61, 194.

1. Chris-tian's life in God is hid - den, But soon the
2. We who here in weakness la - bor The Lord will
3. Thou hast walked the path be - fore us; We fol - low

morn - ing shall be bid - den; The dark of night shall
raise to bliss and fav - or, If but our faith and
Thee, till Thou re-store us Joined through our love and

pass a - way. Oh, when He ap - pears in glad - ness, Our
love are true. En - e - mies will fear and trem - ble, While
faith to Thee. When Thy king-dom is es - tab - lished, Its

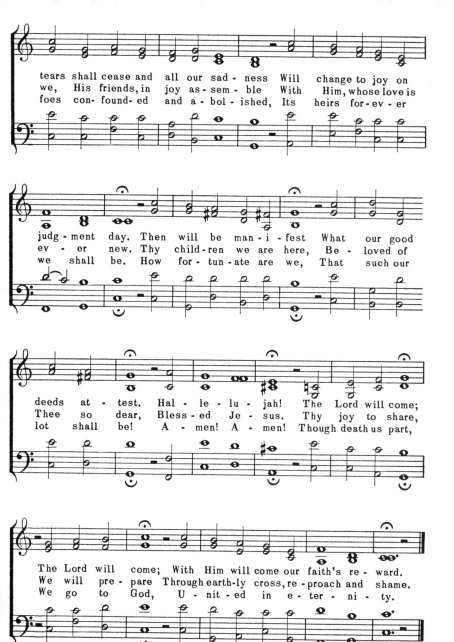

tears shall cease and all our sad - ness Will change to joy on
we, His friends, in joy as - sem - ble With Him, whose love is
foes con - found- ed and a - bol - ished, Its heirs for - ev - er

judg - ment day. Then will be man - i - fest What our good
ev - er new. Thy child - ren we are here, Be - loved of
we shall be. How for - tun - ate are we, That such our

deeds at - test. Hal - le - lu - jah! The Lord will come;
Thee so dear, Bless - ed Je - sus. Thy joy to share,
lot shall be! A - men! A - men! Though death us part,

The Lord will come; With Him will come our faith's re - ward.
We will pre - pare Through earth-ly cross, re - proach and shame.
We go to God, U - nit - ed in e - ter - ni - ty.

97.

60. CHRIST, THE RESURRECTED
59, 61, 194.

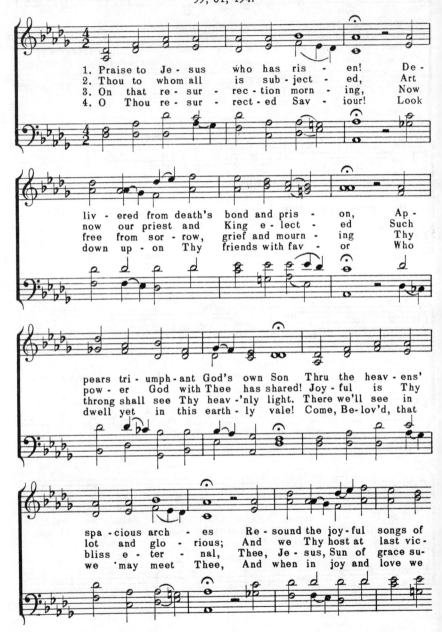

1. Praise to Je - sus who has ris - en! De -
2. Thou to whom all is sub - ject - ed, Art
3. On that re - sur - rec - tion morn - ing, Now
4. O Thou re - sur - rect - ed Sav - iour! Look

liv - ered from death's bond and pris - on, Ap -
now our priest and King e - lect - ed Such
free from sor - row, grief and mourn - ing Thy
down up - on Thy friends with fav - or Who

pears tri - umph - ant God's own Son Thru the heav - ens'
pow - er God with Thee has shared! Joy - ful is Thy
throng shall see Thy heav -'nly light. There we'll see in
dwell yet in this earth - ly vale! Come, Be - lov'd, that

spa - cious arch - es Re - sound the joy - ful songs of
lot and glo - rious; And we Thy host at last vic -
bliss e - ter - nal, Thee, Je - sus, Sun of grace su -
we 'may meet Thee, And when in joy and love we

glad - ness, And peace doth glow a - round God's throne.
to - rious, Shall e - qual glo - ries find pre - pared.
per - nal, Be - hold Thy face. O sac - red sight!
greet Thee, Thy glo - ry un - to us re - veal!

Praise Him Who ev - er lives, Who life and com - fort
Up - on Thy al - tar, Lord, Thy blood for all was
For that new Fa - ther - land Our bod - ies by Thy
O bless - ed shall all be Who are by faith in

gives, Christ the Sav - iour, And to our God! Death's dark a-
poured For re - mis - sion; In pure-ness we For - ev - er
hand Shall be trans-formed; Then we'll be free. Re -deemed by
Thee Res - ur - rect - ed. All who from death To life are

bode Is ban - ished by His con - q'ring rod.
free. Thy ho - ly priest-hood now shall be.
Thee In whom all things re - newed shall be.
brought, Sus - tain their faith, O Son of God!

61. ALL DEVOTED TO ONE

59, 60, 194.

1. One there is to whom we're cleav - ing, Who for us bit - ter death re - ceiv - ing, Has pur - chased us with His own blood. Now our bod - y, heart, af - fec - tion Are Thine, O man of great af - flic - tion, And

2. Not of us is Thy e - lec - tion; Our num - ber is Thy own se - lec - tion Through Thy e - ter - nal plan of grace. All our strength is naught but weak - ness, But he who comes to Thee in meek - ness Shall

3. Sav - iour, all Thy works so ho - ly Didst Thou be - gin so meek and low - ly, And we are weak as Thou dost see. But we know Thou wilt de - fend us; The light of Thine eyes Thou wilt lend us; Our

in Thy love re - pose is good. Ac - cept us as Thine
help and strength from Thee em - brace. Let not our own will
trust in Thy great strength shall be. The mus-tard seed so

own. Pre- pare for Thy re - nown All Thy chil - dren.
reign: Our pov - er - ty is gain For Thy king - dom;
small At length will grow with - al Great and might - y,

O do not hide Thy grace - ful light which
The poor and weak Thy ref - uge seek And
Since Thou, O Lord, Its keep - er art To

shines from Thy sweet face so bright.
bear re - proach, con - tempt and shame.
whom its care God doth im - part.

62. THE FRUIT OF THE SPIRIT

211.

1. The light and strength of faith, Lord, give me, Where-
2. My hope in Thee will nev - er van - ish; O
3. Thy suf - f'ring leads me to sub - mis - sion, And
4. If I must tar - ry here a sea - son, I

by the Spir - it's fruit is shown; A fruit- ful branch, O
let Thy cross its an - chor be, And may by it all
to the low - li - ness of heart! Who seeks Thee must a -
live be - cause it pleas-eth Thee; So, too, when death shall

Sav - iour, make me, Which from the one true vine is
fear be ban - ished; My com -fort I shall find in
void pride's great - ness; The proud and vain are far a -
call, Thy rea - son Shall cause my soul con - tent to

grown! Thou art my rock and firm foun - da - tion, The
Thee! The world in van - i - ty a - bid - eth, But
part From Thy hu - mil - i - ty and meek-ness; Yet
be. O let my life in Thee be hid - den; Thy

Sav - iour who has brought sal - va - tion.   I   build   my
my   heart, Lord, in   Thee con - fid - eth,   Thou fount   of
he   who   knows his   need and weak-ness   Thou from   the
death en - cour - age   me when bid - den   To   leave this

faith on   Thy word   true! When   I   must stand a - mid temp-
light, and grace un - told. I'll   e'er em - brace Thee with af -
dust dost   el - e - vate. En - grave Thy like - ness on   my
vale of   mis - e - ry.   I   bow my   will   to Thine, dear

ta - tion; Let me not miss Thy min - is - tra -
fec - tion. Thou wilt not leave me   in   af - flic -
spir - it, That I   Thy hum - ble - ness in - her -
Sav - iour; Up - on this truth I   pon - der ev -

tion; Thy cov - 'nant Lord, in   me   re - new.
tion, For Thy love   nev - er wax - eth cold.
it   And hast - en   on   to heav - en's gate.
er: Naught, naught shall break our u - ni - ty.

103.

63. THE MAGNET
64.

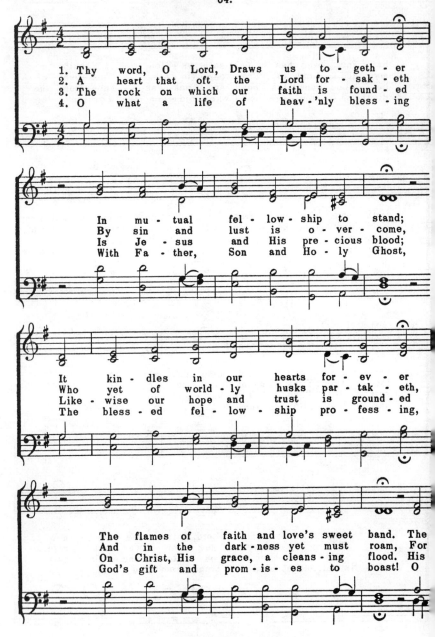

1. Thy word, O Lord, Draws us to-geth-er
2. A heart that oft the Lord for-sak-eth
3. The rock on which our faith is found-ed
4. O what a life of heav-'nly bless-ing

In mu-tual fel-low-ship to stand;
By sin and lust is o-ver-come,
Is Je-sus and His pre-cious blood;
With Fa-ther, Son and Ho-ly Ghost,

It kin-dles in our hearts for-ev-er
Who yet of world-ly husks par-tak-eth,
Like-wise our hope and trust is ground-ed
The bless-ed fel-low-ship pro-fess-ing,

The flames of faith and love's sweet band. The
And in the dark-ness yet must roam, For
On Christ, His grace, a cleans-ing flood. His
God's gift and prom-is-es to boast! O

word   of   grace,   which   brought sal - va - tion
such   no   bless - ings   are   pro - vid - ed;
Word   the   pre - cept   we   ac - know - ledge,
here   are   flames of   sweet   af - fec - tion;

And   fel - low - ship   with Thy great throng,
But   all   who   on   the Lord be - lieve
Our   dai - ly   du - ty from the Lord,
God   giv - eth   to   His ho - ly throng

Who   praise the   Lamb   with harp and   song, Ex -
In   Je - sus   faith   and life re - ceive, Can
This   is   what   we   with one ac - cord   Call
The   ful - ness   of   His bless - ing strong. Here

tends   to   all   its   in - vi - ta - tion.
with   His   bod - y be   u - nit - ed.
fel - low - ship and   real   com - mun - ion.
dwell - eth God in   love's   per - fec - tion.

5. The Father doth caress His children,
   Inspiring trust and faithfulness;
   The Son in love adorns the sinner
   With His eternal righteousness;
   With unction comes the Holy Spirit,
   Anointing us with joy and peace.
   Our hearts in sweet repose increase,
   And godly power we inherit.

105.

64. FOLLOWING JESUS

63.

1. With all our heart, O Lord, we praise Thee,
That Thou up-on this earth-ly sphere Hath chos-en
Thee a ho-ly peo-ple, To ho-nor and
ex-alt Thee here. Un-to this ho-ly con-gre-

2. O God, Thou hast from man-y na-tions
And man-y tongues Thy bod-y called, In which resound praise and ob-la-tions, And where Thy word
is spread a-broad. Thou giv-est through Thy blood, dear

3. On truth this sa-cred house is build-ed.
The firm and might-y Word of God; By an-gels
it is ev-er shield-ed; His light and spirit is its rod. The mem-bers' life is love in

4. In char-i-ty the mem-bers la-bor,
They go with Je-sus hand in hand; In love with
broth-er and with neigh-bor, As one they all
u-nit-ed stand. Re-main-ing ev-er true and

ga - tion Full man - y mor - tals Thou dost
Sav- iour, Un - to the pris -'ners lib - er -
Je - sus, Firm faith their on - ly source of
low - ly, They strive for peace, though men up -

lead, To be their Sav - iour and their
ty, In - vit - est in Thy house to
strength Through which they con - quer all at
braid; In tri - als they are un - dis -

head, And of - fer sin - ful men sal - va - tion.
be, All who in faith in Thee find fa - vor.
length; True hope, their com -fort, nev - er ceas - es.
mayed, De - vot - ed to their Sav - iour whol - ly.

5. They gladly bear the cross of Jesus,
   Fear not its burden or distress;
   Beneath it, pride and envy ceases,
   It leaves no time for idleness.
   Although at times they feel discouraged,
   They look upon their pilgrim way
   To Christ, their Saviour, and their stay,
   And bear their load, renewed with courage.

6. Thus gladly they pursue their journey,
   Serene and joyful day by day;
   They stand in Jesus' care and keeping,
   Refreshed by His word on their way.
   Then flow, ye tears, though oft in sadness,
   Yet fruits of sweetness shall arise,
   For out of love's sweet paradise
   Flows comfort, causing tears of gladness.

65. ONE THING IS NEEDFUL

1. One thing's need - ful! Then, Lord Je - sus, Keep this one thing in my mind; All be - sides, though first it please us, Soon a griev - ous yoke we find, Be - neath which the heart is still fret - ting and

2. Wilt thou find this one thing need - ful? Seek not 'mid cre - at - ed things; What is earth - ly leave be - hind thee; O - ver na - ture stretch thy wings. For where God and man both in one are u -

3. Thus my long - ings, heav'n - ward tend - ing, Je - sus, rest a - lone on Thee; Help me, thus on Thee de - pend - ing; Sav - iour, come and dwell with me! Al - though all the world should for - sake and for -

4. Wis - dom's high - est, no - blest treas - ure, Je - sus, is con - cealed in Thee! Grant that this may still the meas - ure Of my will and ac - tion be. Hu - mil - i - ty there and sim - pli - ci - ty

striv - ing, No true, last - ing hap - pi - ness
nit - ed, With God's per - fect ful - ness the
get Thee, In love I will fol - low Thee,
reign - eth And heav - en - ly know -ledge and

ev - er de - riv - ing; The gain of this
heart is de - light - ed; There, there is the
nev - er to quit Thee, Lord Je - sus, both
wis - dom ob - tain - eth; O, if I of

one thing all loss can re - quite, And
worth - i - est por - tion and best, My
spir - it and life is Thy word. Where
Christ have this know - ledge di - vine, The

teach me in all things to find true de - light.
One and my All and my joy and my rest.
is there a joy which Thou dost not af - ford?
ful - ness of heav - en - ly wis - dom is mine.

66. THE SCHOOL OF THE CROSS
67, 158, 179.

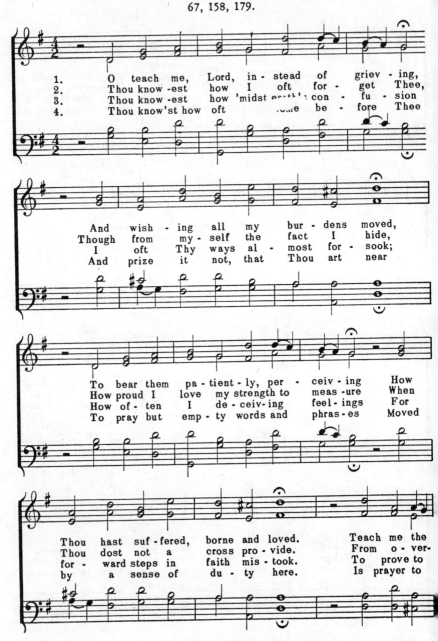

1. O teach me, Lord, in-stead of griev-ing,
2. Thou know-est how I oft for-get Thee,
3. Thou know-est how 'midst earth's con-fu-sion
4. Thou know'st how oft come be-fore Thee

And wish-ing all my bur-dens moved,
Though from my-self the fact I hide,
I oft Thy ways al-most for-sook;
And prize it not, that Thou art near

To bear them pa-tient-ly, per-ceiv-ing How
How proud I love my strength to meas-ure When
How of-ten I de-ceiv-ing feel-ings For
To pray but emp-ty words and phras-es Moved

Thou hast suf-fered, borne and loved. Teach me the
Thou dost not a cross pro-vide. From o-ver-
for-ward steps in faith mis-took. To prove to
by a sense of du-ty here. Is prayer to

art of keep-ing si-lent, That calm, con-tent-ed
con-fi-dence to save me, To show me plain-ly
me my in-ward dam-age, That I was far from
bring to me a bless-ing? Am I to feel that

I re-main; Cross bear-er, Thee, I would re-
what I am, Thou must pro-vide a cross to
Thee a-stray, Hast Thou a cross up-on me
Thou dost hear? A cross must on my soul be

sem-ble, O change to love my bitter-est pain!
shame me, For on-ly thus my pride shall wane.
lad-en, Up-on a dark and thorn-y way.
press-ing; Thou to my brok-en heart art near.

5. O Lord, Thou knowest every secret,
Thou seest, hearest, knowest all.
My sighs and groans, although yet sleeping,
Thou in advance by name dost call.
O grant that Thou, Lord, and Thy purpose
My foremost thought in life may be;
Yea, in Thy silence take and hide me,
Or I shall ne'er from sin be free.

6. Lord, in Thy presence naught is lacking,
No wish denied, but all is right;
Transformed to love is all my burden,
The yoke is eased, the load seems light.
For in Thy stillness nothing threatens
The soul amidst earth's woe and pain.
To me Thy grace shall be sufficient,
The cross shall be my greatest gain.

7. No more complaining, no more grieving,
But grateful praise shall be my lot;
Although chastised, amid oppression,
Thy love and grace forsake me not.
The paths that seem to us the darkest
Are blessings rich, although disguised;
All things for good shall work together
To them that love Thee, Jesus Christ.

111.

67. GOD'S POWER REVEALED IN THE CLOUDS

66, 158, 179.

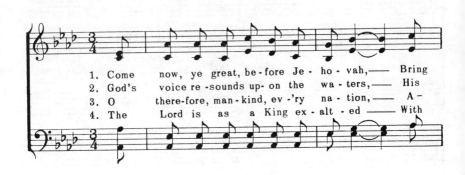

1. Come now, ye great, be-fore Je-ho-vah,—— Bring
2. God's voice re-sounds up-on the wa-ters,—— His
3. O there-fore, man-kind, ev-'ry na-tion,—— A-
4. The Lord is as a King ex-alt-ed —— With

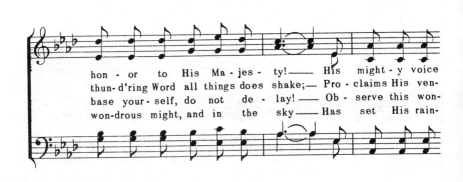

hon-or to His Ma-jes-ty!—— His might-y voice
thun-d'ring Word all things does shake;—— Pro-claims His ven-
base your-self, do not de-lay! —— Ob-serve this won-
won-drous might, and in the sky—— Has set His rain-

is heard with thun-der; Sink down in-to the dust and
geance to His hat-ers And caus-es earth and rocks to
drous in-di-ca-tion That soon will come a judg-ment
bow as a tok-en That grace and mer-cy now is

112.

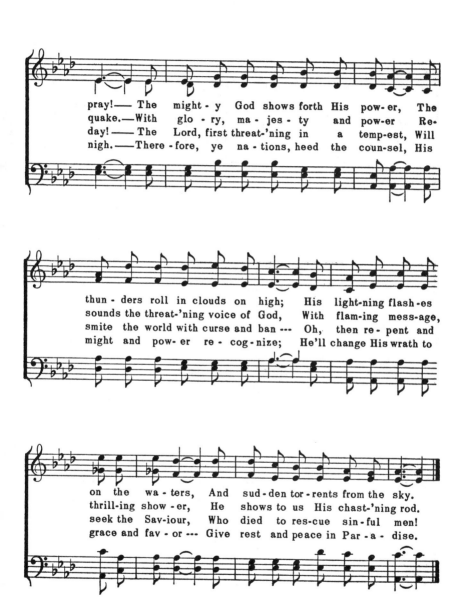

pray!— The might-y God shows forth His pow-er, The
quake.—With glo-ry, ma-jes-ty and pow-er Re-
day! — The Lord, first threat-'ning in a temp-est, Will
nigh. —There-fore, ye na-tions, heed the coun-sel, His

thun-ders roll in clouds on high; His light-ning flash-es
sounds the threat-'ning voice of God, With flam-ing mess-age,
smite the world with curse and ban --- Oh, then re-pent and
might and pow-er re-cog-nize; He'll change His wrath to

on the wa-ters, And sud-den tor-rents from the sky.
thrill-ing show-er, He shows to us His chast-'ning rod.
seek the Sav-iour, Who died to res-cue sin-ful men!
grace and fav-or --- Give rest and peace in Par-a-dise.

113.

68. WALKING WITH GOD
69.

1. God is ev - er pres - ent! Let us now a -
2. O maj - es - tic Be - ing, Prais - es now we
3. We re - nounce with pleas - ure And in full - est
4. Make us tru - ly hum - ble, From the world re -

dore Him, And in rev -'rence come be - fore Him!
of - fer And our will - ing serv - ice prof - fer!
meas - ure, Ev -'ry earth - ly joy and treas - ure.
tir - ed, Gen - tle, mild, with peace in - spir - ed!

"Ho - ly, ho - ly, ho - ly!" An - gel bands are
Might we as the an - gels Stand in sac - red
Life and soul and bod - y, We in con - se -
As the ten - der flow - er Will - ing - ly un -

114.

sing - ing,   And   in - ces - sant   prais - es   bring -
near - ness   And   be - hold   Thy   face   in   clear -
cra - tion   Give   to   Thee,   a   full   pos - ses -
fold - eth,   To   the   sun - light   gent - ly   yield -

ing!   Bow   Thine   ear,   Lord,   and   hear,   As   we
ness!   Grant   that   we,   Day   by   day,   Un - to
sion.   Thee   a - lone   Will   we   own   As   our
eth,   May   we   be   Glad   and   free,   Heav'n- ly

in   sub - mis - sion   Of - fer   our   ob - la - tion!
Thee   be   pleas - ing   And   in   love   in - creas - ing!
God   and   Fa - ther,   Wor - ship -ping   no   oth - er.
light   re - ceiv - ing,   Thou   Thy   work   a -chiev - ing.

5. Come, Lord, dwell within us,
As on earth we tarry;
Let us be Thy sanctuary!
Let Thy holy presence
Fill us with Thy glory;
Love and praise shall tell the story!
May our heart Ne'er depart
From a true devotion,
For Thou art our portion.

69. BROTHERLY LOVE
68.

1. En - ter ye Love's King - dom, All God's own pos - ses - sion,
2. Yield in true sub - mis - sion And in love be fer - vent,
3. If the Sav - iour's King - dom Is to grow and flour - ish
4. Ab - ba, lov - ing Fa - ther, Son and Ho - ly Spir - it,

Who in Christ have found sal - va - tion. Learn from your Re -
Each to be the oth - er's serv - ant; Love is void of
With God's rich - est bless - ings nour - ished, May our love be
Heal each fault and each de - mer - it. False con - ceit and

deem - er, Each to love his broth - er And in love to
en - vy, Full of kind for - bear - ance And un - lim - it -
burn - ing, And God's love re - turn - ing; Je - sus, bless our
an - ger, Self - es - teem and mal - ice Mort - i - fy through

serve each oth - er! Heed with care; Glad - ly bear
ed en - dur - ance, Love in - crease! Nev - er cease
ar - dent yearn - ing! Though our foes Should op - pose,
Thy pure mo - tives! We de - ride Sa - tan's might,

All who seek His fa - vor, Though they faint and wa - ver.
Love's sweet flame to cher - ish, Lest it wane and per - ish!
If we stand u - nit - ed, They shall be re - quit - ed.
As 'round Thee we gath - er, Call - ing Thee our Fa - ther.

116.

70. LOVE AND LOVING

71.

1. O, the fount of truth and grace Found in lov-
2. With-out love the bur-den great On our shoul-
3. Those who un - to Christ the Lord Do sur -ren-
4. Thus with grace our soul and mind Is in -spir-

ing, If with - in the bonds of peace, We are
der Would our weak and fee - ble state Crush and
der All their mind and thought and word In love
ed; In our la - bor joy we find As de -

liv - ing! With - out love we can - not live;
smoul - der; But in love it grow - eth light,
ten - der Shall, by faith and love im - pelled,
sir - ed, Meet - ing kin - dred mind - ed souls

This is truth — ful, Love should make life fruit - ful.
And we of - fer Still to toil and suf - fer.
Bold - ly jour - ney On the nar - row path - way.
Is re - viv - ing, Hum- bling and en - liv - 'ning.

117.

70.

1. Joy - ful songs of praise we bring Thee, our Sav -
2. God, by His own gift of grace Did re - lieve
3. Saints and an - gels here and there Sing Thy prais -
4. God's true chil - dren, heav - en's guests, All ye church -

iour! Of Thy good - ness we will sing
us, And our sin - ful - ness ef - face
es For this new - born sin - ner's share
es; Live hence - forth in right - eous - ness,

And Thy fa - vors! Heart and mind in
Which did grieve us. Je - sus by His
In Thy prom - ise; God gives him e -
As His pur - chase! Had not God re -

ar - dor fill With Thy prais - es,
Fa - ther's will, Made a - tone - ment,
ter - nal life! We em - brace him
vealed His love Us to cher - ish,

For our hope in Je - sus.
Saved from death and tor - ment.
And in love en - fold him.
We in death would per - ish.

5. May our hearts and souls unite
   In affection!
   May our faith be glowing bright,
   And correction
   Come unto us from the fount
   Of the Spirit
   We from Christ inherit.

6. May each newborn child to Him
   Be devoted;
   Be each one to Christ the King
   Consecrated!
   From Him we received the gift.
   Thanks and praises
   We return, Lord Jesus!

7. Creatures new, Lord, we are Thine,
   Thy possession.
   That men share Thy life divine,
   Was Thy mission.
   He who bows at Babel's shrine,
   Homage giving,
   No new life is living.

8. May the world in us perceive
   Love's true fervor,
   With which Jesus' members cleave
   To each other.
   All the brethren who believe,
   Daily striving,
   Christlike to be living!

72. PURE AND HOLY LOVE
18, 47, 48, 49.

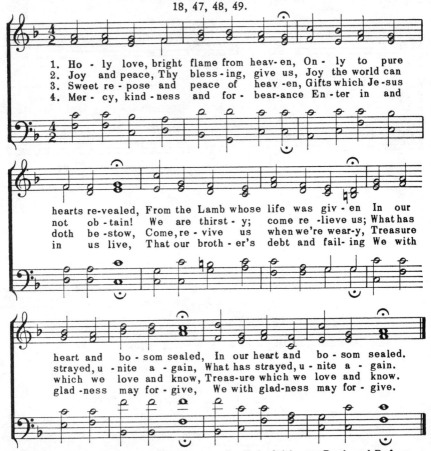

1. Ho-ly love, bright flame from heav-en, On-ly to pure hearts re-vealed, From the Lamb whose life was giv-en In our heart and bo-som sealed, In our heart and bo-som sealed.

2. Joy and peace, Thy bless-ing, give us, Joy the world can not ob-tain! We are thirst-y; come re-lieve us; What has strayed, u-nite a-gain, What has strayed, u-nite a-gain.

3. Sweet re-pose and peace of heav-en, Gifts which Je-sus doth be-stow, Come, re-vive us when we're wear-y, Treasure which we love and know, Treas-ure which we love and know.

4. Mer-cy, kind-ness and for-bear-ance En-ter in and in us live, That our broth-er's debt and fail-ing We with glad-ness may for-give, We with glad-ness may for-give.

5. Meekness, friendship, truth's attire,
Likeness after God's own will,
May both friend and foe desire
What our soul and spirit fills.
What our soul and spirit fills.

6. Goodness, kindness, love most tender,
Do Thy helping hand extend;
Thy protection do Thou render
And Thy foe in love defend,
And Thy foe in love defend.

7. Holy faith, our Rock and Refuge,
Give us courage to be true
And to fight a valiant conflict,
Till the conq'ring host we view,
Till the conq'ring host we view.

8. Tranquil silence, gentle whisp'ring,
Glory, where Jehovah reigns,
Show us, when the scorners mock us,
Thy reward for vict'ries gained,
Thy reward for vict'ries gained.

9. Love of Jesus, love of brethren,
Heal our souls from ev'ry smart!
Grant to us Thy purest motives
And a pure, unspotted heart,
And a pure, unspotted heart.

73. THE FLAME OF JESUS' LOVE
171.

1. O that Thy ar - dent flames were kin - dled, Un- fath - om -
2. Al - read - y it doth burn with bright-ness; See here and
3. And still this heav'n - ly spark ig - nit - eth So man - y
4. All self - es - teem and pride de - stroy - ing, Re-moves im-

a - ble depth of love! May all the u - ni - verse ac -
there in west and east, To Thee the Lamb as ran - som
cold and life - less hearts; It fills the long- ing soul with
pure and guil - ty stain; The streams of Je - sus' love en-

know - ledge That Thou art King and Lord a - bove.
of - fered, A glo - rious pen - te - cost - al feast.
glad - ness And heals from sin and Sa - tan's darts.
joy - ing, By which we God's rich grace ob - tain.

5. Thou never ceasing, living fountain,
   Almighty witness, ever true,
   Thy grace and love may not be wasted,
   Inflame our hearts with love anew!

6. O link together what has scattered,
   Complete Thy temple! keep Thy vows!
   Illuminate with sacred brightness
   The holy church, Thy Father's house!

7. Revive, inflame, redeem, enlighten
   Ere long all peoples through Thy word;
   Appear to ev'ry tribe and nation
   As Saviour, Prince of Peace, and Lord!

8. Then from the lips of countless numbers
   The songs of Jubilee will flow;
   Thy fame shall sound from ev'ry region
   And all the ransomed saints will glow.

74. GOD'S DIVINE COMPASSION

1. I rev - 'rence love's great pow'r un - end - ing,
2. How dost Thou show'r on me Thy fa - vor!
3. I feel that with - out Thee I per - ish,
4. My heart and life are Thine for - ev - er;

Which in Christ Je - sus is re - vealed; To Grace, it-
How doth Thy Spir - it yearn for me! Drawn gent-ly
I feel that I am all Thine own; No earth - ly
O Sav - iour, Thou my on - ly prize! Thy sav - ing

self so free - ly spend-ing To love a worm like
on by love's sweet sa - vor, I come to yield my
treas - ure may I cher - ish; My life is fixed on
blood, which fail - eth nev - er, Was shed that God - ward

me,   I   yield.   I'll sink all thought of self ef -
all   to   Thee;   As   Thou, en - dear - ing love dost
Thee a - lone.   Sweet rest and joy Thou e'er pro -
I   might   rise.   To Thee, our dire, deep fall's sal -

fac - ing   In - to love's o - cean, all em - brac - ing.
hold me,   So in   my   heart I   will en - fold Thee.
vid - est;   Glad - ly I   fol - low where Thou guid - est.
va - tion,   Of heart, of all,   I   make o - bla - tion.

5. I loved and lived in bondage weary,
   When for myself I lived apart.
   I knew Thee not through years so dreary,
   Yet Thou sought'st me with loving heart.
   O, could each sinner know this blessing,
   Thine would he be, his love confessing.

6. Now praise we all the name of Jesus,
   Bright fountain whence love's joy proceeds,
   The stream which here from sin's stain frees us
   And yonder God's blest legions feeds.
   They bend the knee, Thy praise repeating;
   We fold our hands, Thy grace entreating.

7. O Jesus, may Thy name eternal
   Deep in our souls its impress leave!
   May we of Thy sweet love supernal
   In heart and mind the stamp receive!
   Let all our words, let each endeavor,
   Jesus, naught else, proclaim forever!

123.

75. GIVE THANKS UNTO THE FATHER

25, 220, 221, 227.

1. God of un - lim - it - ed com - pas - sion,
2. For Thy most won - der - ful re - demp - tion,
3. For Thy most ho - ly, truth - ful Spir - it
4. For sol - ace in Thy prom - ise giv - en

Thou nev - er - end - ing fount of love!
For the a - tone - ment of our wrong,
By which our spir - it's life is shown,
That Thy rich grace will nev - er end;

With count-less hosts in meek sub - mis - sion
For Thy most gra - cious in - vi - ta - tion
For light and pow - er we in - her - it
When moun-tains fall and rocks are riv - en

We praise Thee now, O Lord a - bove,
And for Thy Word with prom - ise strong.
As Thy al - might - y work is known,
Thy cov -'nant and Thy truth shall stand.

For grace and pa - tience Thou hast shown
Yea, for the com - fort of Thy Word
For the as - sur - ance there we find
Tho' earth and heav - en sink and fall,

Ere this cre - at - ed world was known.
Our hearts bring thanks to Thee, O Lord.
Brings praise our new - born heart and mind.
Yet God shall live, faith - ful to all.

5. Yea, lips and heart shall ever praise Thee,
Yet heart and lips shall ever plead:
Let not my faith grow weak or waver,
But build me on this ground indeed;
On Thy support I will depend
In faith to stand until life's end.

6. Let me in love live pure and holy
And keep me without spot or stain;
Grant that my heart be meek and lowly,
And may no idle joy or pain
E'er sever me from Thy great love,
Until I find Thy rest above.

7. No death nor sorrow, fear nor suff'ring,
All that this world and hell include,
Shall ever part me from my Saviour
Nor from His love and brotherhood.
I trust the God of Faith and truth
With saints above my heart to soothe.

76. BROTHERLY LOVE
75, 145, 220, 221.

1. Where - ev - er, Lord, true love is wan - ing,
2. O this con - fes - sion, Lord, I bring Thee,
3. En - fold us with Thy lov - ing mer - cy;
4. Love's first fruits, Lord, do ev - er nour - ish,

O in - ter - vene ere 'tis too late; And may Thy
In truth and deed it must be told That if the
O ho - ly Lord, wake us from sleep, That we by
For they are pure, sin - cere and true! They cause all

grace ef - fect new ar - dor, Thy Spir - it, Lord, new
flame of love has van - ished, The heart be - comes both
Thy good Spir - it's guid - ance May on - ward tread the
self - ish - ness to per - ish, All ev - il in our

love cre - ate! For if the flame of love should
void and cold. God's love will con - quer all at
path - way steep; That for per - fec - tion we may
hearts sub - due; Love is the God - like qual - i -

126.

die, The light of faith ex -tinct would lie.——— The
length; It gives His chil-dren life and strength.— It
strive, The bless-ed - ness of love re - vive!——— The
ty In which His chil-dren we may be,——— In

light of faith ex - tinct would lie.
gives His chil - dren life and strength.
bless - ed - ness of love re - vive!
which His chil - dren we may be.

Lo, where the love of God has vanished,
The holiness of life is lost;
The love of self has not been banished
And love no more can cover faults;
Here peace with God will fade away
And wantonness soon brings dismay.

True love doth fellowship desire,
It seeks a faithful brother-heart;
True solace here we can acquire,
Where hand in hand and heart in heart
In mutual harmony are bound.
And Christ's love has a dwelling found.

This charity is friendly, sparing:
It looks for brotherly accord,
Is ever patient and forbearing
And seeks not honor or reward;
Is clothed in sweet humility,
From ev'ry taint of evil free.

8. This charity is soon entreated;
Is not insistent on its right,
Is never proud or self-conceited
But finds enjoyment in the light
Of truth, and righteousness, and peace.
True charity shall never cease.

9. True charity no ill is seeking,
Is ready to give others aid;
And if the world is vengeance wreaking,
It trusts in God all unafraid,
Retaining still its confidence
That God will be a sure defense.

10. True love by God has been selected,
Where it is found, there dwelleth He;
In all who are with God connected
Love floweth as within a sea;
Where real and true love holdeth sway,
A child of God is found alway.

77. JESUS, COME, O COME TO ME

132, 133, 181.

1. Je - sus, come, O come to me, Lord, I pray, a - bide with me. Come, Thou art my soul's de - light, And with me do Thou a - bide.
2. Thou - sand times I long for Thee; Noth - ing else can com - fort me; Thou - sand times I cry to Thee; Je - sus, Je - sus, come to me.
3. Pleas - ures on this earth a - bound, Yet my heart no joy has found. But Thy pres-ence, Lord, to me Shall my joy for - ev - er be.
4. To no oth - er be it told That I would my heart un - fold; On - ly Thou may en - ter in, On - ly Thou may reign with - in.

5. Only Thou, O Son of God,
Will I call my crown, my lot;
Thou O Lamb, didst die for me;
Thou my bridegroom e'er shalt be.

78. FAITH, HOPE, AND LOVE

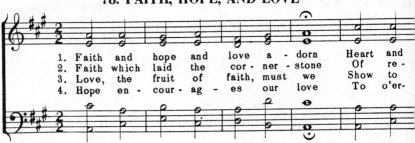

1. Faith and hope and love a - dorn Heart and
2. Faith which laid the cor - ner - stone Of re -
3. Love, the fruit of faith, must we Show to
4. Hope en - cour - ag - es our love To o'er-

life of all true Chris - tians; With these must each
demp-tion's true foun - da - tion, Looks to Je - sus
God and to our neigh - bor; Yield to dis - ci -
come all trib - u - la - tion And will in the

child of God Be en - dowed in full sub -
Christ a - lone, Makes with heart and lips con -
pline each day, Will - ing for the Lord to
deep - est flood An - chor on the firm foun-

mis - sion. All who wish to serve God tru -
fes - sion Of His Spir - it's faith - ful train-
la - bor. No af - flic - tion e'er can sev -
da - tion. What we here en - dure with sad-

ly Must show forth these vir - tues ful - ly.
ing, Bears the cross with - out com - plain - ing.
er Us from Je - sus Christ for - ev - er.
ness, Hope will change to joy and glad - ness.

O preserve this faith in me,
Gracious Lord, in Thy good pleasure;
Shame all those who mightily
Seek to rob me of this treasure;
Let the bruised reed not be broken,
Nor be quenched the flax, still smoking!

May my charity be pure
Not a sham or pretense merely,
O bestow Thy power sure,
That my love may shine out clearly;
Help me love Thee, heavenly Father,
And in Thee, my every brother.

7. Set my hope on solid ground;
Strengthen it in every trial;
May it flourish and abound,
And in danger shun denial.
Let it see past heaven's portal
And find rest in things immortal.

8. Faith and hope will pass away
When believing ends in seeing;
Then our love will enter in,
Where it first came into being.
There my love in endless action
Shall attain sublime perfection.

129.

79. THE UNION OF HEARTS

12, 13, 42, 45.

1 When pure and up-right hearts, By flames of
2. Then shall this vale of tears On earth be-
3. This un-ion of our hearts Shall stand through
4. This God-made un-ion then Shall nev-er

love ig-nit-ed, Are by the bond of faith
come an E-den When joined in spir-it we
grace in Je-sus; We walk the path of life,
more be brok-en, Where faith and love have been

More firm-ly yet u-nit-ed, The
In prayer look up to heav-en, Then
While cheer and trust in-creas-es. Where
The ho-ly cov-'nant's tok-en Where

light of hope beams forth In ra-diance
bear we joy-ful-ly This earth-ly
God in truth a-bides, Where two join
God the seal does give, The hope shall

far	and	nigh,	In -	vites	us	to	par -
toil	and	care;	We	put	our	trust	in
hand	and	heart,	We	find	a	three - fold
e'er	re -	main,	Though	part - ing	be	our

take	The	bless - ings	from	on	high.
God	And	all	com - plaints	for - bear.
cord,	Not	light - ly	rent	a - part.
lot,	To	meet	in	heav'n	a - gain.

5. And then, what blissful joy
   Will bind such hearts together,
   When after parting's grief
   They meet again in heaven,
   Who through this earthly vale
   Did journey hand in hand,
   Joined in the bond of grace
   By love's most sacred band!

6. This covenant shall then
   Endure and stand forever;
   There neither grief nor pain
   Shall come to part or sever.
   There God shall e'er abide
   With us our truest friend,
   Our hearts in Him unite
   Forever, without end.

131.

80. LOVE BEGETS LOVE
53, 81, 183, 249.

1. Love, who fash - ioned me, the like - ness Of Thy
2. Love, by which I was se - lect - ed Ere I
3. Love, which for my sin did suf - fer And which
4. Love, which o - ver - came and con - quered My per -

God - head here to bear Me from fall and from trans -
saw the light of day; Love, whose good - ness was re -
died, that I might live; Love, which grace to all does
verse and way - ward heart; Love, by which I'm bound and

gres - sion Didst re - store with ten - der care: Love, I
flect - ed In man's like - ness and ar - ray; Love, I
of - fer And e - ter - nal peace does give; Love, I
an - chored That from Thee I would not part; Love, I

give my - self to Thee, Thine to be e - ter - nal - ly.
give my - self to Thee, Thine to be e - ter - nal - ly.
give my - self to Thee, Thine to be e - ter - nal - ly.
give my - self to Thee, Thine to be e - ter - nal - ly.

5. Love, that ever shall continue
Step by step doth gently lead;
Love, that sayeth: "Peace be with you,"
And for me doth intercede;
Love, I give myself to Thee,
Thine to be eternally.

81. THE HOUR OF PRAYER
53, 80, 82, 183.

1. It is here, the pre - cious mom - ent Which u - nites our
2. Tho' we are but fee - ble chil - dren, Cour-age we through
3. Not a - lone for self we're plead - ing As we bow be -
4. "Great,"Thou saidst it, "is the har - vest!" Lord,more reap-ers

hearts in prayer, When the peo - ple of God's cov - 'nant
grace re - ceive Thou didst lib - er - ate the sin - ners,
fore Thy throne; While for all we're in - ter - ced - ing,
then a - rouse! Gath- er what the foe has scat-tered,

'Round the throne of grace ap - pear. Hear, O Lord, our
All who in Thy blood be - lieve. All who hum - bly
Thy re - deem -ing grace make known! Man - y, Lord, Thou
Lord, a -gain in - to Thy house! O, may soon this

hum - ble prayer, Un - to us Thy bless - ings share!
seek Thy face There will find a - bun - dant grace.
art a - ware, Lan -guish yet in Sa - tan's snare.
earth so wide Be a tem - ple of Thy light!

5. Lord, Thy kingdom's humble servants
With new grace and zeal endue!
Wake the lifeless; make them fervent;
Consecrate Thy house anew!
Gather, Shepherd, true and great,
Far and near all who have strayed.

133.

82. HAPPINESS OF THE GODLY

53, 80, 81, 183.

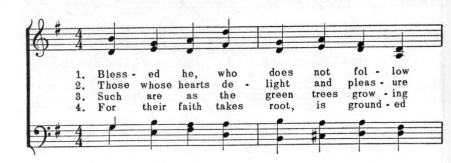

1. Bless - ed he, who does not fol - low
2. Those whose hearts de - light and pleas - ure
3. Such are as the green trees grow - ing
4. For their faith takes root, is ground - ed

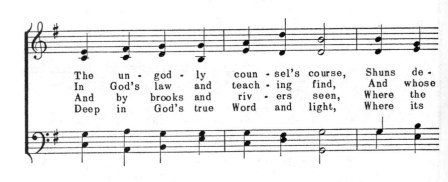

The un - god - ly coun - sel's course, Shuns de -
In God's law and teach - ing find, And whose
And by brooks and riv - ers seen, Where the
Deep in God's true Word and light, Where its

ceit - ful thoughts and ac - tions And the way of
souls find joy and pas - ture In His ways and
fruits are nev - er tar - dy And whose leaves are
life's sup - port is found - ed And love's flame be -

sin ig - nores;	Who the mock - ers' horde does spurn
mer - cies kind;	All such lives a true light show,
ev - er green,	Where the sun - rays and the heat
comes more bright,	Where their hope does bloom and grow

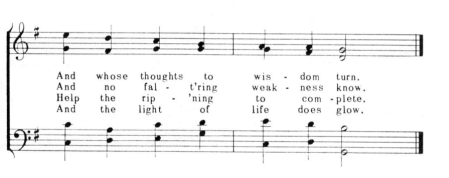

And whose thoughts to	wis - dom turn.
And no fal - t'ring	weak - ness know.
Help the rip - 'ning	to com - plete.
And the light of	life does glow.

5. But of such are not the mockers
   Of ungodly, wicked mind,
   Who in trials and afflictions
   Are as chaff before the wind;
   As the grass that is today
   Soon does fade and pass away.

6. Scorners, who the Lord would flatter
   In the judgment shall not stand;
   Likewise they who discord scatter
   Perish as the sinking sand;
   Sinful ways shall not endure,
   But the righteous way is sure.

83. THE PENITENT'S CONFLICT
50, 154, 178.

1. Life has be - come so gloom - y, So
2. We bear for Him a long - ing When
3. Thus we can feel how griev - ous Life
4. The Lord at all times choos - es The

griev - ous is our woe, As if the
left a - lone, op - pressed; If we could
with - out God would be; How wretch - ed
time His gifts to share; He sends a

Lord in heav - en, No spark of love would
but em - brace Him, For - ev - er hold Him
and how help - less, How full of pov - er -
ray of sol - ace To ban - ish grief and

show. As yet no par - don giv - en, Earth
fast! With weep - ing pleas and wres - tles, As
ty, We here would starve and fam - ish If
care; He pours His gen - tle bless - ing In -

136.

can no peace af - ford; Yet wea - ry hours thus
Ja - cob moved in soul, Un - til it wins the
not our weep - ing soul The Lord in love would
to the with - 'ring heart, And leads thru gloom and

striv - en Are bless - ings from the Lord.
con - flict, And faith can make it whole.
nour - ish, Would com - fort and con - sole.
sad - ness To bright ways heav - en - ward.

5. Our hearts would prove unfaithful,
   Would tire of Jesus' love,
   If He the heavy burden
   'Neath which on earth He strove
   For us and our transgressions
   In His meek lowliness,
   Should not lay on our shoulders
   To share His sore distress.

6. Therefore, learn thou His guidance
   Meekly to understand,
   When times of gloom and sadness
   Befall thee in this land.
   Soon shall descend from heaven
   His rich grace, as the dew,
   And make the dreary desert
   A meadow green and new.

84. THE REAL LONGING FOR HOME

50, 83, 178.

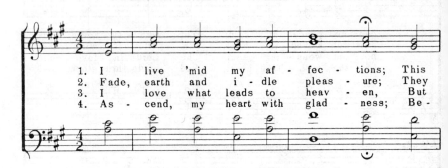

1. I live 'mid my af - fec - tions; This
2. Fade, earth and i - dle pleas - ure; They
3. I love what leads to heav - en, But
4. As - cend, my heart with glad - ness; Be -

world I do not love; With long - ings
are the soul's dis - tress; They glit - ter
not to that be - low; The world, its
yond there's joy and love; En - dure all

true I jour - ney To heav - en's home a -
from a dis - tance, Yet who will them ca -
lust - ful tu - mult And all it can be -
pain and sad - ness To gain the rest a -

138.

bove;   There   dwells my   soul im - mor - tal;
ress,   Ac - cepts but   filth for   jew - els
stow,   Be - neath my   feet   I   tram - ple
bove!   Let   oth - ers choose what's earth - ly,

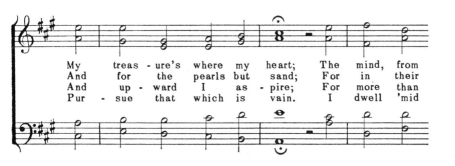

My   treas - ure's where my heart;   The   mind, from
And   for   the   pearls but sand;   For   in   their
And   up - ward I   as - pire;   For more than
Pur - sue that which is vain.   I   dwell 'mid

earth - ly por - tal, A - ris - es heav - en - ward.
mag - ic po - tion There is but death at hand.
world - ly wis - dom Thy king - dom I de - sire.
my   de - vo - tions, For thus death is but gain.

85. THE LORD'S PRAYER
50, 154, 178.

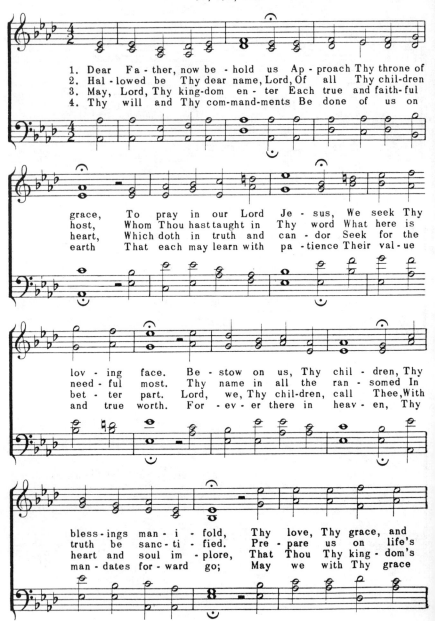

1. Dear Fa - ther, now be - hold us Ap - proach Thy throne of
2. Hal - lowed be Thy dear name, Lord, Of all Thy chil-dren
3. May, Lord, Thy king-dom en - ter Each true and faith-ful
4. Thy will and Thy com-mand-ments Be done of us on

grace, To pray in our Lord Je - sus, We seek Thy
host, Whom Thou hast taught in Thy word What here is
heart, Which doth in truth and can - dor Seek for the
earth That each may learn with pa - tience Their val - ue

lov - ing face. Be - stow on us, Thy chil - dren, Thy
need - ful most. Thy name in all the ran - somed In
bet - ter part. Lord, we, Thy chil-dren, call Thee, With
and true worth. For - ev - er there in heav - en, Thy

bless - ings man - i - fold, Thy love, Thy grace, and
truth be sanc - ti - fied. Pre - pare us on life's
heart and soul im - plore, That Thou Thy king - dom's
man - dates for - ward go; May we with Thy grace

140.

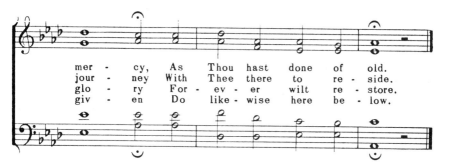

mer - cy, As Thou hast done of old.
jour - ney With Thee there to re - side.
glo - ry For - ev - er wilt re - store.
giv - en Do like - wise here be - low.

5. Our daily bread, Lord, give us
For body, soul, and mind,
Thy words of life so precious,
So pure and so refined.
We pray Thee for Thy favor,
Our Lord on heaven's throne;
Thy bread of heaven's flavor
Can please our hearts alone.

6. Forgive us our transgressions,
Where we, O Lord, have not
In words, in deeds, or patience
Done as Thy word has taught.
They are unworthy servants
Who do no more at best
Than what laws and commandments
Require of them, then rest.

7. Let us, Thy children, mindful,
Obey Thy words with cheer;
Let none of us be idle,
Nor indolent while here.
And as Thou, Lord, hast mercy,
Where we not right have done,
So are we ever ready,
Forgiving everyone.

8. When Satan gives oppression
And night and darkness fall,
Give courage and discretion
To conquer over all;
And when in tribulations,
Grant us new strength and power;
And with Christ's inspiration,
Prepare us for the hour.

9. The glory and the kingdom
Forever Thine shall be,
Almighty King and Sov'reign,
In all eternity!
Put to extermination
Those pow'rs of wicked life.
O, may for all creation
Redemption soon arrive.

10. And now in termination,
Amen, so it shall be.
Our prayers and supplications
Shall bring response from Thee.
Thou art the true and faithful,
The God of Covenant!
In Thee our heart is joyful,
Our God of Hosts so grand.

86. THE LORD WILL PROVIDE

87.

1. Though trou - bles as - sail And dan - gers af -
2. Though of - ten the heart With storms be op -
3. His call we o - bey As A - bram of
4. When Sa - tan ap - pears, Ob - struct - ing our

fright, Though friends should all fail And
pressed, Af - flic - tions do smart, By
old, Not know - ing our way, But
path And fills us with fears, We

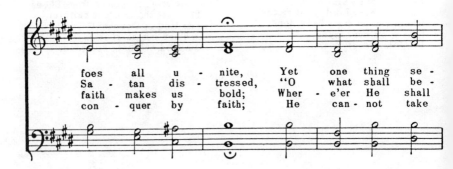

foes all u - nite, Yet one thing se -
Sa - tan dis - tressed, "O what shall be -
faith makes us bold; Wher - e'er He shall
con - quer by faith; He can - not take

cures	us	What-	ev	-	er	be	-	tide,	This
fall	us?"	We	wear	-	i	-	ly	sighed;	Still
lead	us,	The	way	He	doth	guide;	He
from	us,	Though	oft	he	has	tried,	The

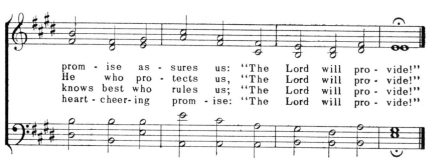

prom	-	ise	as	-	sures	us:	"The	Lord	will	pro	-	vide!"
He	who	pro	-	tects	us,	"The	Lord	will	pro	-	vide!"
knows	best	who	rules	us;	"The	Lord	will	pro	-	vide!"
heart	-	cheer-	ing	prom	-	ise:	"The	Lord	will	pro	-	vide!"

5. He tells us we're weak,
   Our hope is in vain;
   The good that we seek
   We shall not obtain;
   Yet when such temptations
   Our patience have tried,
   In this we find solace:
   "The Lord will provide!"

6. Though merit and strength
   We do not possess,
   And honor and wealth
   Our souls would distress;
   In Thy name, Lord Jesus,
   We'll ever abide,
   And thus we say: "Amen,
   The Lord will provide!"

87. FAITH'S CONFIDENCE
86.

1. While Fear hints, "There's some - thing God will de -
2. Be - gone, un - be - lief, my Sav - iour is
3. His love in time past for - bids me to
4. Though dark be my way, since He is my

ny," "No good thing," is Faith's de -
near, And for my re - lief will
think He'll leave me at last in
guide, 'Tis mine to o - bey, 'tis

ci - sive re - ply; What — e'er He with -
short - ly ap - pear By faith let me
trou - ble to sink; Each sweet Eb - en -
His to pro - vide; Though cis - terns be

holds is most wise - ly de - nied; How
wres - tle, and He will per - form; With
e - zer I have in re - view Con -
brok - en, and crea - tures all fail, The

144.

full   is   the   prom - ise,   "The Lord will pro - vide."
Christ in   the   ves - sel,   I   smile at   the   storm.
firms   His   good pleas - ure   to   help me   quite through.
word   He   has   spok - en   shall sure - ly   pre - vail.

5. Since all that I meet shall work for my good,
The bitter is sweet, the medicine food;
Though painful at present, 'twill end before long;
And then, Oh, how pleasant the conqueror's song.

6. Why should I complain of want or distress,
Temptation or pain? He told me no less:
The heirs of salvation, I know from His word,
Through much tribulation must follow their Lord.

7. How bitter that cup, no heart can conceive,
Which He drank quite up, that sinners might live.
His way was much rougher and darker than mine.
Did Jesus thus suffer and shall I repine?

8. Though troubles assail, and dangers affright,
Though friends should all fail and foes all unite,
Yet one thing secures us, whatever betide,
The Scriptures assure us the Lord will provide.

9. How firm a foundation, ye saints of the Lord,
Is laid for your faith in His excellent word!
What more can He say than to you He hath said,
You who unto Jesus for refuge have fled?

88. OUR PILGRIM WAY

1. Be our jour - ney and our way
2. Of this we are con - fi - dent
3. He that wa - ter for His own
4. He who in His ten - der care

Of temp - ta - tions full; Be our earth - ly
And we hold it fast, That the Lord, though
Out of rocks did bring, And the food for
Holds the world and all, And with - out whose

pil - grim - age But an hum - bling school,
heav - ens rend, Keeps us to the last.
proph - et lone Sent on rav - en's wing;
will no hair From our head may fall;

Yet we are of joy - ful mind,
Though our strength so oft in - deed
He who with few fish and bread
To whom great is not too great,

146.

Trust - ing not there - on What our - selves we do or find, But that Christ is strong.
Threat - ens to take wing, We keep faith, there is no need, We still have our King.
Mul - ti - tudes did feed, Has He not, when all is said, Help in ev - 'ry need?
Small is not too small, Could He real - ly come too late, Or not heed our call?

5. He that opened heavens, hath
   Out of such great love,
   For us plainly marked the path
   To the realms above;
   He who keeps that home prepared,
   Would He e'er allow
   Those for whom he surely cared
   All to perish now?

6. Nay, that shall not be our lot,
   God is ever kind;
   Keeps His promise, breaks it not,
   Comforts heart and mind.
   Though you may see trouble nigh --
   Pilgrim, do not fear,
   Look in faith to God on high
   For your help is near!

147.

89. THE SEVEN WORDS OF JESUS ON THE CROSS

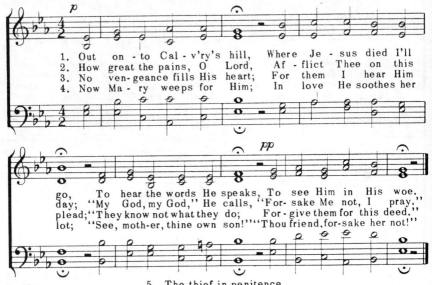

1. Out on-to Cal-v'ry's hill, Where Je-sus died I'll
2. How great the pains, O Lord, Af-flict Thee on this
3. No ven-geance fills His heart; For them I hear Him
4. Now Ma-ry weeps for Him; In love He soothes her

go, To hear the words He speaks, To see Him in His woe.
day; "My God, my God," He calls, "For-sake Me not, I pray."
plead; "They know not what they do; For-give them for this deed."
lot; "See, moth-er, thine own son!" "Thou friend, for-sake her not!"

5. The thief in penitence
   Is pardoned ere he dies:
   "Today shalt thou yet be,
   With Me in Paradise."

6. "I thirst," He cries in pain,
   For there is no distress,
   Which Christ, the Friend of Man,
   Endured not at His death.

7. He bows His head and cries,
   "'Tis finished, all is done,
   O God, receive my soul."
   Life's victory is won.

90. FOLLOW ME!

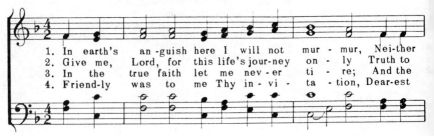

1. In earth's an-guish here I will not mur-mur, Nei-ther
2. Give me, Lord, for this life's jour-ney on-ly Truth to
3. In the true faith let me nev-er ti-re; And the
4. Friend-ly was to me Thy in-vi-ta-tion, Dear-est

seek nor crave a crown of hon - or, When my Lord a crown
guide me through this world so lone - ly And Thy Spir - it for
fruit of faith, the ho - ly fi - re, Love un -tar- nished,Lord,
Lord! So, in my hum - ble sta - tion Heav -en- ward my steps

of thorns did wear. Will not seek the flow'r - y path of
to lead the way. Give a heart that will- ing - ly will
O give to me. With-out it I can- not for - ward
shall e'er pro - ceed; Therefore lend un - to Thy low - ly

ro - ses, When our ho - ly Lord and Sav - iour, Je - sus,
fol - low On the path so steep and straight and nar - row
jour - ney; Love a - lone can lead to love e - ter - nal;
serv - ant From a - bove Thy grace and love so fer - vent;

There on Cal - va - ry the cross did bear.
Where Thy ho - ly feet once led the way.
On - ly love leads through this world to Thee.
Strength-en and di - rect my wea - ry feet.

et a clear and hopeful view be given   6.Yea, upon this earth I am a stranger,
nto me into Thy blissful heaven,   Burdened with a cross and many dangers,
hen on earth no rest from toil I find.   Am a pilgrim, poor and unbeknown.
 this vale of anguish and affliction   Be the cross my pilgrim journey's token
ve me constant peace and pure affection Till my earthly house at last be broken,
nd a trusting, heaven-gladdened mind.   And I reach that dear and heav'nly home.

91. THE HEAVENLY MIND

92.

1. Heav - en - ward, e'er heav - en - ward
2. Heav - en - ward di - rect thy soul
3. Heav - en - ward the Lord would have
4. Heav - en - ward thy ref - uge take

Let us wend our way! What the right - eous
Ev - 'ry morn a - new! Swift our pil - grim -
Thee to set Thy aim; Be not anx - ious;
When op - pressed with care, For thy God will

seek is there Found with - out de - lay,
age doth roll; This, O man, is true!
do not crave Earth - ly wealth or fame.
ne'er for - sake Nor leave in de - spair.

But not on earth. Joy here al - ter -
O plead and pray: God, who called me
From such ab - stain! On - ly what with
Why this dis - tress? In the realms of

150.

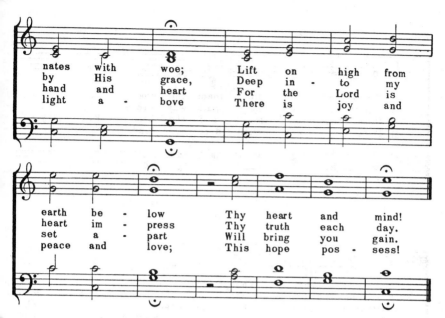

nates	with	woe;	Lift	on	high	from
by	His	grace,	Deep	in -	to	my
hand	and	heart	For	the	Lord	is
light	a -	bove	There	is	joy	and

earth	be -	low	Thy	heart	and	mind!
heart	im -	press	Thy	truth	each	day.
set	a -	part	Will	bring	you	gain.
peace	and	love;	This	hope	pos -	sess!

6. Heavenward walk by thy side
All the Lord's elect,
And with heav'nly foretaste do
What their Lord directs.
O join the throng!
Strive with zeal while here below;
Walk life's way through pain and woe;
In God be strong!

7. Heavenward His hand doth guide
Through the desert waste;
Draws thee closer to His side,
Makes thy spirit chaste.
He will destroy
Every earthly vanity,
And will lead thee finally
Into His joy.

7. Heavenward through all contempt
Our dear Saviour trod;
Follow Him, where'er He went,
As a child of God.
Hold fast to Him!
Silently thy burden bear;
Change thy murm'ring into prayer;
The vict'ry win!

8. Hallelujah! Heavenward,
Let thy thanks ascend;
Thou shalt also join thy Lord
At the journey's end.
Then thou shalt be
Where all pain is turned aside,
There to praise Him, glorified
Eternally.

9. "Hallelujah," thou wilt sing
When thy Lord shall come,
Joyfully His own to bring
To His heav'nly home.
Great is the Lord!
For the cross He took a throne,
Made His victory thine own!
Praised be the Lord!

151.

92. FORWARD

91.

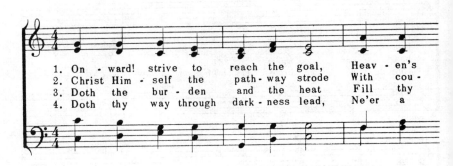

1. On - ward! strive to reach the goal, Heav - en's
2. Christ Him - self the path - way strode With cou -
3. Doth the bur - den and the heat Fill thy
4. Doth thy way through dark - ness lead, Ne'er a

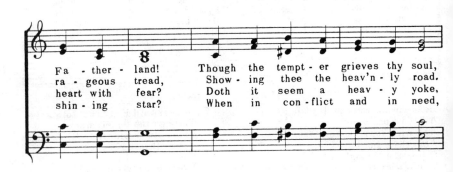

Fa - ther - land! Though the tempt - er grieves thy soul,
ra - geous tread, Show - ing thee the heav'n - ly road.
heart with fear? Doth it seem a heav - y yoke,
shin - ing star? When in con - flict and in need,

Je - sus guides thy hand. So, safe - ly
Fol - low with - out dread! O trust in
What thou hast to bear? O, then be -
Seems His help a - far? He is thy

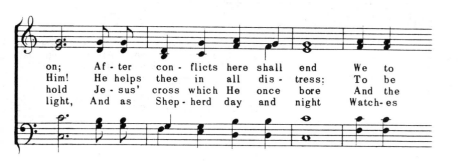

on; | Af - ter | con - flicts | here | shall | end | We | to
Him! | He helps | thee | in | all | dis - | tress; | To | be
hold | Je - sus' | cross | which | He | once | bore | And | the
light, | And | as | Shep - herd | day | and | night | Watch- es

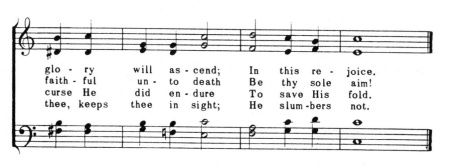

glo - ry | will | as - cend; | In | this | re - | joice.
faith - ful | un - to | death | Be | thy | sole | aim!
curse He | did | en - dure | To | save | His | fold.
thee, keeps | thee | in | sight; | He | slum - bers | not.

5. And when death shall come at last
   Thou shalt feel no dread;
   When thy mortal pain is past,
   Thou shalt see our Head
   In radiance new.
   When our conflict here doth end,
   Into glory shall ascend
   The Christian true.

153.

93. TRUST IN GOD

28, 29, 30, 94.

1. God, my hope and con - so - la - tion, Ev - er Thou my
2. All things be to Thee com - mit - ted; All Thou do - est
3. Lead me, Lord, as Thou best know - est How be - fore Thee
4. Though I meet with pain and sor - row, Oft must feel how

ref - uge be! In Thy care I'll find pro - tec - tion,
is well done; If for death or life I'm fit - ted,
I should live; If but Thou my foot - step guid - est,
hard it be Through af - flic - tions here to strug - gle,

Though no oth - er light I see. Oft on rug - ged
Thy com - mands I'll nev - er shun. Though the bur - den
Joy and bless - ings I re - ceive. If in grace with
Yet my God shall faith - ful be. Thou dost help my

road of sad - ness I find com - fort, joy and
oft be griev - ous, Thou dost com - fort and re -
Thee I'm stand - ing, Dan - gers fade at Thy com -
bur - den car - ry; Should I com - fort - less then

154.

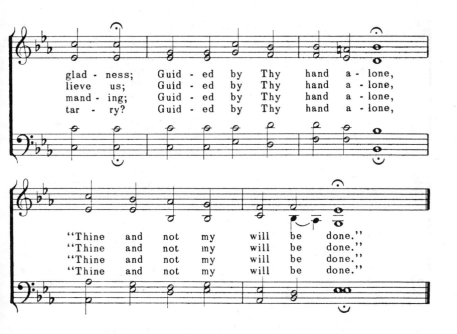

glad - ness;   Guid - ed   by   Thy   hand   a - lone,
lieve   us;   Guid - ed   by   Thy   hand   a - lone,
mand - ing;   Guid - ed   by   Thy   hand   a - lone,
tar - ry?   Guid - ed   by   Thy   hand   a - lone,

"Thine   and   not   my   will   be   done."
"Thine   and   not   my   will   be   done."
"Thine   and   not   my   will   be   done."
"Thine   and   not   my   will   be   done."

5. In Thy hands I am committed,
   Father, with content repose;
   Ev'ry charge shall be acquitted;
   Turned to bliss shall be my woes.
   When at last from heaven's portal,
   I review my life-path mortal,
   I shall utter, deeply moved,
   "O how truly Thou hast loved!"

155.

94. THE SHIP OF FAITH

28, 93, 186, 217.

1. Though great dan - gers oft sur - round us Pass - ing through life's storm-y sea, Where the clouds of gloom and dark - ness Hov - er o'er our heads, and we Through the temp - est must keep row - ing, In dis - tress and

2. Yet the Lord is ev - er near us; He doth guide our ves -sel's course; He would test our love and firm - ness, Giv -ing storm and wind their course. That our faith be shown in clear - ness, Seem-ing - ly He

3. He is Lord; when He com - mand - eth Storms a - bate, and o -cean waves Will, al - though they rage with mad - ness, Gent- ly cease; for He who saves Gives re - pose; and in dis - trac - tion It is He who

4. There - fore, trust - ing in God on - ly, Place your con - fi - dence in Him; He is near, though we feel lone - ly, Help de -lays and light grows dim. Be con - soled and trust in Je - sus, In this Rock your

scarce - ly know - ing Whe - ther we the poor, un -
hides His near - ness; If we plead with fer - vent
gives pro - tec - tion; He will ne'er His own for -
strength in - creas - es; Let your faith rest in His

known, Of our Lord are left a - lone.
will, He will bid the sea be still.
sake, Nor His ho - ly cov -'nant break.
blood, Fear - ing nei - ther storm nor flood.

Should our faith and courage falter
In the tempest of this world,
Fervent prayer upon the altar
Is an anchor that will hold
In the wounds of Jesus surely,
Grounded on His blood securely,
And ascends, through faith alone
To His holy, sacred throne.

Oh, this anchor is united
By the endless chain of love,
That extends from earth beneath us
To our Father's home above;
Jesus draws in love so tender,
Till we all the radiant splendor
Of that peaceful harbor see
Where our home fore'er shall be.

7. Jesus' cross - that is the symbol
Of the banner that we bear;
Under this, what need to tremble?
Who need falter or despair?
He that in this sign believeth,
There a heavenly crown receiveth;
After the victorious fight
Cometh he to realms of light.

8. Therefore, on, beloved pilgrims!
Faithfully your way pursue;
Yonder for you as His children
Lies that peaceful haven, too.
There the little bark arriveth,
After tempest it surviveth;
For your compass, Holy Writ,
Keeps thy bark and guideth it.

95. CHALLENGE TO THE NOMINAL CHRISTIAN

28, 93, 94, 186.

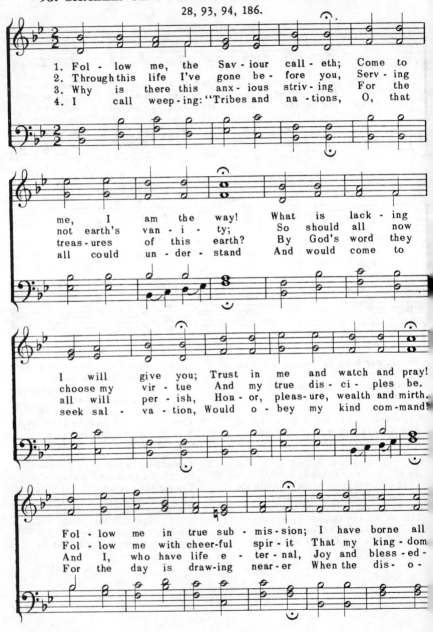

1. Fol - low me, the Sav - iour call - eth; Come to
2. Through this life I've gone be - fore you, Serv - ing
3. Why is there this anx - ious striv - ing For the
4. I call weep - ing: "Tribes and na - tions, O, that

me, I am the way! What is lack - ing
not earth's van - i - ty; So should all now
treas - ures of this earth? By God's word they
all could un - der - stand And would come to

I will give you; Trust in me and watch and pray!
choose my vir - tue And my true dis - ci - ples be.
all will per - ish, Hon - or, pleas - ure, wealth and mirth.
seek sal - va - tion, Would o - bey my kind com - mand!

Fol - low me in true sub - mis - sion; I have borne all
Fol - low me with cheer - ful spir - it That my king - dom
And I, who have life e - ter - nal, Joy and bless - ed -
For the day is draw - ing near - er When the dis - o -

your trans - gres - sion; Learn of me; both great and
ye in - her - it. Yea, for - sake the high - way
ness su - per - nal, Find so few who will o -
bey - ing hear - ers Who the truth have not be -

small, Meek - ly, hum - bly hear my call.
broad; Fol - low me on heav - en's road.
bey On the straight and nar - row way!
lieved, In false hope they were de - ceived.

5. When the words by prophets spoken,
Their fulfillment then shall find:
"Lo! Their vision I have broken
And confused their heart and mind!"
Woe to ev'ry willful being
Who is constantly pursuing
A perverse and sinful way,
And in selfish pride does stay.

6. Therefore, all ye human beings,
Hear today the Saviour's word;
He came for the poor lost sinner
Who with joy His message heard.
Come, believe! Be meek and lowly,
For His Word is true and holy;
Who believes Him is made free
Here and in eternity.

7. Sing, all ye who are persuaded
By the power of His call!
O, be glad; for you are aided
By His hand through dangers all.
Not a sparrow ever falleth
Lest it be that God alloweth;
So rejoice exceedingly
For His kingdom yours shall be.

8. Walk thus, cheering one another,
Little flock, e'en to the end;
If ye see a stumbling brother,
Helpful word and hand extend;
Filled with God's own mighty fullness,
Follow Christ in holy stillness;
Sing to Him a "Gloria!"
And rejoice, "Hallelujah!"

96. IN TIME OF PERSECUTION

167, 196.

1. Though their foes may try them, Christ's true friends de-
2. And when Sa - tan rag - es And a - gainst us
3. Will his cru - el ac - tion Bring him sat - is-
4. For a sea - son Sa - tan May our down - fall

fy them And to Him ad - here; Though the
stag - es Tor - ture, fire and death, Has - tens
fac - tion? No, the Chris-tian's blood Yields the
threat - en, But be not a - fraid! For the

arch - foe, Sa - tan, God's own chil-dren threat - ens,
to de - fy us And with - al des - troy us,
fruits most pleas - ing, Bless-ings still in - creas - ing
Lord of heav - en Hath the prom-ise giv - en

They will have no fear. God gives strength To
Armed with spite and wrath, Yet we know Each
From the face of God. Wrath and sword Have
Of en - dur - ing aid. His right arm Will

160.

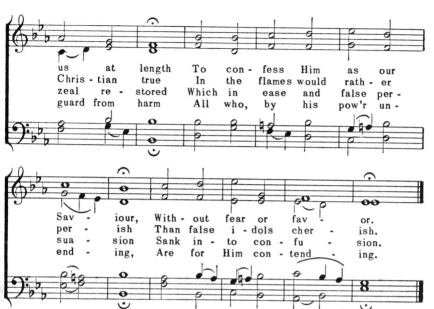

us at length To con - fess Him as our
Chris - tian true In the flames would rath - er
zeal re - stored Which in ease and false per -
guard from harm All who, by his pow'r un -

Sav - iour, With - out fear or fav - or.
per - ish Than false i - dols cher - ish.
sua - sion Sank in - to con - fu - sion.
end - ing, Are for Him con - tend - ing.

5. So stand fast, ye faithful;
Though the foe seem dreadful,
Help is at your side.
Christ in triumph rising,
Haughty foes despising,
Will defeat their pride.
Though, behold, A lion bold,
Or a Nero should o'ertake you,
God will not forsake you!

6. Though proud seas endeavor
Our small bark to sever
From its Faithful guard,
Though great storms are roaring;
Though great billows soaring,
May distress it hard,
Christ, the Lord, Will help afford;
In the very darkest hour
He will show His power.

7. Though my foes are pressing
And my ship distressing,
God is e'er my shield;
It shall not be shattered;
God the waves will scatter;
It will never yield.
Then at last, All danger past,
With our Pilot, Christ, commanding,
Find its heav'nly landing.

8. Should our vessel flounder,
Peter nigh go under,
Jonah near be lost;
Should a Paul be drifting,
Still God's arms are lifting
All the tempest-tossed;
Noah found A landing-ground;
He and his by God were cherished,
Though the whole world perished.

9. O, be glad, my brothers;
Brave the hate of others;
And be not dismayed.
Though vain men assail you,
Let your faith not fail you;
Still be unafraid.
God hath shown More power alone
Than great hosts in armor trusting,
For your downfall lusting.

10. Let from every angle
Storms our ships entangle;
God is in command!
It will not go under
Or through weakness founder,
But come safe to land;
For at last, The storms all pass,
Christ, our great and mighty Pilot,
Will to heaven guide it!

97. THE GOSPEL
96, 196.

1. Word which God has spo - ken, Word of peace - ful to - ken, Gos - pel of the Lord! Fount of ben - e - dic - tion, Com - fort in af - flic - tion, Ho - ly Spir - it's sword!

2. Un - to ev - 'ry na - tion Thou dost bring sal - va - tion Through Thy bless-ed light, Till the un - der - stand - ing Of Thy truth ex - pand - ing Shall dis - pel the night.

3. All is now ac - com - plished; God has sent re - demp - tion By His lov - ing Son; Christ His life has giv - en, To the cross was driv - en, For us life has won.

4. Je - sus' in - vi - ta - tion Calls to ev - 'ry na - tion: "Draw nigh and be - lieve! God your sins will par - don Lest your hearts should hard - en In your un - be - lief.

Source of might, Of life and light!
God's own light, O star so bright!
Christ ful - filled The Fa - ther's will,
Come to me; I'll make you free

Joy - ful mes - sage of God giv - en, Sent to us from heav-en!
Send to man - y hearts Thy ra-diance, Who yield in o - be-dience.
To His hon - or, praise and glo - ry. What a joy-ful sto - ry!"
From your bond-age and op - pres-sion. Let me take pos-ses-sion!"

5. See how sinners revel,
   Serving death and devil;
   Numberless are they
   Who in lofty places
   Bow to idol faces,
   Shameful homage pay;
   Yet some time Shall brightly shine
   On the hills our Saviour's healing,
   Valleys reconciling.

6. Though mid strife and tumult,
   Men will heap their insult
   On the blood of Christ;
   Ye who love the Saviour,
   Bearing ill-will ever,
   Being much despiséd,
   Soon 'tis past, And they at last
   Who have served, endured, and waited
   Shall be vindicated.

7. See the mighty nations,
   Whose imaginations
   Are an idle dream,
   Christ's own name now bearing,
   Yet for Him not caring;
   Yea, they Him blaspheme;
   Trust the Lord; Such are abhorred,
   And one day will crash in pieces.
   Then the evil ceases.

8. See the lowly churches,
   Which by Christian virtues
   Satan's power defy,
   Where the true salvation,
   Preached with consecration,
   Leads to life on high.
   Great shall be The small ye see
   When all to their Saviour plighted,
   Once shall be united.

9. In His grace rejoicing
   And His praises voicing
   We have peace with God;
   Heart and soul we offer
   Him who once did suffer
   And our pardon bought.
   Love Him here; And without fear
   Praise His holy name forever
   As our God and Saviour!

98. CALL TO BEGINNERS
167, 196.

1. Be not thou dis - cour - aged, Though the tempt - ers flour - ish; Him who calls, o - bey! Fol - low, though they threat - en, For the Sav - iour's serv - ants Call: Do not de - lay. Don't re -

2. See'st thou oth - ers wan - der Who the Sav - iour slan - der, Dead in un - be - lief, Who are ev - er seek - ing With their ev - il speak - ing, Christ's fold to de - ceive; Do not

3. Yield to Him sub - mis - sion Who for thy trans - gres - sion Died up - on the cross! Do no long - er tar - ry; You must haste and hur - ry; Tar - di - ness is loss. When at

4. We must shun the teach - ing Of those who are preach - ing Sin - ful greed and lust, To the Beast al - le - giance, To God dis - o - be - dience, Whose re - ward is just. Wrath and

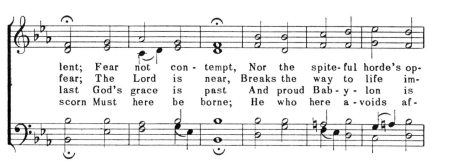

lent; Fear not con - tempt, Nor the spite- ful horde's op-
fear; The Lord is near, Breaks the way to life im-
last God's grace is past And proud Bab - y - lon is
scorn Must here be borne; He who here a - voids af -

pres - sion; Hold fast thy con - fes - sion!
mor - tal; Strive to find the por - tal!
ban - ished, All hope will have van - ished.
flic - tion For - feits God's af - fec - tion.

5. Therefore onward hurry;
Do not longer tarry
Here in Babel's land!
He who here stays captured
Ne'er shall be enraptured
With that sacred band.
Up and strive For endless life;
Do not fear the roaring lion;
Fear the God of Zion.

99. BATTLE AND VICTORY

104, 119, 243, 253.

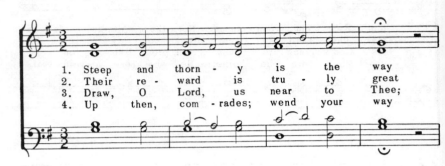

1. Steep and thorn - y is the way
2. Their re - ward is tru - ly great
3. Draw, O Lord, us near to Thee;
4. Up then, com - rades; wend your way

Lead - ing us to full per - fec - tion;
Who, un - to the end en - dur - ing,
Draw to Thee each val - iant fight - er.
Through the wil - der - ness with cour - age;

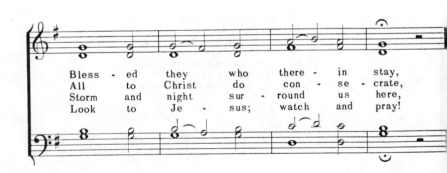

Bless - ed they who there - in stay,
All to Christ do con - se - crate,
Storm and night sur - round us here,
Look to Je - sus; watch and pray!

Bat - tling   un - der   Christ's   di - rec - tion.
Flee   the   world - ly   lust   al - lur - ing.
But   a - bove   'tis   calm   and   bright-er.
God   pre - pares   you   for   the   con - flict;

Blest   is   he   who   runs   the   race,
They   who   hope   un - fail - ing - ly
There,   be - yond   death   and   the   tomb,
In   the   weak   He   shows   His   might,

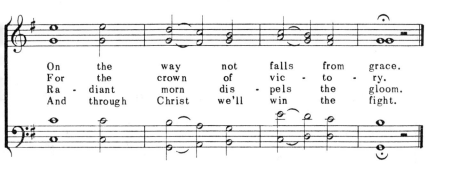

On   the   way   not   falls   from   grace.
For   the   crown   of   vic - to - ry.
Ra - diant   morn   dis - pels   the   gloom.
And   through   Christ   we'll   win   the   fight.

167.

100. THE SUPREME SACRIFICE

99, 119, 253.

1. God with us! We need not fear;
   Je - sus crowns with life e - ter - nal;
   Faith - ful let us be while here,
   Till God ends our pil - grim jour - ney;

2. See, our Sav - iour leads the way;
   Tri - umph marks His ev - 'ry foot - step;
   Fol - low Him in glad ar - ray
   Brave - ly with cou - ra - geous ef - fort!

3. Fierce - ly shall our foe ap - proach;
   Man - y breth - ren brave are fall - ing;
   For God's king - dom they en - dure;
   Life e - ter - nal is their call - ing.

4. Do not fear the tempt - er's wrath,
   Though the man of sin be rag - ing;
   Soon to Judg - ment he must pass;
   And then, breth - ren, we shall en - ter

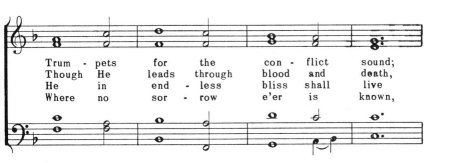

Trum - pets for the con - flict sound;
Though He leads through blood and death,
He in end - less bliss shall live
Where no sor - row e'er is known,

Up, ye val - iant, stand your ground!
He' - roes nev - er lose their faith.
Who for Christ his life will give.
Where all dread and fear have flown.

5. We behold the heav'nly throng
Who in ages past have suffered
Persecution, hate, and wrong,
Who for God their lives have offered;
Look beyond, behold their course;
Strive as they, to heaven's doors.

101. GOD'S EXALTATION
104, 119, 243, 253.

1. Our great God, we praise Thee now,
2. Ev - 'ry - thing shall sing Thy praise;
3. Great and small shall sing Thy praise
4. And Thy church with - in the pow'r

Laud - ing Thee with ex - ul - ta - tion;
Cher - u - bim and ser - aphs' voic - es
O - ver all Thy great cre - a - tion.
Of Thy Spir - it's in - spi - ra - tion

The whole earth be - fore Thee bows
Praise and hon - or to Thee raise.
To Thee, Fa - ther, God of grace,
Sings to Thee, our God and King;

And a - dores Thy great cre - a - tion.
And the an - gel host re - joic - es,
Sings the ho - ly con - gre - ga - tion,
Thou our joy and con - so - la - tion.

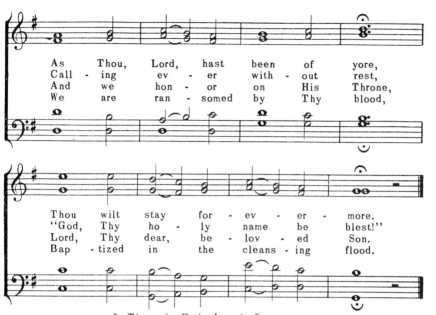

As Thou, Lord, hast been of yore,
Call - ing ev - er with - out rest,
And we hon - or on His Throne,
We are ran - somed by Thy blood,

Thou wilt stay for - ev - er - more.
"God, Thy ho - ly name be blest!"
Lord, Thy dear, be - lov - ed Son.
Bap - tized in the cleans - ing flood.

5. Thou, the Father's only Son,
Cam'st to give mankind redemption;
From Thy throne Thou didst descend
Here to make Thy habitation.
Grace and mercy came from Thee,
And from sin we now are free.

6. Open now is heaven's gate;
And our Saviour's interceding
Reconciles us unto God
When in faith He hears our pleading.
Fin'lly comes Thy Judgment day,
Time and hour we can not say.

7. Lord, protect Thy children all;
Hear their humble supplication.
Thou didst for our ransom, Lord,
Bear the cross and tribulation.
When our transient life is gone,
Take us to our heav'nly home.

8. Graciously behold Thy flock;
Help and bless Thy heirs forever.
Lead us in Thy righteous paths;
From the enemy deliver.
Hear our earnest pray'r and plea:
Lord, Thy coming we would see.

171.

102. THE ASSURANCE OF TRUE FAITH
103.

1. My faith gives joy and sweet - est rest, Leads
2. Lord, for Thy fold Thou dost pre - pare A
3. My praise and thanks I give to Thee, For
4. Thy ho - ly Word does teach - ings give In

me to heav - en and the blest, To Thee, my
right un - to Thy king - dom there, A treas - ure
through Thy grace Thou mak - est me An heir by
faith, and hope, and love to live; For this, O,

God and Fa - ther. The com - fort of mor -
and pos - ses - sion. The sec - ond death I
Thy a - dop - tion. With - in the Word Thy
Lord, I thank Thee. Should I not seek with -

tal - i - ty Pre - serve with stead-fast faith in
need not fear, For im - mor - tal - i - ty is
truth I find Which sanc - ti - fies my life and
in this time A fore - taste of the joys di -

me; I'd fol - low Thee for - ev - er. Sal -
near; Thy death gives us sal - va - tion. I
mind And brings me to per - fec - tion. Yes,
vine And for Thy home pre - pare me? Sal -

va - tion is the no - blest part; Im -
am re - deemed! Thy mor - tal pain Has
born a - new in heart I feel; Thy
va - tion is the no - blest part; Im -

press this deep - ly on my heart.
brought for me e - ter - nal gain.
Spir - it, Lord, does this re - veal.
press this deep - ly on my heart.

103. BLEST ETERNITY
102.

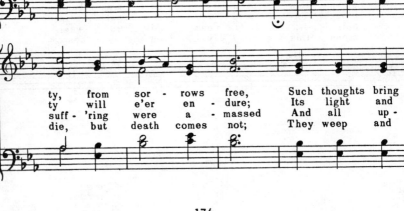

1. O word of joy, E - ter - ni - ty,
2. No splen-dor here can be un - furled
3. It mat - ters not that we en - dure,
4. Be - hold the plight of the con - demned,

Which holds such charms and joy for me,
Which will re - main, but with the world
As mar - tyrs al - so did of yore,
How sad their fate with - out an end,

O Life with - out ces - sa - tion! E - ter - ni -
Shall fall in - to de - struc - tion; E - ter - ni -
The cross and much af - flic - tion. Al - though our
Those cast in - to per - di - tion! They ev - er

ty, from sor - rows free, Such thoughts bring
ty, will e'er en - dure; Its light and
suff - 'ring were a - massed And all up -
die, but death comes not; They weep and

peace that I can be Re - lieved from earth's vex-
joys, di - vine - ly pure, Are free from all cor-
on the bal - ance placed, We'd find this full con-
bear the sad - dest lot In mourn - ful, lost con-

a - tion; They fill my heart with sweet - est cheer,
rup - tion; Yea, God to us did this re - veal
vic - tion: E - ter - nal life doth far out - weigh
di - tion. How great will then that glo - ry be

When trials and grief as - sail me here.
With - in His word of sweet ap - peal.
All trials for which it doth re - pay.
For us who from this will be free!

. Throughout the long eternity
The ransomed host shall dwell with Thee;
They never shall grow weary.
Rejoicing with the angels there,
The blest inheritance they share
In peace and endless glory.
As angels, they from manna live,
Which Christ, true to His promise, gives.

6. Ah, how I long now to depart
To satisfy my weary heart
With Thee, O life immortal!
When can I soon to Thee ascend
To where my thoughts do daily wend
And enter heaven's portal?
I would forget this world and strife
And work for sweet eternal life.

175.

104. AT THE GRAVE OF THE BELIEVER
99, 119, 253.

1. Mor - tal shell, So now thou art
2. There - fore rest thou calm - ly here;
3. 'Tis His will that we have life
4. Christ Him - self lived here be - low;

In thy cool grave calm - ly sleep - ing;
Rest se - rene - ly in the gloam - ing,
Still in bod - ies mor - tal flow - ing;
In a pil - grim's hut He tar - ried.

From earth did thy soul de - part
Till the time for us draws near,
All who won the crown through strife,
Great - er far than ours, we know,

To take com - fort in Christ's keep - ing.
When our feet are tired of roam - ing.
Once be - neath this yoke were groan - ing.
Were the bur - dens that He car - ried.

176.

Thou wilt break thy grave's dark walls
And we in the grave a - bide,
Death takes us to God at last,
Firm in con - flict let us be

And a - rise when Je - sus calls.
Where all cares are laid a - side.
As it did those of the past.
With our eye fixed, God, on Thee.

5. What is life passed in this frame,
   This short space with gloom o'erclouded,
   Toward life with immortal fame?
   Yet on this short hour enshrouded
   Hangs, Thou God of mystery,
   Either death or life with Thee.

6. Thou on whom our all we stake!
   Ours indeed will be life's measure,
   When our eye in death does break,
   Thou wilt give us then this treasure.
   Son of Man and God, our Friend,
   Thou on us Thy peace didst send.

7. Lord, to Thee, not to the world,
   We belong --Thou shalt awake us.
   This pow'r of the better world
   Let us taste when death does take us.
   May we here in faith abide
   And in death with Thee reside.

177.

105. FAITHFUL UNTIL DEATH REMAIN!

99, 104, 120, 253.

1. Faith-ful un-til death re-main! For the crown of life be striv-ing. Break through bonds of woe and pain, In His prom-ise e'er con-fid-ing, Which through grace is

2. There no crown shall e'er a-dorn Him who wav-ers in the bat-tle. He who bears re-proach and scorn, Keep-ing faith-ful in the strug-gle, Shall re-ceive the

3. If this treas-ure you a-wait, In the con-flict grow not wea-ry. Peace a-bounds in Je-sus' path, Though the way seems oft-en drear-y. We must toil through

4. Have you vowed to serve the Lord, 'Neath His ban-ner ev-er fight-ing? Flee the e-vil of this world, Sa-tan and his pow-er smit-ing; Till the vic-tor

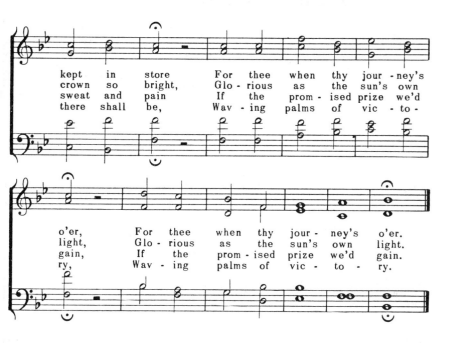

kept in store | For thee | when thy | jour - ney's
crown so bright, | Glo - rious | as the | sun's own
sweat and pain | If the | prom - ised | prize we'd
there shall be, | Wav - ing | palms of | vic - to -

o'er, | For thee | when thy | jour - ney's | o'er.
light, | Glo - rious | as the | sun's own | light.
gain, | If the | prom - ised | prize we'd | gain.
ry, | Wav - ing | palms of | vic - to - | ry.

5. Thus our duty is made plain,
Trusting and in God abiding.
Faithful to thy Lord remain;
Till your eyes in light beholding,
See prepared there for the blest
:: Shining crowns of righteousness. ::

179.

106. THE WAY AND THE REWARD
55, 109, 153, 177.

1. Two ways, O man, are there for thee; There are two des-ti-na-tions. Up-on the path to heav'n we bear The cross and trib-u-la-tions. The oth-er path with joy a-bounds, And yet no in-ward

2. E-ter-ni-ty is draw-ing near; O, seek your soul's sal-va-tion! Up-on the nar-row path of life There's mer-cy and pro-tec-tion. E-ter-nal is the great re-ward, If on the path-way

3. If on the path you do re-main Where sin the mor-tals cher-ish, And God's rich mer-cy you dis-dain, Your hopes will sure-ly per-ish. Woe un-to you, if here you stay, With un-be-liev-ing

4. O, why not turn, and heed the call, And come in true sub-mis-sion! His par-don's free to one and all; In Him you'll find re-mis-sion. For you have lived, who-e'er you be, In world-ly thought and

peace	is	found;	It	leads	thee	to	de -	struc -	tion.
of	the	Lord	You	fear	not	the	af -	flic -	tions.
heart	o -	bey	The	pow'r	of	sin	and	dark -	ness.
van -	i -	ty,	Which	lead	in -	to	per -	di -	tion.

In God's good word you'll surely find
The way to life immortal.
Through Jesus' death the pathway leads
To heaven's open portal.
Upon the cross His life He gave,
And triumphed over death and grave;
He bore your soul's transgressions.

8. His way at first may seem too hard,
Too steep, and full of sorrow;
Yet peace e'en now is its reward,
And bliss in God's tomorrow.
Who through the narrow gate doth press,
An inner peace will he possess,
And very joy in living.

If thou wouldst own the gift of grace
And heaven's joy inherit,
Then walk by faith before His face,
Led by the Lord's own Spirit.
Thou must with Christ be crucified,
And all thy sins and all thy pride
Upon His cross must perish.

9. The broader way at first may seem
As through a pleasant pasture,
But in its path great dangers teem;
It ends in dark disaster.
In righteous anger God will cast
Into great agony at last
The unrepentant sinner.

In true repentance, die to sin,
In Jesus' name believing!
Baptized into His death with Him,
Full pardon be receiving!
Who dies with Christ will with Him rise,
A new life's way before him lies,
The road of life with Jesus.

10. Therefore, O soul, consider well
What there shall be your portion,
And choose while yet you live on earth
The way of full salvation!
If in the Lord your hopes do rest,
Then with this treasure you are blest.
Woe to the unbelievers!

106, 153, 177.

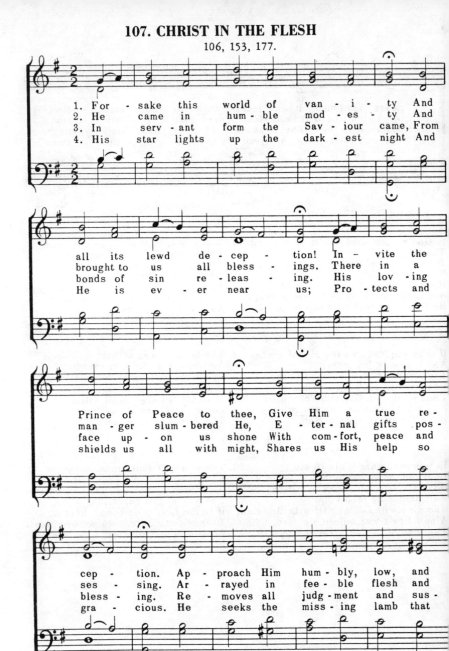

1. For - sake this world of van - i - ty And
2. He came in hum - ble mod - es - ty And
3. In serv - ant form the Sav - iour came, From
4. His star lights up the dark - est night And

all its lewd de - cep - tion! In - vite the
brought to us all bless - ings. There in a
bonds of sin re - leas - ing. His lov - ing
He is ev - er near us; Pro - tects and

Prince of Peace to thee, Give Him a true re -
man - ger slum - bered He, E - ter - nal gifts pos -
face up - on us shone With com - fort, peace and
shields us all with might, Shares us His help so

cep - tion. Ap - proach Him hum - bly, low, and
ses - sing. Ar - rayed in fee - ble flesh and
bless - ing. Re - moves all judg - ment and sus -
gra - cious. He seeks the miss - ing lamb that

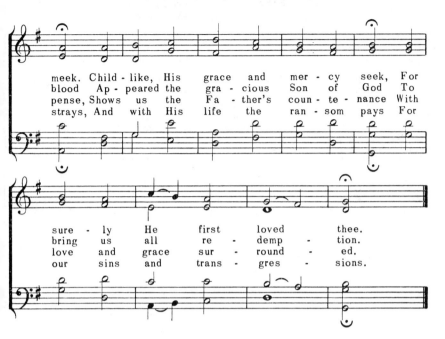

meek. Child - like, His grace and mer - cy seek, For
blood Ap - peared the gra - cious Son of God To
pense, Shows us the Fa - ther's coun - te - nance With
strays, And with His life the ran - som pays For

sure - ly He first loved thee.
bring us all re - demp - tion.
love and grace sur - round - ed.
our sins and trans - gres - sions.

5. If thou to life wouldst find the way,
   Then search the Scriptures ever.
   They show that, through Christ's death, man may
   Have life that endeth never!
   Lo! On the cross His life He gave
   And then was laid into the grave
   Because of thy transgressions.

6. What's needful most keep well in mind,
   Within His fold remaining.
   Be eager for His bread refined,
   Life's fount thy soul sustaining.
   With faith in Him look heavenward;
   Repentant seek His loving heart,
   His arms for thee are open.

7. And though upon the raging sea
   By storms thou shalt be driven,
   Thine anchor, guard and shield is He;
   His love to thee is given.
   He is thy Light in night and grief,
   Thy sword the vict'ry to achieve.
   He never will forsake thee.

108. THE FIELD AND THE FRUIT

55, 106, 109, 153.

1. Con - sid - er, man, that heart of thine, Thy
2. Is now thy heart an o - pen way Of
3. No life and grace canst thou ob - tain Thy
4. And though thy heart is dull and cold From

life and deeds be - hold - ing. Do thorns there
wide and broad di - men - sions From which those
soul to feed and nour - ish, If thus o'er -
sin - ful - ness so hard - ened, Where - in that

grow, or fruits di - vine? Are weeds there - in re -
e - vil birds of prey Can rob all good in -
trod - den and de - stroyed This pre - cious seed shall
seed can - not take hold, And can - not thus be

sid - ing? The fruits will tru - ly man - i -
ten - tions? O, be sin - cere! It is no
per - ish. Or if that seed but reach the
strength - ened. 'Tis true up - on a ston - y

fest   What   seeds   have   in   thy   heart   been   cast,   If
jest;   If   thorns and   weeds thy   heart   in -   fest,   Then
ear   And   not   thy   heart, there is   great   fear   This
heart   That   seed   can -   not   take   root   and   start, And

God's   or   the   de -   stroy - -   er's.
sad   is   thy   con -   di   - -   tion!
seed   shall   be   un -   fruit - -   ful.
there - fore   it   must   per - -   ish.

. Until thy heart is broken down
And through God's word made tender,
The seed, which thereupon is sown,
Can find no place to enter.
Oh, lose no time, but now repent!
Have faith that God His grace will lend,
And thou wilt surely conquer!

. Or is it only thoughts of greed,
Of wealth and earthly splendor
That fill thy heart so that this seed
Can find no place to enter?
Oh, man, take heed! If that be so,
Then in thy heart no fruits will grow
That lead to life eternal.

. A heart that's always on the chase
For wealth and riches striving,
Will have no welcome and no space
For this good seed reviving,
Or lovest thou but vain display,
Which soon will fade and pass away,
And leave thy soul no shelter?

8. But still they're some found here below
Whose hearts like fields are fruitful,
Wherein that seed will start and grow
In hearts upright and truthful.
The seeds which in these hearts are sown
Will thrive until good fruit is grown;
They are the true believers.

9. He who has ears, Oh, let him hear
And give it due reflection,
For while this day of grace is near
Seek for thy soul protection!
O, pray that while this day does last
Good seeds into thy heart be cast
And that they grow and prosper!

10. Oh, my Lord Jesus, Thee I pray,
My heart for Thee make useful;
And for Thy seed prepare the way.
Grant that it may be fruitful!
Yea, fruits of virtue, grace and love,
That follow me to heav'n above --
For this, O Lord, I pray Thee!

109. GRATITUDE FOR DELIVERANCE
55, 106, 153, 177.

1. If God with-in these e-vil days His mer-cy
2. The en-e-my is wrath-ful still, But God with
3. We thank Thee, Lord, we are re-deemed! Our soul they

were not shar-ing, No strength or grace could
wise di-rec-tion Has saved us from the
could not cap-ture, For as a bird from

we ob-tain; Our hearts would be de-
world-ly lure And giv'n our soul pro-
nets re-leased, We have es-caped in

spair-ing. A rem-nant small, a hand-ful
tec-tion. For un-be-lief with man-y
rap-ture. The bonds are loosed, and we are

we, By many haugh - ty men to be De -
woes Has thus in - creased, and o - ver - flows The
free, And strength- 'ning grace we find in Thee, The

spised and per - se - cu - ted, De -
world, as does a riv - er, The
God of earth and heav - en, The

spised and per - se - cu - ted.
world, as does a riv - er.
God of earth and heav - en.

110. THE LORD, MY LIGHT AND SALVATION

1. O Lord, my light, In Thee I shall pre-vail; With Thee I am se-cure. I need not fear, Though Sa-tan would as-sail; His trials I shall en-dure. The en-e-my I am not

2. One thing I seek Far more than tongue can tell: That in Thy ho-ly place With Thee, my God, I might for-ev-er dwell To praise Thee for Thy grace. O, Lord, I wish to see Thy

3. Thou art my tow'r; In time of great dis-tress I seek Thy realm of light; There I re-joice; With-in this vale of tears, Sus-tain me with Thy might. Un-to Thy name I'm hon-or

4. Lord, do Thou hear My plead-ing and my pray'r! Thy word dwells in my heart. Thy grace does flow From Thy blest home on high. The shield of faith Thou art. Be-fore Thy coun-te-nance ap-

fear - ing;	In	stead - fast	faith	to	Thee	I'm
splen - dor!	Pre - pare	me	now	that	I	may
bring - ing,	And	joy - ous -	ly	Thy	prais - es
pear - ing,	In	truth	and	spir - it	Thee	I'm

near - ing.	Thou	art	my	light.
en - ter	Thy	man - sion	bright.
sing - ing;	Hal - le - lu -	jah!
near - ing;	Oh,	hear	my	pray'r!

5. Oh, lead Thou me
Upon the narrow way,
Lest I should stray from Thee!
In Thee alone I place my trust each day;
No mortal can help me.
In Thee, my Lord, I am confiding;
For me a home Thou art providing
In realms of light.

111. THE CALL FOR LABORERS

1. A - wake, Thou soul's first in - spi - ra - tion; Let watch - men stand be - fore the tem - ple door! With con - stant zeal and firm de - vo - tion, A - gainst the

2. Is thus the pi - ous flame ex - tin - guished, The flame of faith di - vine and fer - vent love? Who'll call the souls un - to the Mas - ter, And lead them

3. O, that Thy fire were bright - ly burn - ing And all with faith and love might be in - spired! If all this world were for Thee yearn - ing, For in Thy

4. The prom - ise of true pas - tors giv - en; Hearts like Thine own do Thou in - them in - still. Thy ho - ly Word was nev - er brok - en; We know that

en	-	e	-	my	they	do	im -	plore.	Their
to		the		cross	and	Lord	a -	bove?	Where
blood	sal	-	va -	tion	is	ac -	quired!	O,
Thou	this		prom -	ise	wilt	ful -	fill.	The

peal	-	ing	calls	through -	out	the	world	re - sound; Sal-
is	-	the	Spir -	it's	wit -	ness	in	this day? De-
Lord,	Thou	King,	and	Sav -	iour,	hear	our	plea And
en	-	e -	mies	be -	fore	Thy	hand	shall fall; Thou

va	-	tion,	Lord,	in	Thee	a -	lone	is found.
ny	-	ing	self,	the	Lord	we	should	o - bey.
grant	our	wish	and	speak,	"So	shall	it	be!"
art	for	-	ev -	er	King	and	Lord	of all.

191.

112. THE WATCHMEN'S CALL

1. Call and cry, ye watch - men, bold - ly;
2. Tru - ly stones could not help cry - ing
3. There -fore rise, all ye, His serv - ants;
4. Speak the gos - pel of sal - va - tion

Call a - loud and spare them not!
If the watch - men's call would cease,
For E - li - jah's spir - it pray!
Bold - ly in the wil - der - ness!

Je - sus wants a faith - ful wit - ness;
And the ver - y rocks a - bout us,
If as Lord ye would ad - dress Him,
In the Sav - iour's blood there's heal - ing.

Teach - ers not con - fess - ing Je - sus
Ev - 'ry one a cry - ing wit - ness
Faith - ful - ly ye must con - fess Him,
Grace and par - don He's re - veal - ing

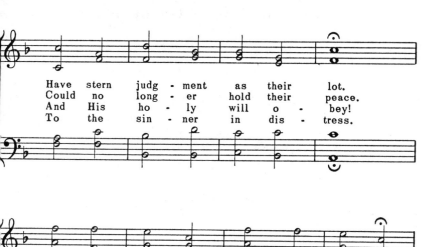

Have stern judg - ment as their lot.
Could no long - er hold their peace.
And His ho - ly will o - bey!
To the sin - ner in dis - tress.

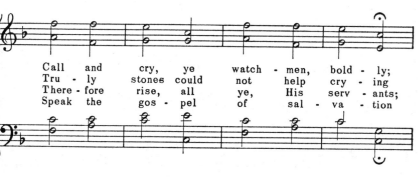

Call and cry, ye watch - men, bold - ly;
Tru - ly stones could not help cry - ing
There - fore rise, all ye, His serv - ants;
Speak the gos - pel of sal - va - tion

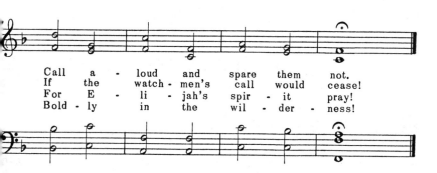

Call a - loud and spare them not.
If the watch - men's call would cease!
For E - li - jah's spir - it pray!
Bold - ly in the wil - der - ness!

113. THE MINISTERS OF THE GOSPEL

57

1. Should I re - strain the Spir - it's course For
2. Should praise of man be more to me Than
3. O Lord, be - hold the frown of them Who
4. Shall I to please the blind - ed throng With -

fear of man so fee - ble? Though Sa - tan's
God's most bless - ed fa - vor? And though man
still re - ject Thy mer - cy! Could I at -
hold Thy word so truth - ful? Or thus to

hosts are rag - ing here, Should I not be more
might re - ject His word, The Truth re - mains for -
tain a bless - ed end, If I would now for -
soothe the ears of men Of their re - proach be

faith - ful? Awed by a mor - tal's frown, shall
ev - er; Un - chang-ing, sure, it does im -
sake Thee? And could I live with Thee on
mind - ful, To gain earth's gild - ed joys, or

194.

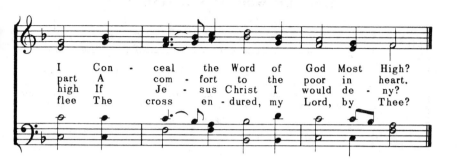

I   Con - ceal   the Word of God Most High?
part A   com - fort to the poor in heart.
high If   Je - sus Christ I would de - ny?
flee The cross en - dured, my Lord, by Thee?

5. What then is he whose scorn I dread,
Whose wrath or hate dismaying?
It is but mortal man I know,
His frown I am not fearing.
He is an heir of death, a slave
To sin, a bubble on the wave!

6. Yea, let men rage; my God is still
My refuge and my tower.
I shall arise to my reward,
Awakened by His power,
Since in all pain Thy tender love
Will still a consolation prove.

7. O, may I seek the souls who stray
And save them from destruction,
And through Thy holy love still lead
Them to Thy congregation.
May pray'rs and pleadings penetrate
To warn them of their lost estate.

8. The mortal man may quite disown
And speak in bold derision
Against my labors and my name;
Yet blest is my condition.
The love of God dispels the fear
And makes my faith in Him more dear.

114. OUR WISH IN PARTING
115, 118.

1. We tar - ry in this blest and tran-quil un - ion,
2. Our souls have been u - nit - ed in sweet un - ion
3. O, may the Chris-tian love be ev - er glow-ing
4. And so, fare - well to you, be - lov - ed broth-er,

And thus u - nit - ed speak the fare - well word. Ye
And man - y pre - cious ho - urs have gone by. Our
With - in our hearts; this is our Sav - iour's will! Though
As now we part and say our fond "fare - well!" Should

loved ones, now the part - ing hour is near - ing,
thoughts a - rose to Christ, our Lord and Sav - iour,
cross or pain or scorn or death be - fall us,
we, a - gain be meet - ing one an - oth - er,

The fare - well greet - ing sounds in one ac -
And He our hearts with love did sanc - ti -
May faith and love to Him be con - stant
Then may we find that in you still doth

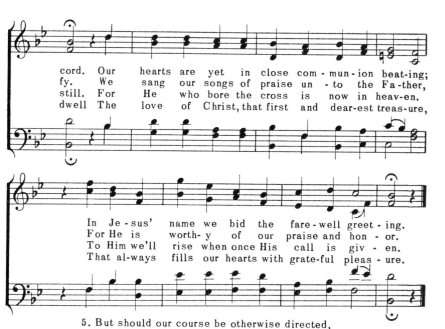

cord. Our hearts are yet in close com - mun - ion beat-ing;
fy. We sang our songs of praise un - to the Fa-ther,
still. For He who bore the cross is now in heav-en.
dwell The love of Christ, that first and dear-est treas-ure,

In Je - sus' name we bid the fare - well greet - ing.
For He is worth- y of our praise and hon - or.
To Him we'll rise when once His call is giv - en.
That al-ways fills our hearts with grate-ful pleas - ure.

5. But should our course be otherwise directed,
   Should we on earth no more each other see,
   Should death approach more quickly than expected,
   Then may the Lord unite us lovingly
   In yonder realm of peace and joy forever,
   Where sun and moon need not be shining ever.

6. Our hands to you in brother-love extending,
   Beloved friends, accept our fond farewell;
   God speed you on until your journey's ending,
   On to His throne where you His praise will tell!
   We look beyond to those untroubled regions,
   In hope to join the Lamb and all His legions.

7. Farewell, meanwhile, farewell, for we are leaving.
   Let not God's Word despised, neglected be!
   E'er faithfully unto your Saviour cleaving,
   His Word, your all in all eternally.
   Let none be found pervert in his behavior,
   But hold ye fast to Christ, our blessed Saviour.

8. So fare ye well! Our hands are joined in parting.
   This may our final farewell greeting be.
   O, let us look unto our Lord and Saviour,
   Who'll lead us into all eternity!
   O, may God's grace, our bond of love completing,
   Protect us all; this is our farewell greeting!

115. THE ARMOR OF GOD
114, 118.

1. Put on the ar - mor of the Lord and
2. When days of trib - u - la - tion are ap -
3. The shield of faith be thine in ev - 'ry
4. So pray ye now, and nev - er cease your

Sav - iour. The en - e - my with art - ful
pear - ing, Call on the Lord; His grace will
con - flict, And from this pre - cious treas - ure
pray - ing Un - to the Lord, and in your

guile is nigh. The hearts of men are oft de -
strength-en thee. Though pow'rs of dark - ness round thee
nev - er part. Though fier - y darts a - round thee
prayer en - dure; For, broth - er, now there can be

ceived by Sa - tan; In God's own strength we
here are rag - ing, God's ar - mor shall your
here are fall - ing, The shield of faith shall
no de - lay - ing! Well for him who in

198.

ev - er	must	re - ly.	Not	on - ly	flesh	and
strength and	ref - uge	be.	Your	loins	be	gird - ed
quench each	fier - y	dart.	The	Spir - it's	sword	and
Je - sus	stands se - cure!	Al - though	a	thou - sand

blood	are	we	sub - du - ing,	But	e - vil
with	God's	truth and	vir - tue,	And	may the
hel - met	of	sal - va - tion	Shall	shield thee
ar - rows	fall	a -round you,	Your	en - e -

spir - its	with	their	hosts pur - su - ing.
Spir - it's	light	shine	bright - ly o'er	you.
in	each	trial and	trib - u - la - tion.
my	shall	nev - er - more con - found	you.

5. You know the way which Christ has marked so clearly,
The way of self-denial that He trod;
O love Him more and evermore sincerely
Who bore the cross for us, the Son of God!
O hear Him from the seat of mercy pleading
With us, His sheep, who need His tender leading!

6. I am the Way, the Truth, and Life eternal.
Whoe'er believes in me shall never die.
Accept the Word which God has kindly given,
The Word of Truth with grace to sanctify.
The Word, as balm, for wounded hearts has healing,
And thus in Thee new life and light revealing.

116. THE FAITHFUL SHEPHERD, JESUS CHRIST

1. The Lord, He is my shep - herd true, Who lead - eth me se - cure - ly On pleas - ant pas - tures to and fro With joys and bless - ings sure - ly. He leads me to the fount of

2. His Word is bread un - to my soul, My in - ner man re - stor - ing. Up - on life's pil - grim jour - ney here My heart to Him goes soar - ing. He safe - ly leads me with His

3. A might - y fort - ress is His name, Where suc - cor nev - er fail - eth. In dai - ly con - flict here on earth Where Sa - tan's might as - sail - eth, I trust in my dear Shep - herd's

4. Not mere - ly 'gainst our flesh and blood This con - flict is en - act - ed; 'Gainst Sa - tan's whole in - fer - nal brood Our bat - tle is di - rect - ed. Yet I feel nei - ther fear nor

life	My	soul	to	com - fort	and	re - vive.
hand	Through	pil - grim's	dale	to	heav - en's	land.
might	And	to	this	strong-hold	take	my flight.
fright,	For	Je - sus	is	my	strength and	might.

5. His staff is ever my support
   On pathways lone and dreary;
   My consolation is His Word;
   And, lest I might grow weary,
   A table is prepared for me
   In presence of mine enemy.

6. Lo, He anoints my head with oil
   And heals my wounded spirit;
   He stays my soul, and after toil
   He never fails to cheer it.
   He makes my cup to overflow
   That I, refreshed, may onward go.

7. This Shepherd ne'er forsakes His fold
   In joy nor yet in sorrow,
   But shares to us His love untold
   Each day and each tomorrow.
   Then let us follow to the end
   And with Him enter heaven's land.

8. Then haste, this faithful Shepherd claim
   Whose care is ever present,
   Who calls His faithful ones by name
   To pastures green and pleasant.
   He finds them all where'er they roam;
   He leads the way and brings them home!

117. DOST THOU LOVE ME?

1. "Dost thou love Me?" the Sav - iour said To Pe - ter, His true serv - ant, When o'er the fold He gave him charge And His di - vine com - mand - ment. The Sav - iour did him thus re - mind That scorn and

2. It is no art in peace - ful days Our love to be re - veal - ing, When all is well with life and soul, When here no wolves are rag - ing. But when the e - vil days ap - pear, When tri - als,

3. The Lord be - holds us in our grief, And asks in true af - fec - tion, "Dost thou love Me, my fol - low - er, In sor - row and af - flic - tion? Thoug grief may press on ev - 'ry side, Will yet thy

4. The com - mon an - swer that we hear, And oft in deep - est sad - ness, "Thou know - est, Lord, I hold Thee dear, Thou art my Joy and Glad - ness." And then the Lord doth ask a - gain, "Wilt thou love

tri -	als	he	would	find,	E'en	death	and	per - se -
grief	and	pain	draw	near,	Will	yet	our	love be
love	in	Me	a - bide?	Wilt	thou	in	per - se -
Me	a -	mid	great	pain?	Will	in	the	fier - y

cu -	tion	Would	be	the	shep	-herd's	por - tion.
fer -	vent,	A -	bid - ing	as	His	serv - ant.
cu -	tion	Still	keep	thy	firm	de -	vo - tion?"
tri -	al	Thy	love	know	no	de -	ni - al?"

5. "Then, follow Me, and feed My sheep
On pastures green and pleasant,
And o'er them faithful vigil keep,
For wolves are always present;
Preserve and guide them on their way
That leads through death to endless day,
In love for them here living
And for them your life giving."

6. The faithful shepherds do not flee
When hungry wolves are nearing;
Ah, no, their duty then they see
Unto their sheep adhering.
Their sheep will follow after them
When first they here the Cross of shame
Upon their backs have taken,
And shame leaves them unshaken.

7. Afflictions here on earth abound
And burdens we must carry.
Through Jesus' death we shall attain
The Kingdom of His glory.
Through many conflicts we must go,
And bear our mutual grief and woe,
For trials oft are given,
Whereby our faith is proven.

118. GOD'S GLORY MAGNIFIED BY HIS WORKS
114, 115.

1. Lord, Thou Cre - a - tor, glo - rious is Thy king - dom! In all the world we sing of Thy great fame. The hosts of heav'n with all the true and faith - ful chil - dren now em - ploy - ing, E - ter - nal - Thou art pre -

2. The might and plan of foes Thou art de - stroy - ing, As gra - cious won - der in Thy cov - 'nant new, The mouths of Thine own chil - dren now em - ploy - ing,

3. O Lord, how won - drous is Thy strength and kind - ness Which Thou to mor - tal man dost yet re - veal! Thy love is shown to us in all its full - ness, For through Thy

4. Thy blood has made a - tone - ment for Thy chil - dren; Thy grace and love to them has e'er been shared. How pre - cious are the words which Thou hast spok - en: "My king - dom

Tune arranged from "My God And I" with permission of copyright owner.
Copyright 1957 by Kalnin, Mohr and Apsit.

204.

ly shall praise Thy ho - ly name. Thou art ex -
par - ing Thee a pow - er, too, Un - to Thy
grace our guilt no more we feel. True in - no -
for the meek has been pre - pared!'' The sin - ful

alt - ed there in heav - en's splen - dor, And kings and
hon - or and un - to Thy glo - ry, Where- by, at
cence is still Thy ad - o - ra - tion, And chil - dren
man is called to Thy al - le - giance, And as Thy

pow - ers shall to Thee sur - rend - er.
length Thy foes must bow be - fore Thee.
have Thy spe - cial in - vi - ta - tion.
child is led un - to o - be - dience.

When I behold Thy strength and mighty power,
Thou, God and Ruler of the hosts of light,
The moon and stars and all Thy works so wondrous
Proclaim Thy glory and Thy sovereign might!
How wonderful, O Lord, is Thy creation!
We worship Thee in holy admiration.

O, what is man that Thou shouldst him remember,
The son of man, that Thou for him shouldst care,
That Thou to him Thy saving grace shouldst render,
Yea, that Thou didst his very nature share?
Thou hast Thyself, Thy precious lifeblood given,
An offering to ransom him for heaven.

7. Though for a moment Thou hast him forsaken,
With praise and honor Thou dost him receive.
To light and life Thou dost him then awaken;
O, who can this Thy love divine perceive?
Thou grantest righteousness and grace, O Saviour,
And leadest him on heavenly ways forever.

8. Thou wilt again exalt him in high measure,
When he the battle of the faith has fought;
And once again Thou wilt in him find pleasure,
When Thou hast him unto Thy glory brought.
O Lord, our Ruler, may Thy praise forever
Be sung by choirs of all Thy children ever!

119. ARISE, FOR THE LIGHT COMETH!

99, 104, 120, 253.

1. One flock and a shep-herd dear! What a glor-ious vis-i-ta-tion When Thy day will once ap-pear To re-store us full sal-va-tion. Let His light wake

2. Watch-man, is the day a-far? See the morn-ing light is gleam-ing; Light from the bright morn-ing star Through the dark-est clouds is stream-ing. Stran-gers blind-ed

3. Come Thou, Shep-herd, faith-ful One; May Thy light dis-pel the dark-ness! From Thee and Thy lit-tle fold Err-ing lambs have strayed so help-less. Lit-tle flock, now

4. See the dark clouds pass a-way With the morn-ing light's ap-pear-ance. Thirst-ing stran-gers kneel to pray By the fount of life in rev-'rence, Till they see the

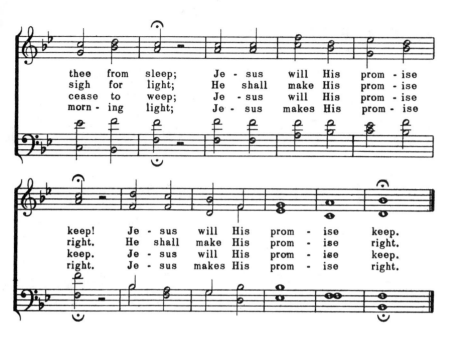

thee from sleep; Je - sus will His prom - ise keep! Je - sus will His prom - ise keep.
sigh for light; He shall make His prom - ise right. He shall make His prom - ise right.
cease to weep; Je - sus will His prom - ise keep. Je - sus will His prom - ise keep.
morn - ing light; Je - sus makes His prom - ise right. Je - sus makes His prom - ise right.

5. See the graves asunder rent
   With their dead to life appearing!
   Angel of the covenant
   Now proclaims His day is nearing!
   Jesus calls: "Let there be light!"
   Jesus makes His promise right.
   Jesus makes His promise right.

6. O, behold that glorious day!
   Jesus Christ, our Sun and treasure,
   Giving light and wisdom still,
   Peace and joy in fullest measure!
   See the light! Awake from sleep!
   Jesus will His promise keep!
   Jesus will His promise keep!

120. JESUS LIVES!
99, 104, 119, 253.

1. Je - sus lives! I live with Him. Death no more my soul shall fright - en. Now He lives, and at His call, From death's sleep I shall a - wak - en; I am glo - ri - fied in Thee;

2. Je - sus lives! O'er all the world Pow'r su - preme to Him is giv - en. With my Sav - iour I shall live; I shall reign with Him in heav - en. Thus in God con - fid - ing still;

3. Je - sus lives! Do not de - spair: He shall show His great com - pas - sion To the sin - ner who re - pents; Per - fect shall be his re - mis - sion. Thou shalt hear the sin - ner's plea;

4. Je - sus lives! And I shall find Life in Him and full sal - va - tion. Ne'er op - pose Him; He shall then Make your heart His hab - i - ta - tion. Weak - ness is o'er - come in Thee;

208.

This	my	con - fi - dence	shall	be.
He	His	prom - ise	will	ful - fill.
This	my	con - fi - dence	shall	be.
This	my	con - fi - dence	shall	be.

5. Jesus lives! No pow'r of night
From the Lord my soul shall sever.
Sorrows may come o'er the way,
Yet I'll cling to Him forever.
Light and faith I find in thee;
This my confidence shall be.

6. Jesus lives! Henceforth is death
But the gate to life immortal;
This shall calm my trembling breath,
When I pass its gloomy portal.
Faith shall cry, as fails each sense:
Jesus is my confidence.

7. Jesus, my Redeemer, lives!
Hence I shall to life awaken.
O what joy this message gives!
How then can my hope be shaken?
For how could our blessed Head
Rise and leave His members dead?

8. By the bond of hope and love
I am bound unto the Master.
Faith looks up to Him above,
Rests on Him through all disaster.
Even death now cannot keep
From my Shepherd me, His sheep.

9. Who here suffers, sighs, and yearns,
There will walk in glorious splendor;
Here my flesh to dust returns,
There it will arise in grandeur.
Sown here in mortality;
There it's risen gloriously.

10. Then rejoice, His children dear,
In His guidance and protection;
Death may come, but do not fear:
There shall be a resurrection
When the final trump shall call,
From the graves awaking all!

121. CHRIST THE RESURRECTED

134, 135, 138, 139.

1. We wel - come now the He - ro, Who lay in calm re - pose, For o - ver death He tri - umphed And from the grave He rose.

2. O Lord, Thou hast now con - quered That strong and craft - y foe; This giv - eth faith and com - fort, For God is with us now!

3. The peace, which Thou hast brought us, All fear has put to flight; The right - eous now in cho - rus Are sing - ing with de - light!

4. May we with con - so - la - tion, Thy tro - phies with Thee share. O, that this great sal - va - tion, Ex - tend here ev - 'ry - where!

5. Our sins have all been buried
   There in the grave with Thee.
   Oh, what a blessed comfort;
   We fear no enemy!

6. Lord, for this great salvation
   Be Thou forever praised,
   That after life's temptations
   To heaven we'll be raised.

7. We shall without despairing
   Go with Thee to the grave,
   And we Thy face beholding,
   May be forever safe.

8. Extend Thy banner o'er us,
   And guide us to the goal!
   Beyond the grave and darkness
   To heaven lead our souls.

9. What is there now to harm us?
   Of death we have no fear;
   We have in our Lord Jesus
   Found grace and mercy here!

1. Thine is the light! From Thee true wis - dom
2. Thine is the strength! True teach - ers for Thy
3. Thy Spir - it, Lord, Re - news our faint - ing
4. Thy bless - ings flow Up - on the seeds of

comes, Which leads our hearts a - right. Thou art the
fold Thou dost pro - vide, O Lord! Thou dost im -
souls; Its help we do im - plore. Our hearts oft
truth Which in our hearts re - main. The shift - ing

Fount, From which all grace does flow And brings us
part Sal - va - tion's strength and pow'r To him who
seem To sink in deep re - pose Till it does
wind De - stroys the germ of life And blows a -

to Thy light. Our souls, O Lord, Thou dost en -
speaks Thy word. He plants and wa - ters, light be -
zeal re - store. For through the Ho - ly Spir - it's
way the grain. If in our hearts Thy seed has

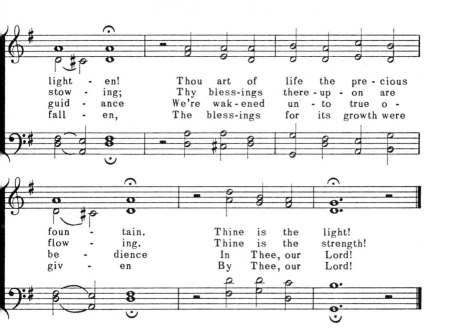

light	-	en!	Thou	art	of	life	the	pre - cious
stow	-	ing;	Thy	bless-ings	there - up -	on	are
guid	-	ance	We're	wak-ened	un - to	true	o -
fall	-	en,	The	bless-ings	for	its	growth	were

foun	-	tain.	Thine	is	the	light!
flow	-	ing.	Thine	is	the	strength!
be	-	dience	In	Thee, our	Lord!
giv	-	en	By	Thee, our	Lord!

5. The fruit is Thine!
   The tender germs of life
   Oft perish in distress.
   Salvation's fruit is ripened by Thy grace,
   And thou alone canst bless.
   If in our youth we learn Thy wisdom
   And reap the harvest in the autumn,
   Thine is the fruit!

6. The praise be Thine,
   Thou, Lord of righteousness;
   Salvation comes from Thee!
   In time of grace awaken us with zeal
   That we may faithful be!
   May we return to Thee rejoicing,
   With Thy Redeemed ones ever singing:
   Hallelujah!

123. HEAD AND MEMBERS
124, 164, 230, 248.

1. We praise Thee, Lord, with pow'r to save!
2. My soul is ev - er prais - ing Thee!
3. I'm rec - on - ciled to God through Thee.
4. From judg - ment and dam - na - tion free,

Thou didst a - rise from death and grave.
I am re - deemed e - ter - nal - ly.
Sal - va - tion's strength is crown -ing me.
Be - liev - ing I do wor - ship Thee!

Thou hast dis - pelled the pow'rs of night;
From heav - en's throne to earth - ly strife
With God Thou reign - est with - out end;
Thou liv - est and I'm ev - er Thine,

Our life is now re - vealed in light.
Thou didst de - scend to give us life.
Thou art my Sav -iour and my friend.
And now e - ter - nal life is mine.

214.

5. I shall, when Thou, O Lord of All,
   Shall come with pow'r the dead to call,
   Arise from death and leave my grave
   To dwell with Thee forever safe.

6. Before Thy throne and in Thy sight,
   Forever like the angels bright,
   In realms above the saved shall shine.
   O what a glory shall be mine!

7. O dwell within me, Lord, I pray!
   I'll strive to live for Thee each day.
   O, may my faith in Thee be true;
   Unto Thy image me renew!

8. Since Jesus rose, there's strength and life
   To help me through this earthly strife.
   O, Saviour, grant that I may be
   Thy faithful servant, pure and free!

9. Be Thou my comfort, light and share,
   My life, salvation, here and there.
   O, may my soul to Thee ascend,
   When here my pilgrimage shall end!

10. O, thou redeemed, do glorify
    The Saviour, who now lives on high!
    And there He intercedes for thee;
    He lives in all eternity!

124. RESURRECTION AND SPIRITUAL LIFE
123, 164, 230, 248

1. O Thou who in the grave didst lay, O sac - red
2. How did Thy hum-ble flocks re - joice When they saw
3. O Lord, Thou liv-est for us now; Our Lord and
4. And now in Spir-it Thou dost call From heav - en

be to us this day, For on this day our Lord a-
Thee and heard Thy voice! O Lord, may we, though on this
Je - sus Christ art Thou! We know that Thou canst hear and
to us one and all: "May peace be with thee, child of

rose In glo - ry from His death re - pose.
earth, Share with them all their peace and mirth!
see, When we sing songs of praise to Thee!
mine, For heav - en's king - dom shall be thine."

5. Lest we forget Thy name we ask
   That pleasure be to us our task.
   Thou livest for us now and we
   Have faith to end our days in Thee.

6. Thy Spirit's seal, O Lord, we pray
   Renew and strengthen in each day!
   And through Thy love so pure and kind,
   Draw up to heaven heart and mind.

7. Thy Spirit animate each heart;
   God's holy love to us impart.
   Give us Thy likeness, pure and fair;
   For heaven's kingdom us prepare!

8. May, Lord, Thy holy love to us
   Keep our hearts true and virtuous.
   Thou image of the Father dear,
   Make us like Thee, so pure and clear!

125. CHRIST, OUR LEADER

1. Draw us to Thee, O Lord; may we Still
2. Draw us to Thee; our plea shall be, Freed
3. Draw us to Thee; our course shall be Wher -
4. Draw us to Thee, for weak are we; In

jour - ney on to heav - en. In one ac - cord Thro'
from this earth's af - flic - tions. By Thy great might, In
ev - er Thou shalt lead us. Thy light re - veal, That
Thee we seek pro - tec - tion. Lord, we are Thine; Thy

Christ our Lord May grace to us be giv - en.
won - drous light, We'll strive for full per - fec - tion.
we may feel Thy mer - cy in its full - ness.
hand di - vine Can save us from de - struc - tion.

5. Draw us to Thee, and then shall we
   Prepare us for Thy kingdom.
   Do make us pure; To live secure,
   We'd share in Thy salvation.

6. Draw us to Thee, and we shall see
   The victor's crown of glory,
   Which we shall gain, If we remain
   Thy children, pure and lowly.

7. Draw us to Thee, and then shall we
   Ascend to Thee in heaven.
   Our praise shall be, Eternally
   To Thee, our Saviour, given!

217.

126. JOY ON THE SABBATH DAY

1. O how wel - come is the sab - bath, Joy - ous
2. Hear the words of ex - hor - ta - tion From the
3. Ye re - deemed, con - tin - ue prais - ing, Joy - ful -

Day for all the ran - somed! Day of peace and
Mas - ter of cre - a - tion. We can feel His
ly your voi - ces rais - ing, Thank-ing God for

day of rest, Con - se - crat - ed to God's blest.
love for all. Heed, o - bey His ten - der call.
His great love, Man - i - fest - ed from a - bove.

4. He, who never has denied us,
But abundantly supplied us,
Took our sins and guilt away
And provides for us each day.

5. May this be a day of blessing!
In Thee, Lord, we are rejoicing.
He's the sun, whose radiance bright
Fills our hearts with warmth and light.

6. Lord, may we in fullest measure
Seek to do Thy will with pleasure.
Let us ever live for Thee,
Free from sin and vanity.

7. Father, through Thy word awaken
Us to faith and true devotion!
Zeal to serve Thee do Thou give;
Show us that Thy Son still lives.

8. For Thy fervent love we pray Thee!
May we ever striving daily
On the sorrowing bestow
Words of comfort in their woe.

9. Precious Teacher, leave us never!
We would follow Thee forever
Praying, seeking, trusting Thee,
Till Thy glory we shall see.

127. PROVE YE EVERY SPIRIT

1. Prove ye, prove ye ev'- ry spir - it, As the Mas - ter
2. Thus their right- eous-ness be - hold - ing, All in out- ward
3. Though the wolves be ev - er rag - ing, Thou Thy fold art

did com - mand it; Know their works, not words a - lone, Men, as
form un - fold-ing, In - ward-ly they will ap - pear Hos-tile
still de - fend-ing. When such spir- its do as- sail, We, who

trees, by fruits are known. Are their fruits, their works and
to Thy chil - dren here. He who lives in true o -
know Thee, will pre - vail. Lord, do Thou dis - pel con-

teach-ing Based on doc - trines Christ was preach-ing? Do they
be - dience Can dis -cern the voice and pres - ence Of such
fu - sion, Err - ing ones free from de - lu - sion. Sav-iour,

love and teach the truth? Will their wis- dom God ap - prove?
stran-gers which draw near; May we flee when they ap- pear.
may Thy fold in - crease, Grant us com-fort, joy and peace!

128. BAPTISM AND COMMUNION

1. O God be praised, who reigns a - bove,
2. Our heav - y debt He did for - give
3. He cleansed us from each sin - ful stain
4. The wed - ding gar - ment white as snow

For grant - ing us sal - va - tion! We
And gave us rai - ments spot - less. His
Through pre - cious blood of Je - sus. He
He gave us in bap - tis - m. Through

have through Je - sus Christ, His Son,
Spir - it did our souls re - vive;
did u - nite us then with Him,
right - eous - ness in Him we have

Ob - tained re - gen - er - a - tion.
Our hearts were filled with glad - ness.
From Ad - am's fall re - deemed us.
To a new life a - ris - en.

220.

5. In this pure garment, white and fair,
   Of heavenly perfection
   He calls us to His supper there;
   O, blessed invitation!

6. Ye children of the Lord, rejoice
   In true and holy union,
   That ye are called to sup with Him
   In such divine communion.

7. A mansion He has now prepared
   For us in heaven's glory,
   And with the robe of righteousness
   He clothes us pure and holy.

8. Rejoice, thou holy Church of God,
   Christ's advent now is nearing!
   For He shall come to call His bride
   With angel hosts appearing.

9. Your wedding robes keep free from stain;
   Your soul guard from deception.
   Thou wilt enjoy with Jesus there
   A glorious reception.

10. O, blest are they who here receive
    The Bridegroom's invitation
    And who endure unto the end
    All trials and tribulation!

11. And after all the many griefs
    Through which they here are going,
    In glory they shall then rejoice
    With crowns of beauty glowing.

12. O, therefore Zion, God's own host,
    Hold fast to faith's assurance;
    Stay true, and thou shalt then receive
    A crown for thy endurance!

129. THE HEART, GOD'S SANCTUARY

1. O Lord of Hosts, how pleas-ant is
2. O, how my soul does long to live
3. My soul had strayed a - way from Thee,
4. My err - ing soul, which once was lost,

The ci - ty where Thy name in glo - ry
With - in the por - tals of Thy Sanc - tu -
But now in peace - ful rest it is a -
With - in Thy blood and wounds has found re -

dwell - eth! When Thou in - to the mor - tal
ar - y! O, Lord, my soul re - joic - es
bid - ing. To Thee I turned and found a
demp - tion. I hum - bly fall be - fore Thy

hearts dost turn, How blest are they in
fer - vent - ly. To Thee I give all
safe re - treat, Just as a swal - low
mer - cy seat And find my sol - ace,

whom Thy Spir - it rul - eth! They shall re - joice in
hon - or, praise, and glo - ry! I'll wor - ship Thee through
to its nest re - turn - ing. How sweet to rest, thus
rest and full sal - va - tion. With Thee, my God and

all e - ter - ni - ty Who live for Thee.
all my pil - grim days With thanks and praise.
kept in ev - 'ry hour From Sa - tan's pow'r!
King, I would a - bide, What - e'er be - tide!

5. O blessed are all they who dwell
Within Thine house, who praise Thee now and ever.
O blessed is the man, he doeth well,
Whose rest Thou art, whose heart is Thine forever;
For he, who Thee as his sure strength doth know,
May safely go.

6. In peace, he treads this vale of tears,
Where troubles rise and there is so much sorrow;
There is no need or anguish that he fears;
He trusts in God, thus facing each tomorrow.
Thou crownest him with blessings rich, divine,
For he is Thine.

7. Lord God of hosts, now hear our prayer;
Our God our Shield, we daily do implore Thee;
For it belongs, O Lord, unto Thy care
To keep the kingdom of Thy Son before Thee;
When Satan threatens, Thou art Sun and Shield,
To Thee we yield.

130. SONG OF PRAISE FOR REDEMPTION
131.

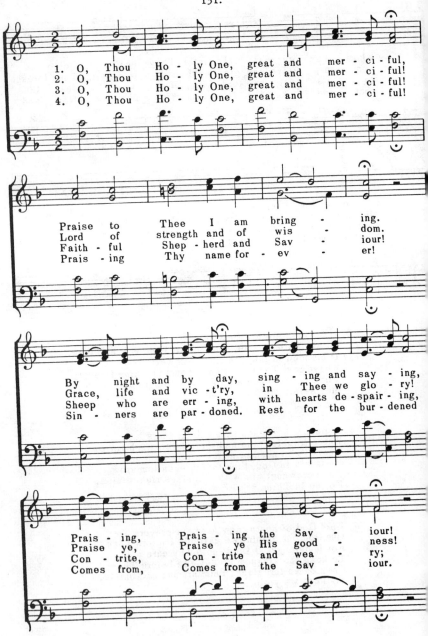

1. O, Thou Ho - ly One, great and mer - ci - ful,
2. O, Thou Ho - ly One, great and mer - ci - ful!
3. O, Thou Ho - ly One, great and mer - ci - ful!
4. O, Thou Ho - ly One, great and mer - ci - ful!

Praise to Thee I am bring - ing.
Lord of strength and of wis - dom.
Faith - ful Shep - herd and Sav - iour!
Prais - ing Thy name for - ev - er!

By night and by day, sing - ing and say - ing,
Grace, life and vic - t'ry, in Thee we glo - ry!
Sheep who are err - ing, with hearts de - spair - ing,
Sin - ners are par - doned. Rest for the bur - dened

Prais - ing, Prais - ing the Sav - iour!
Praise ye, Praise ye His good - ness!
Con - trite, Con - trite and wea - ry;
Comes from, Comes from the Sav - iour.

224.

An - gels re - joic - ing, their choirs are prais - ing,
See - ing His glo - ry, tast - ing His mer - cy,
Such art Thou seek - ing, the right - eous keep - ing
Joy be in heav - en; mer - cy is giv - en!

Laud - ing, Laud - ing the Sav - iour!
Praise ye, Praise ye His good - ness!
In Thy, In Thy great mer - cy.
Thanks to, Thanks to the Sav - iour!

5. O, Thou Holy One, Thou All-gracious One,
   King of heavenly glory!
   Sins Thou dost banish; then they all vanish.
   Adam's, Adam's sin is past.
   Grace Thou revealest; all our wounds healest,
   Moses', Moses' law is past.

6. O, Thou Holy One, Thou All-gracious One!
   Thou alone art my Portion!
   Thy Spirit's power grants every hour
   To us, to us salvation!
   Freed by Thee, Saviour, I would not waver,
   Yielding, yielding my all to Thee.

7. O, Thou Holy One, Thou All-gracious One!
   Thou dost grant holy seasons!
   Our heart rejoices; we lift our voices:
   Praise Thee, praise Thee forever!
   There we will meet Thee, with all who love Thee,
   Praise Thee, praise Thee forever!

8. O, Thou Holy One, Thou All-gracious One,
   Father, Saviour and Counsellor!
   There I'll be living where Thou art giving
   To Thine, to Thine full glory.
   Those who live for Thee, by Thee made worthy,
   Shall shine, shall shine in glory!

225.

131. EXALTATION

130.

1. O Thou Ho - ly One, great and
2. O Thou Ho - ly One, great and
3. O Thou Ho - ly One, great and
4. O Thou Ho - ly One, great and

mer - ci - ful! Lord of all and Cre -
mer - ci - ful! We al - so are Thy
mer - ci - ful! Je - sus, Sav - iour of
mer - ci - ful! Spir - it of love and

a - tor! Thee we are
chil - dren. Thy mer - cy
man - kind! Friend of the
wis - dom! Com - fort us

near - ing,   Bless - ings de - sir - ing,   Help
plead - ing,   In   Thee con - fid - ing.   Help
chil - dren,   Sav - iour of   sin - ners.   Help
ev - er;   Show   us   the   Fa - ther; Reign

us, Help us, Je - ho - vah!
us, Help us, O   Fa - ther!
us, Help us, Lord Je - sus!
Thou, Reign Thou, with - in   us!

5. O Thou Holy One, great and merciful!
Comfort and keep us ever!
Thou, our Consoler, Helper and Father,
Share us, Share us Thy blessings!

132. APPROACH TO THE THRONE OF GOD

77, 181, 133.

1. To Thee, Sav - iour, we draw near, With our
2. Mor - tals in this world can find Joys that
3. Pre - cious is Thy king - dom there, What can
4. Je - sus, come, we do im - plore! Thine we'd

thanks we now ap - pear. Hear Thou, Lord, our child - like
cheer the car - nal mind, And what men shall count as
now with it com - pare! Grace, O Lord, in Thee, we
be for - ev - er - more. Give us now Thy Spir - it's

plea; Grant what we shall ask of Thee.
gain, All such pleas - ures are in vain.
find, Joy and peace for heart and mind.
seal; Thus Thy prom - is - es re - veal.

5. Lord, Thy gospel does resound
With its news the world around.
Nations hear the blessed word,
Grace and peace from Christ, the
(Lord.

6. Open Thou the hearts of men!
Let Thy kingdom come, and then
Check Thou every cunning might,
Turn to day the darkest night!

7. In Thine heralds, power inspire,
Patience, wisdom, love's true fire!
Though they here must sow in tears,
Yet the richest fruit is theirs.

8. Zion, thank Thy Lord anew;
What you pray He'll gladly do,
For His mercy does appear
To us all, both far and near.

9. Brethren, sing through all the days
Songs of love and hymns of praise.
Jesus Christ our joy shall be
Here and in eternity.

133. THE CITY OF GOD
77, 132, 181.

1. Tri - umph, O Thou cit - y fair, Which the
2. Though the en - e - mies as - sail, Fear - less
3. Doth the na - tions' wrath in - crease? Let them
4. All thy foes the Lord pur - sues, Till at

Sav - iour does pre - pare For the right - eous
shall Thy flock pre - vail, For the Lord of
rage -- bear thou in peace! Suf - fer in a
length He all sub - dues, Lays the world be -

fold so pure! They are ev - er kept se - cure.
glo - ry bright Gives thee lib - er - ty and light.
pa - tient mood; Bleed! for fruit - ful is thy blood!
neath His yoke, Who His ven - geance did pro - voke.

5. He who will not to Thee turn,
   And Thy pard'ning graces spurn,
   Shall not see Thy glory bright,
   But great woe and endless night.

6. "Jesus lives!" my song shall be.
   He upholds and comforts me.
   Though all hell oppose my ways,
   God defends me. Him I'll praise!

7. And Thy fold in one accord
   Worships Thee, our King and Lord!
   When the storms are raging sore,
   Be our refuge evermore!

Music arranged from "Hand In Hand With Jesus."
Composer, L. D. Huffstuttler
Copyright owner, Stamps-Baxter Music & Printing Co.
Used by permission

229.

134. THE GRACE OF GOD

121, 135, 138, 242.

1. May grace be with us ev - er, The grace of Christ, the Lord, May He, as here we jour - ney, jour - ney, His grace to us af - ford.
2. While on this nar - row path - way For grace we do de - pend Up - on the Lord and Sav - iour, Sav - iour, Who'll lead us to the end.
3. For grace we still are trust - ing In Christ who can re - new Our hearts when sad and wea - ry, wea - ry; We know the Lord is true.
4. Though sor - row be in - creas - ing In faith we look to Thee. Thou art the bless - ed Sav - iour, Sav - iour; Thy com - ing we would see!

5. Thy grace we need forever,
   Without it we would fail.
   In patience we shall conquer, conquer,
   Through faith we shall prevail.

6. No loss are we sustaining
   What we for Christ deny.
   For He in love and mercy, mercy,
   His grace shall e'er supply.

7. O Lord may it be pleasing,
   Though oft on Thee we call;
   Thy mercy we are pleading, pleading;
   Thy grace be with us all!

135. ABIDE WITH US

121, 134, 138, 139.

1. A - bide with us, Lord Je - sus; Thy grace on
2. A - bide with us, dear Sav - iour! For Thee our
3. A - bide with Thy true bright - ness, Thou pre - cious
4. A - bide with heav'n-ly bless - ings, O rich - est

us be - stow; And guard that ne'er can
hearts pre - pare, That hence - forth and for -
light di - vine! And gird us with up -
Lord of peace! May grace, each heart pos -

harm us, The e - vil, craf - ty foe.
ev - er Sal - va - tion we may share.
right - ness, To truth our hearts in - cline!
ses - sing, A - bun - dant - ly in - crease!

5. Thy wings for our protection
Be o'er us, Lord, unfurled!
O, guard us from deception
Of Satan and the world!

6. Abide with Thy devotion;
Thy children ever bless!
Grant Thy heroic courage,
Help us through all distress!

136. THE PILGRIM'S SONG
121, 134, 137, 242.

1. Come chil - dren, join in sing - ing Sweet
2. He is the faith - ful Shep - herd, Our
3. His word our souls does nour - ish; It
4. It shows us our rich treas - ure Which

prais - es to our Lord, Who blest us
Rock and Ref - uge true, Who lov - ing -
is so sweet and pure, Gives faith and
God doth now pre - pare, Re - fresh - es

with sal - va - tion Through faith in His good
ly doth lead us, Whose word doth us re -
strength in con - flict, All tri - als to en -
us with pleas - ure, Its com - forts we do

word. Who blest us with sal - va - tion
new. Who lov - ing - ly doth lead us,
dure. Gives faith and strength in con - flict
share. Re - fresh - es us with pleas - ure,

232.

Through	faith	in	His	good	word.
Whose	word	doth	us	re -	new.
All	tri -	als	to	en -	dure.
Its	com -	forts	we	do	share.

5. Our hearts are filled with praises;
   Our zeal it does renew,
   :: Removes all fear and doubting,
   Gives motives pure and true. ::

6. It has great fascination
   For us on earth below,
   :: And in all tribulation
   Doth heaven's cheer bestow. ::

7. And when with troubles burdened,
   We'll tell our Friend so dear.
   :: He hears our earnest pleading;
   With help He'll soon appear. ::

8. He graciously beholds us
   And leads us in His way,
   :: And joyfully we'll journey
   To heaven day by day. ::

9. So let us journey onward
   To heaven and the blest,
   :: For after strife and toiling
   We'll reach the land of rest. ::

137. OUR LOVE SHALL NOT DIMINISH

121, 134, 139, 242.

1. Our love shall not di - min - ish Nor fade nor wax a - way; Bind us till life we fin - ish And in the grave we lay.

2. Our love shall not di - min - ish; It is our Lord's com - mand, And free us from all blem - ish, Be - fore our God to stand.

3. Though all this world be fleet - ing, True love will still a - bide, And when our jour - ney's end - ing, Lord, lead us to Thy side.

4. Yea, great - er love shall be there More per - fect and com - plete, When freed from pain and sor - row, Our Lord and God we meet.

D.S. al fine.

5. Earth's trials and temptations
Make true love manifest,
:: To gain for us salvation
And heaven's joy and rest.::

6. Pure love leads to perfection,
Joy of our soul and guide,
:: Gives us true satisfaction,
And leads to heaven's light. ::

138. JESUS IMMANUEL
121, 134, 137, 139.

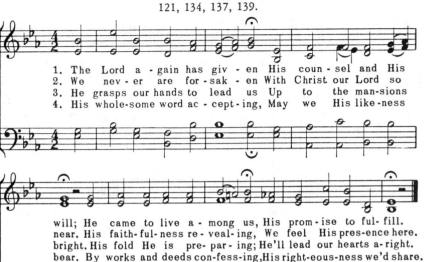

1. The Lord a - gain has giv - en His coun - sel and His
2. We nev - er are for - sak - en With Christ our Lord so
3. He grasps our hands to lead us Up to the man - sions
4. His whole-some word ac - cept-ing, May we His like -ness

will; He came to live a - mong us, His prom-ise to ful- fill.
near. His faith- ful- ness re - veal- ing, We feel His pres-ence here.
bright. His fold He is pre- par- ing; He'll lead our hearts a- right.
bear. By works and deeds con-fess-ing, His right-eous-ness we'd share.

5. May we in silence striving,
In Christ each vict'ry gain,
And with the Spirit's guidance,
Submissive still remain.

6. So march then boldly onward;
Our Saviour's in the lead!
He, as a faithful shepherd,
Sustains us in our need.

7. We shall not be regretful
We trod the narrow way.
We know the Lord is faithful,
Whose call we did obey.

8. We earnestly are striving
For that which brings us peace,
Renouncing sin, abhorring
The world's iniquities.

9. Protect, O Lord, Thy children,
As we still tarry here,
That we in realms of glory
May then with Thee appear.

10. Our songs of praise ascending
In heaven's melody,
There in Thy glorious kingdom
We'll ever worship Thee.

235.

121, 134, 137, 138.

1. Oh, what is more de - light - ful, And in what blessed state,
2. We live in bless-ed near-ness To Thee, Lord, day by day,
3. Our lips may be in si - lence, Yet prays our heart to Thee;
4. With mer-cy and with good-ness Our hearts are oft re-freshed,

When we our souls and bod - ies To God do con - se - crate?
As if our eyes be - hold Thee; And joy at-tends our way.
Our thoughts are e'er as - cend - ing To heav-en con-stant-ly.
And when we need His pres - ence He an-swers our re-quest.

When we our souls and bod - ies To God do con - se - crate?
As if our eyes be - hold Thee; And joy at-tends our way.
Our thoughts are e'er as - cend-ing To heav- en con-stant-ly.
And when we need His pres-ence He an-swers our re-quest.

5. Around His footstool bowing
   As children dear are we,
   :: And when our tears are flowing
   Straight to His heart we flee.::

6. And when we do grow weary
   He bringeth us to rest;
   :: We in our graves do tarry,
   And sleep there with the blest.::

7. There freed from earthly burdens,
   With no more pain or ache,
   :: Till in the glorious morning
   He calls: "Awake! Awake!"::

8. What further shall transpire
   May unto us but seem,
   :: While we are rising higher,
   As if but in a dream.::

9. With angels upward soaring
   Into the realms of light,
   :: Our Saviour there beholding,
   We'll share His glory bright.::

10. There with the angels singing,
    In heaven we shall roam,
    :: With gratitude proclaiming:
    We've reached the soul's bright home.::

140. ENTREATY FOR GOD'S BLESSINGS

1. Spir-it of true love and strength, Spir-it of great splen-dor, Do Thou now and ev-er-more To us bless-ings ren-der. Sin-ners, Lord, un-wor-thy are, Of Thy great com-pas-sion. He who seeks Thee earn-est-ly Shall ob-tain re-mis-sion.

2. Now, O Lord, our hearts in-flame, Grant us all Thy bless-ing! And Thy pres-ence here pro-claim, Us in love em-brac-ing! Speech and si-lence, pray'er and plea, E'en the soul's re-flec-tion, We sub-mit, O Lord, to Thee And Thy wise di-rec-tion!

3. Ho-ly Lamb, Thy pre-cious blood Brings to all sal-va-tion; In this pure and cleans-ing flood Have we found re-demp-tion. When Thy flock was gath-ered there In true sup-pli-ca-tion, In Thy strength Thou didst ap-pear To Thy con-gre-ga-tion.

141. PRAISE AND CONSECRATION

1. For ev-er be praised, God's spir-it of grace, That from Thee I learn How friend-ly my Sav-iour To sin-ners doth turn.

2. If on-ly my thought En-tire-ly were fraught, With soul and with voice To cause, O, my Sav-iour, Thy heart to re-joice!

3. The ho-urs are gone And gain there is none, If they were not spent In trust-ing in Je-sus, Who to us was sent.

4. My spir-it this day Will faith-ful-ly say; Reign Thou in my heart; Thy coun-sel and wis-dom From me not de-part!

5. O blessed are they
In holy array,
Who with eager mind
Salvation in Jesus
Did seek and did find!

238.

142. OBEDIENCE TO THE WORD
143, 163, 169, 216.

1. Thy word, O Lord, for - ev - er is   The mir - ror
2. Can we our im - per - fec - tions see   With - out a
3. His word o - bey and warn - ing take;   His wis - dom
4. Sal - va - tion through our faith is found;   No works of

where we see   Our faults and   du - ties as they
hum - ble sigh?   Should we neg - lect   God's pre - cious
will pre - vail.   For if we   know, and heed it
law we need.   Though bap - tized, yet   our hope is

are,   Our like - ness   un - to Thee.
word,   And light - ly   pass it by?
not,   It is of   no a - vail.
vain   If we His   word don't heed.

5. The wrath of God lies on the world,
On whom its ways pursue,
Yet grace enough is found in God
To live in Him anew.

143. FAREWELL SONG

142, 163, 169, 216.

1. We'll now de - part, ye faith - ful friends; And from this place we'll go; The Lord, in whom our spir - its blend, Will lead us on the road.
2. The Lord our wel - fare al - ways seeks; He grants His word and grace; He com - forts him who sighs and weeps, Con - soles at ev - 'ry place.
3. Let's now de - part in tran - quil joy, And to God's word hold fast. Should Sa - tan come us to an - noy, Our prayers will drive him back.
4. Oh, watch ye faith - ful broth - ers mine, While in this pil - grim's dale; The might - y Word of God di - vine, Your com - pass, will not fail.

5. Ye sisters all, start on the way
   In service for the Lord,
   In watchful striving, fervent prayer,
   You'll find a rich reward.

6. May we be cheerful now and blest,
   And sojourn side by side;
   Our path leads to eternal rest,
   To heaven's paradise.

144. RECEPTIVE HEARERS

1. Faith-ful Sav-iour, we draw near To Thee in de -
2. Sav-iour, come with us a - bide; Lord, for Thee we're
3. Teach us, Lord, that we may be Filled with Thy true
4. Show us how Thy word re - news, Giv - ing us di -

vo - tion. Fill our hearts and minds we pray, With Thy
long - ing! As our teach - er now pre - side; Still our
meek - ness. We would hum - bly fol - low Thee, Striv - ing
rec - tion; How its truth and heal- ing strength Leads to

in - spi - ra - tion. Let Thy word, -- the light di - vine,
ar - dent yearn - ing! May Thy word of truth so great
for Thy like - ness. Fill our hearts with this de - sire;
full per - fec - tion! O, let Thy al - might-y word

In our hearts now bright-ly shine And Thy fold en - light - en.
Man- y souls re - gen - er - ate, Life to all be shar-ing!
May we god - li - ness ac- quire, Like Thee, pure and right-eous.
Make us per -fect in Thee, Lord, through its med - i - ta - tion!

5. Blessed joy to trust in Thee,
   Lord of all creation!
   For in Thee we build our faith,
   Thou, our firm foundation.
   Lord, in faith we look to Thee,
   'Til the blest eternity
   Leads to full salvation.

241.

145. OUR HAPPY LOT

25, 75, 220, 221.

1. Our lot is found in pleas-ant pla-ces; A good-ly her-i-tage is ours, To Him whence come all gifts and gra-ces, Let us give praise with all our pow'rs. He choos-es us of

2. He un-der-took our souls' sal-va-tion; sad con-di-tion moved Him so! And came to us from pure com-pas-sion To raise us from our depths of woe. O, won-der-ful, sur-

3. He saw in us no form of beau-ty, vir-tue, nor in-trin-sic worth. Not one there was that did his du-ty, For all were sin-ners from their birth; Nor was there one in

4. Then, moved at heart with deep com-pas-sion, The Lord stretched out His arm to save; And His own life for our sal-va-tion, And there-with all things, free-ly gave: A-dop-tion, son-ship,

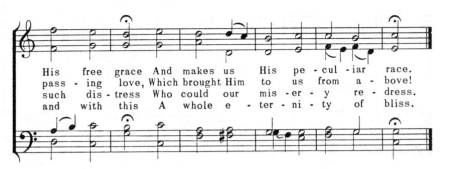

His free grace And makes us His pe - cul - iar race.
pass - ing love, Which brought Him to us from a - bove!
such dis - tress Who could our mis - er - y re - dress.
and with this A whole e - ter - ni - ty of bliss.

5. O, Lord, of goodness so amazing,
   Not one is worthy, no not one.
   We stand in shame and wonder gazing
   At wondrous things which Thou hast done.
   Thy crowning grace and precious blood
   Have reconciled us with our God.

6. We feel quite certain of obtaining
   Nothing but goodness from Thy hand,
   And wend our way without complaining
   Through dreary mist and barren land,
   With heav'n in view, where we shall be
   Joined through eternity to Thee.

7. Our lot is found in pleasant places;
   A goodly heritage is ours;
   And gladly would we share the graces,
   Which God's great goodness richly show'rs.
   Yea, we commend them unto all
   Who would obey the gracious call.

8. It grieves us sore when men refuse them
   And treat God's blessings with disdain;
   Or by neglect forever lose them
   And make the grace of God in vain.
   All ye who thirst come here and buy,
   And Christ will all your wants supply.

243.

146. HOW SHALL IT BE?

180.

1. How shall it be when we at last re - turn - ing
2. How shall it be when trem-bling-ly we lis - ten
3. How shall it be when now the soul, un - fet - tered,
4. How shall it be when we shall hear Him call - ing:

From wea - ry wan - d'rings and from toil and strife, Shall
To an - gel bands who greet us with their song, With
Goes soar - ing up - ward in un - hin-dered flight, Drawn
"Come now, ye bless - ed of My Fa-ther's grace!" And

reach the home for which our heart is yearn - ing
harps of gold which in their ra - diance glis - ten,
on by love to Him whose light has scat - tered
wor - ship - ping, up - on His foot - stool fal - ling,

And en - ter in - to ev - er - last - ing life? When
They praise the Lamb, which saved the blood-washed throng? When
The dark - ness which hid heav - en from our sight? When
We look in - to that kind and smil - ing face? The

from our feet the dust of earth has van - ished, The
far and near the ho - ly place re - sound - eth With
from the eye of faith the veil of dull - ness, As
eyes which shed those bit - ter tears, well know - ing Man's

244.

last sweat from our brow is wiped a - way, Our
"Hal - le - lu -jahs" which the ran -somed sing, The
mist be - fore the morn- ing sun doth fall, And
wretch-ed - ness and hard-ness of his heart; The

eyes be - hold what oft earth's care has ban - ished
ho - ly in - cense of their prayer a - bound - eth,
we the Son of God in all His full - ness
wounds, with that pure, pre-cious blood o'er - flow - ing

And gave to us new cour - age on our way.
Rolls up - ward to the throne of God, the King.
Be - hold up - on His throne, the Lord of All?
Which saved us from death's dread and poi - soned dart!

5. How shall it be, when we in close relation
   With holy saints the streets of heaven tread;
   Where trees of life, fresh as in first creation,
   By waters from the stream of life are fed?
   Where fountains of eternal youth shall flourish,
   The hand of time no more shall work decay,
   No eyes shall close in death, no more souls perish;
   Pain, sorrow and distress have passed away!

6. How shall it be? Oh, what this mortal vision
   Can neither see, nor hear, nor understand,
   Of happiness and glory shall be given
   To those who pass into that promised land!
   Then onward, brethren! Let us hasten thither,
   'Tis worth the hardship and the pain we bear
   To climb this path, for there shall never wither
   The blest inheritance which we shall share!

147. YEARNING FOR HOME

1. Come, come, sweet rest, Which leads to God
2. Hence van - i - ty, E'en world and time!
3. Thou cit - y pure With walls se - cure,
4. And ho - li - ness, That pure white dress,

And brings us to our bless - ed Sav - iour.
My heart longs for its home in heav - en.
With pre - cious jew - els bright - ly beam - ing;
Is there Thy host with grace a - dorn - ing.

In that blest place, Where face to
Here tears op - press, But all dis -
Cel - es - tial lights Are shin - ing
Our thanks and praise To God we'll

246.

face,		The	ran - somed	host	sings	
tress		Shall	change to	joy	when	
bright;		The	light from	God	and	
raise,		With	joy - ful	songs	of	

to	God's	praise	and	fa -	vor.
His	re -	ward	is	giv -	en.
the	blest	Lamb	is	stream -	ing.
grat - i -		tude	re -	sound -	ing.

5. Come, come, sweet rest, Us from distress,
   From cross and sorrow to deliver.
   Eternity where we shall be
   United with eternal joys forever.

148. GOD IS STILL WITH ME
149.

1. No - ah's ark long drift - ed On the
2. Mos - es, brave and daunt - less, Crossed the
3. Jon - ah's hour of tri - al Led through
4. Dan - iel's den of li - ons Teach - es

surg - ing flood, But with eyes up -
sea to land, Lead - ing with him
night and fear; Yet God showed with
true and sure, When on God de -

lift - ed, Trust - ed he in God.
fear - less Hosts of cov - e - nant;
pow - er That His help was near.
pend - ing, We can feel se - cure.

When through - out life's jour - ney Rag - ing
Thus re - signed I'll trav - el Through the
Thus in all dis - tress - es When by
So in all dis - tress - es I can

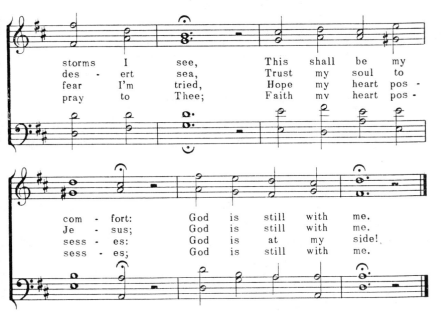

storms	I	see,	This	shall	be	my
des - ert	sea,	Trust	my	soul	to
fear	I'm	tried,	Hope	my	heart	pos -
pray	to	Thee;	Faith	my	heart	pos -

com - fort:	God	is	still	with	me.
Je - sus;	God	is	still	with	me.
sess - es:	God	is	at	my	side!
sess - es;	God	is	still	with	me.

5. Three men in the furnace
   Praised their God on high,
   Stood their foes confounded,
   Silenced scorn and lie.
   In reproach and censure
   I rest calm and free
   On this blessed promise:
   God is still with me.

6. Jesus' death arena
   And His cross and grave
   Teach me wait serenely
   God's will sure and safe;
   My support and pillar
   And my gain is He,
   My strong fort in terror;
   God is still with me.

7. He broke Peter's fetters,
   Opened doors for Paul;
   He will those deliver
   Who trust Him in all.
   So I'll wander gladly,
   Till my home I see,
   And in Zion's mansion,
   God is still with me.

149. OUR BLESSED PORTION
148.

1. Is there an-y pleas-ure In life here on
2. Moved to weep with sad-ness, Were no Sav-iour
3. Tears of joy I bring Thee, Je - sus, Man of
4. I have hap-py ho-urs; With Thee I am

earth? In what lot and meas - ure Have we
here; Joy has come in full - ness, Since Christ
pain, That Thou, Lord, didst call me, To Thy
blest! Find - ing in Thee pow - er, When I

peace and mirth? Here where sin pre - vail - eth,
did ap - pear. He who comes con - fess - ing:
flock or - dain. With Thy love's per - sua - sions
am dis - tressed. I was all un - wor - thy

Fear, dis - tress and need, For naught here a -
"My Lord and my God!" And with joy ex -
Thou my heart didst win, Guid - ed me with
And a way - ward child; Now I have found

rit.

vail	-	eth;	Death	we	all		must	meet.
press	-	ing,	Bless	- ed	is		his	lot.
pa	-	tience,	Have	Thee	still		with	- in.
mer	-	cy	In	Thy	love		so	mild.

5. Is this not a pleasure, Christian, here to be?
   Seek ye all this treasure, Jesus offers free!
   If man knew the blessing, We enjoy in Thee,
   Far more would be willing Now to follow Thee.

6. But with all their pleasure, Christians have their grief;
   Still in every failure, They shall find relief.
   From His home in heaven, God looks down on them,
   When His grace is given, They press on again.

7. Then He shall come gently, - Lead us by His hand
   From our weary journey To the Father-land.
   There when strife is over, Praise to God we'll bring,
   With the righteous chorus "Hallelujah" sing!

150. CAST THY BURDEN ON THE LORD

151.

1. Why wilt thou thus for the mor - row, O, my heart, For thy part as a hea - then sor - row, Where - fore is thy dai - ly weep - ing, When God will, Lov - ing still, Take thee in His keep - ing.

2. God thy life to thee has grant - ed; This is plain; So re - main Now to Him de - vot - ed; In the fu - ture He will ren - der To thee all; None will fall Who to Him sur - ren - der.

3. Wilt thou food have for the mor - row? God in - deed Fills all need; Care thou needst not bor - row. Thou on this canst be re - ly - ing; Dai - ly bread Your own God Rich - ly is sup - ply - ing.

4. Life is more than earth - ly liv - ing, God shall be, We shall see, All that's need - ful giv - ing, As on Him we are re - ly - ing, Ev - 'ry need, As we plead, He will be sup - ply - ing.

5. Take no thought here for thy clothing;
Christ declares: "Have no cares;
Thou shalt lack in nothing!
See the lily in its glory,
Standing there Slender, fair;
Thus God careth for thee!"

6. He who righteousness is seeking
And who still God's own will
Over all is keeping,
Will receive as he requires
Drink and food, Ev'ry good,
As his heart desires.

7. Should my faith by God be tested,
All that's dear To me here
From my hand be wrested,
All these things will work together
For my gain, Even pain
Given by my Father.

8. He is able to be giving
All again; Doth ordain
His Word for our living.
Lo, how many souls, believing,
Now live so, Without woe,
Without care and grieving!

9. Cares commit they to their Saviour;
To His will Bowing still,
To His guidance ever;
What God wills is their true pleasure;
He, their Lord, And His Word,
Their abiding treasure.

10. From them God is naught withholding;
He gives bread In their need,
All their cries beholding.
He with comfort oft is nearest
Quickly hears And appears
When the need is greatest.

11. All to Thee, as truly fitting --
Burdened heart, Care and smart --
Lord, I am committing!
Therefore, Lord, do Thou care for me!
I to Thee Bend the knee;
Silent, I adore Thee.

12. I will thank Thee for Thy favor
Evermore, And therefore
Never, never waver.
To Thy name be thanks and praises;
Take my part; Heal my heart,
Amen, yea, Lord Jesus!

151. WHY ART THOU GRIEVED?
150.

1. Why should sor- row ev - er grieve me? Christ is near. Who can
2. Weak was I and emp- ty- hand - ed When on earth At my
3. My pos- ses-sions and my liv - ing Are not mine; God di-
4. What are all these earth- ly treas-ures But a hand Full of

here E'er of Him de - prive me? Who can rob me
birth My first breath was grant - ed; Help -less, too, when
vine All to me is giv - ing. What He gave will
sand And but fleet-ing pleas -ures. Yon -der are the

of my treas - ure, Which God's Son
death o'er- takes me, Shall I go
I re - store Him; Though be - reft
real pos - ses - sions; Christ pre - pares,

For me won, Suff - 'ring in full meas - ure?
From life's woe, When my breath for - sakes me.
Of each gift, Still shall I a - dore Him.
And He shares Them with- out ces - sa - tion.

5. Lord, Thou Fount of all true pleasure!
I am Thine; Thou art mine.
E'er will I Thee treasure.
I am Thine, for Thou hast bought me;
Lost I stood, But Thy blood
Free salvation brought me.

6. Thou art mine; I love and own The
Light of Joy, e'er shall I
In my heart enthrone Thee.
Saviour, let me soon behold Thee
Face to face. May Thy grace
Evermore enfold me!

152. THE CHILDREN'S PRAYER

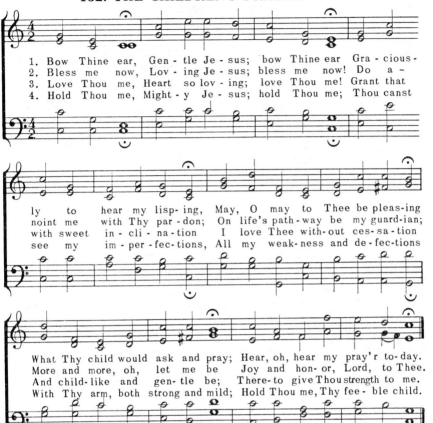

1. Bow Thine ear, Gen - tle Je - sus; bow Thine ear Gra - cious-
2. Bless me now, Lov - ing Je - sus; bless me now! Do a -
3. Love Thou me, Heart so lov - ing; love Thou me! Grant that
4. Hold Thou me, Might - y Je - sus; hold Thou me; Thou canst

ly to hear my lisp - ing, May, O may to Thee be pleas-ing
noint me with Thy par - don; On life's path - way be my guard-ian;
with sweet in - cli - na - tion I love Thee with - out ces - sa - tion
see my im - per - fec - tions, All my weak-ness and de - fec-tions

What Thy child would ask and pray; Hear, oh, hear my pray'r to - day.
More and more, oh, let me be Joy and hon - or, Lord, to Thee.
And child-like and gen - tle be; There-to give Thou strength to me.
With Thy arm, both strong and mild; Hold Thou me, Thy fee - ble child.

5. Comfort me, my Consoler; comfort me!
When at Thy feet I am bowing,
Silently my tears are flowing,
And my troubled heart in me
Thirsting longs for grace from Thee.

6. Heal Thou me In my illness; heal Thou me!
When in times of sore affliction
Send Thy love and pure affection
To my poor and wounded heart;
Heal Thou ev'ry painful smart.

7. Carry me, Faithful Shepherd; carry me,
As Thy lamb in Thy compassion,
In Thy arms with Shepherd fashion.
In faith I on Thee rely;
Bear me to Thy home on high.

153. THE LORD IS MY SHEPHERD
55, 106, 109, 177.

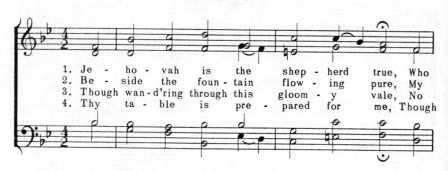

1. Je - ho - vah is the shep - herd true, Who
2. Be - side the foun - tain flow - ing pure, My
3. Though wan - d'ring through this gloom - y vale, No
4. Thy ta - ble is pre - pared for me, Though

gives me full sal - va - tion. This Watch - man
soul is ev - er joy - ful. When cour - age
e - vil am I fear - ing. Thy eyes be -
en - e - mies sur - round - ing. Thou canst dis -

nev - er sleeps or fails, His good - ness is my
fails, I go to drink Its wa - ters clear and
hold my jour - ney here; Thy grace Thou still art
pel my fear and woe With words of cheer a -

256.

por - tion. To ver - dant pas - tures does He
peace - ful. In right - eous paths He lead - eth
shar - ing. Thy rod and staff's con - sol - ing
bound - ing. My head with oil Thou dost a -

lead. My soul on dews of life shall feed, The
me; His guid - ing hand and care I see; He
pow'r, Thy faith-ful - ness and strength each hour Shall
noint. The cup o'er-flows. Thou dost ap - point My

spir - it's grace a - bound - ing.
leads me for His name's sake.
lead me safe - ly on - ward.
long - ing soul to heav - en.

5. Thy goodness and Thy mercy shall
   Abide with me forever.
   Within my Lord's abode I'll dwell,
   Till death this life shall sever.
   And when my pilgrimage is o'er,
   On wings of fervent love I'll soar
   Up to the Father's mansion.

154. AWAKE!

50, 83, 178.

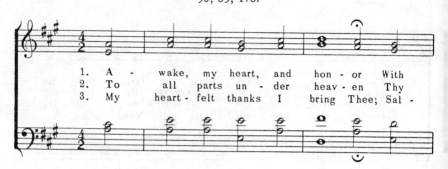

1. A - wake, my heart, and hon - or With
2. To all parts un - der heav - en Thy
3. My heart - felt thanks I bring Thee; Sal -

praise and thanks and might Thy God and
truth and faith ex - tend; We see each
va - tion I have found. As Thou hast

Thy Cre - a - tor, And sen - ti - nel at
morn and e - ven Thy grace of cov - e -
suf - fered for me, In love to Thee I'm

258.

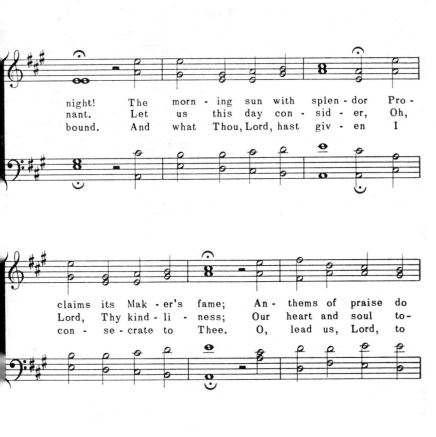

night! The morn - ing sun with splen - dor Pro -
nant. Let us this day con - sid - er, Oh,
bound. And what Thou, Lord, hast giv - en I

claims its Mak - er's fame; An - thems of praise do
Lord, Thy kind - li - ness; Our heart and soul to -
con - se - crate to Thee. O, lead us, Lord, to

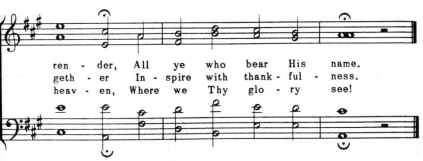

ren - der, All ye who bear His name.
geth - er In - spire with thank - ful - ness.
heav - en, Where we Thy glo - ry see!

155. PARTING HYMN
83, 154.

1. Why should ye all be weep - ing And break my
2. As though to part for - ev - er We press each
3. We say: "I here, you yon - der; You go and
4. Then let us cease from weep - ing And mod - er -

ver - y heart? We're in the Sav - iour's
oth - er's hands; And yet no pow'r can
I re - main," And yet are not a -
ate our woe, For we are in Christ's

keep - ing And shall not there - fore part. No
sev - er Our love's e - ter - nal bands. We
sun - der, But links of one great chain. In
keep - ing With whom we al - ways go. Thus

time nor place can sev - er The bonds which
look quite brok - en - heart - ed And sob our
tones of deep af - fec - tion, "Our ways part
un - der His pro - tec - tion We're led by

us	have	bound;	In	Christ	a - bide	for
last	fare - well,	And	yet	can - not	be
here,"	we say,	Yet	go	in	one	di -
His	sure	hand,	And	in	the	same	di -

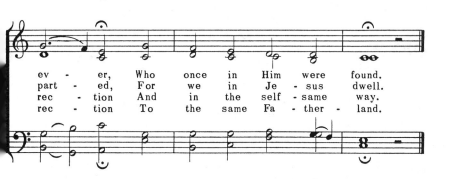

ev - er,	Who	once	in	Him	were	found.
part - ed,	For	we	in	Je - sus	dwell.
rec - tion	And	in	the	self - same	way.
rec - tion	To	the	same	Fa - ther - land.

5. Then not to parting's sorrows
   We dedicate this hour,
   But to renew our union
   With Christ, our rock and tow'r.
   If faith in Him unite us,
   Though parting gives us pain,
   It cannot disunite us
   For we in Him remain.

156. WILLINGLY ENDURE

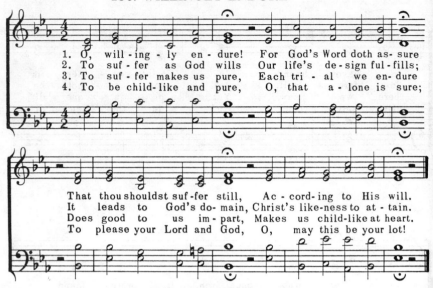

1. O, will-ing-ly en-dure! For God's Word doth as-sure
2. To suf-fer as God wills Our life's de-sign ful-fills;
3. To suf-fer makes us pure, Each tri-al we en-dure
4. To be child-like and pure, O, that a-lone is sure;

That thou shouldst suf-fer still, Ac-cord-ing to His will.
It leads to God's do-main, Christ's like-ness to at-tain.
Does good to us im-part, Makes us child-like at heart.
To please your Lord and God, O, may this be your lot!

5. Then as a child draw nigh;
   He hears your every sigh;
   You shall not leave His face
   Without His blessed grace.

157. AS PANTS THE HART
30, 31, 32, 186.

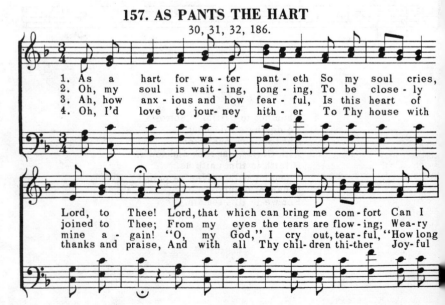

1. As a hart for wa-ter pant-eth So my soul cries,
2. Oh, my soul is wait-ing, long-ing, To be close-ly
3. Ah, how anx-ious and how fear-ful, Is this heart of
4. Oh, I'd love to jour-ney hith-er To Thy house with

Lord, to Thee! Lord, that which can bring me com-fort Can I
joined to Thee; From my eyes the tears are flow-ing; Wea-ry
mine a-gain! "O, my God," I cry out, tear-ful, "How long
thanks and praise, And with all Thy chil-dren thi-ther Joy-ful

find a - lone in Thee.   In Thee is the liv - ing
is   my soul in me.   Day and night, with - out re -
must I   bear this pain? Come and take me, Lord, and
voi - ces to Thee raise, When their knees to Thee they're

wa - ter; Thirs - ty cries to Thee I ut - ter; O, when
lent - ing, Sa - tan is   my soul tor - ment - ing, As he
guide me From the dark - ness where I hide me, From the
bow - ing, And with thanks their hearts o'er-flow - ing, When Thy

shall I by Thy grace See Thee, Sav - iour, face to face?
says with bit - ter scorn: "See, the Lord does from Thee turn!"
depths of in - ner night To the glo - ries of Thy light!"
bless -ing, pow'r and light Fills their hearts with sheer de- light.

5. Yet in sorrow I find comfort;
In the dark, I trust my God;
For my good He but intendeth,
Gratefully His help I'll laud.
When o'er me the floods are passing
And the roaring waves are lashing,
This I know: The Lord is light,
He will help me by His might.

6. Grace and goodness He has promised;
He's a true and mighty Lord.
Nothing then shall ever part us;
He will keep us by His word.
Though I must endure affliction,
Yet I feel my Lord's affection;
He is here my strength in life,
And helps me in ev'ry strife.

158. THE RULER OF ZION

66, 67, 179.

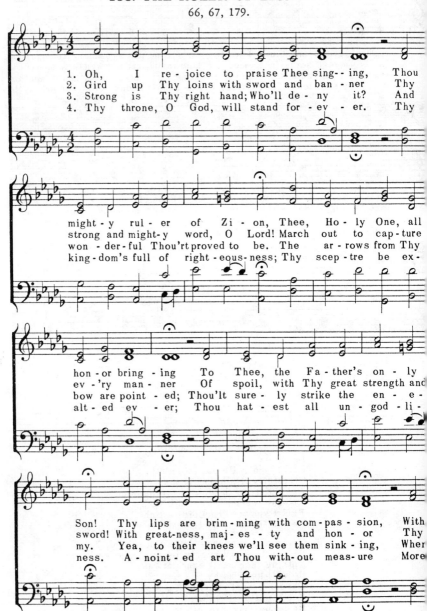

1. Oh, I re-joice to praise Thee sing-- ing, Thou might-y rul-er of Zi-on, Thee, Ho-ly One, all hon-or bring-ing To Thee, the Fa-ther's on-ly Son! Thy lips are brim-ming with com-pas-sion, With

2. Gird up Thy loins with sword and ban-ner Thy strong and might-y word, O Lord! March out to cap-ture ev-'ry man-ner Of spoil, with Thy great strength and sword! With great-ness, maj-es-ty and hon-or Thy

3. Strong is Thy right hand; Who'll de-ny it? And won-der-ful Thou'rt proved to be. The ar-rows from Thy bow are point-ed; Thou'lt sure-ly strike the en-e-my. Yea, to their knees we'll see them sink-ing, Wher

4. Thy throne, O God, will stand for-ev-er. Thy king-dom's full of right-eous-ness; Thy scep-tre be ex-alt-ed ev-er; Thou hat-est all un-god-li-ness. A-noint-ed art Thou with-out meas-ure More

love and fa - vor and with grace;
truth is brought in - to the light;
Thy great might - y voice is heard;
than all Thy as - so - ci - ates;

Shines, Lord of All, in
To those op-pressed, Thou
And when they see Thy
E - ter - nal king-dom

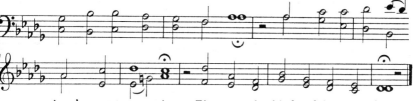

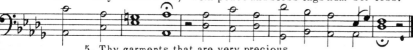

love's sweet pas - sion, Thy gen - tle, kind and lov - ing face.
send - est free - dom, De- stroy-est Sa - tan's yoke with might.
great sword gleam- ing 'Twill put to flight all Sa-tan's horde.
is Thy treas - ure, With peace and bless-ings num- ber- less.

5. Thy garments that are very precious
   Send forth a perfume, pure and rare,
   When Thou dost come from out Thy palace
   In kingly robes beyond compare!
   O Lord, so awesome is the glory
   Of heavenly light and majesty;
   O Victor great, with praise and honor
   Wilt Thou be crowned eternally!

6. Arrayed in garments of Thy splendor
   Kings' daughters now before Thee stand;
   The Bride, in raiment bright with grandeur,
   Is standing at Thine own right hand.
   Beloved Daughter, His voice heeding,
   Now thy devoted Lord adore;
   Forget Thy people and their pleading,
   Thy father's house forevermore!

7. The Bride appears with grace adorned,
   With her great King's most glorious dress.
   Her garments are in gold embroidered,
   With everlasting righteousness.
   Then, in the raiment He made precious
   With His own blood on Calvary,
   He leadeth her into His palace,
   To dwell with Him eternally.

8. In place of fathers, Thou hast children
   Distributed o' er all the world,
   Placed here as rulers; and to conquer
   They follow Thee with flags unfurled.
   We think of Thee with joy and pleasure
   And nations bring their thanks to Thee.
   And in the coming age of ages,
   Resounds our praise eternally.

265.

159. SELF-SACRIFICE

27.

1. Let your whole life be an off - 'ring To God and to Christ the Lord. None who here to Him sur - ren - der Will re - gret it, for His Word Gives us peace, (Gives us peace) And re - lease, (And re-lease) Sweet rest aft - er bat - tles
2. He who sow - eth will be gath - 'ring; O, my loved ones this is true. If but man - y this were learn - ing What the Lord for us would do. If we thus, (If we thus) With - out loss (With-out loss) Sow as He does ask of
3. As the stars in yon - der heav - en Give light to this earth - ly sphere, Thus al - so who in this tu - mult Sows good seed to God's praise here, Clothed di - vine, (Clothed di-vine) He shall shine, (He shall shine) As the stars do all the
4. 'Tis im - por - tant to be striv - ing For this goal, O, child of God, And to re - al - ize the call - ing Where-fore we live on this sod, Not that we, (Not that we) Gath - 'ring be (Gath-'ring be) Rich - es here that on - ly

cease. Gives us peace, (Gives us peace) And re - lease,
us. If we thus, (If we thus) With - out loss
time. Clothed di - vine, (Clothed di-vine) He shall shine,
flee. Not that we (Not that we) Gath - 'ring be

(And re - lease) Sweet rest aft - er bat - tles cease.
(With-out loss) Sow as He does ask of us.
(We shall shine) As the stars do all the time.
(Gath-'ring be) Rich - es here that on - ly flee.

5. No, to work our own salvation,
   For this reason we are here;
   Not to study wicked fashion,
   But to shun all evil here.
   :: For this old world and gold
   Will once vanish, we are told. ::

6. Oh, if we are ever ready
   To serve Jesus day by day,
   Sacrifice our soul and body,
   Bear each burden by the way,
   :: We shall fear, Nothing here,
   For the Lord is always near. ::

7. Oh, my brethren, then surrender
   To your Saviour, give your all;
   Dearly love His every member,
   Keep a childlike heart withal.
   :: Love in peace; never cease;
   This your Lord will greatly please. ::

8. Love should grow anew each morning,
   Love itself in works should show,
   Should each member be adorning,
   Christ in us where'er we go!
   :: Then, well so! Love's pure glow
   Gives to faith the power to do. ::

9. Brethren, O, what bliss we're sharing
   When true love inspires our lives;
   With the weak one gladly bearing,
   Love here for perfection strives;
   :: Fervently Glad we'll be
   Now and in eternity. ::

10. Where the true love is forsaken,
    There is death and emptiness;
    There forgotten is the Saviour;
    Life is then filled with distress.
    :: Then we stray, From the way,
    Stumbling on from day to day. ::

11. Let us then be up and doing;
    Satan would our work undo,
    And, the glow of love subduing,
    Quench our joy in Jesus too,
    :: That we may Not each day
    Live to honor God alway. ::

12. They who love the Saviour dearly,
    And not for vain pleasures seek,
    Glad for that which He providETH;
    Will be happy, blest and meek.
    :: And their peace Ne'er shall cease;
    Heaven will their joy increase. ::

160. THE BELIEVING FAMILY

1, 2, 3, 210

1. I and my house, we are pre-pared, As long as
2. May Thy good Spir-it fur-ther, Lord, Work in us
3. Give to our house the peace with-in, And to all
4. O, let our house be built on stone, Up-on Thy

to us life is shared To serve Thee, Lord, sin-
through Thy might-y Word, And guide our souls for
who a-bide there-in, In love bind us to
ho-ly truth a-lone, That we may nev-er

cere-ly. Thou shalt be Mas-ter of the house, Who
ev-er! O may it shine forth clear and bright, That
geth-er. That we may be pre-pared al-way To
wav-er, And e-ven when the days are dark May

with His bless-ing us en-dows And we may
in our house the one true Light May there be
bear and to en-dure, we pray In hum-ble-
we Thy ho-ly foot-steps mark And fol-low

love Thee dear - ly | Bless all, | Though small
lack - ing nev - er! | Lord, now | Be - stow
ness for - ev - er. | Each soul | Ful - fill
Thee, O Sav - iour! | In Thee | Have we,

As Thy low - ly, | Pure and ho - ly | Con - gre -
Food from heav - en, | Morn and e - ven, | While we're
Love's sweet meas - ure | With great pleas- ure, | There - by
E'en in sad - ness | Last - ing glad - ness | In rich

ga - tion | To Thy great name's ad - o - ra - tion.
liv - ing | And our- selves to Thee are giv - ing.
show - ing | Pleas - ing fruits from tear - ful sow - ing.
meas - ure, | For Thou giv - est heav'n-ly pleas- ure.

5. And finally 'bove all we pray
   That in this house no spirit stay
   But only Thine own Spirit;
   Our conduct here to regulate,
   And perfect order to instate,
   In holy, God-like manner.
   Amen! Amen! Come draw near us,
   Sun of clearness, Truthful witness,
   Shine in heart and soul with clearness.

269.

161. LOOK UPON JESUS

15, 33, 35, 52.

1. O, how joy - ful are Thy mem - bers, Sore - ly
2. Reign then in Thy kind - ly gra - ces O - ver
3. When the cares of life are press - ing Let us
4. Lord, for us the roots un - cov - er Of dis-

tempt - ed Man of care, That up - on this earth Thou
Thy dis - ci - ple band; Pour up - on our pil - grim's
in Thee find re - lief; And on us Thy peace dis -
guised or gild - ed sin; May we then Thy cross dis -

cam - est And for us the cross didst bear!
path - way Bless - ings from Thy lov - ing hand!
pens - ing Drive a - way the deep - est grief.
cov - er Where our vic - t'ry Thou didst win.

All in - firm - i - ties didst car - ry, Al - so
By Thy Spir - it's gen - tle woo - ing, Start in
When temp - ta - tions here as - sail us, Let us
Help us to be faith - ful ev - er; Hold us

ev - 'ry sin - ner's woe; And for ev - 'ry earth - ly
us with-out de - lay Ho - li - ness of life and
look up to the cross; If in strife fear would o'er-
fast, for we are Thine, Till at last we shall for-

dwell - er In - to bit - ter death didst go!
long - ing For the straight and nar - row way!
take us, Be pro - tec - tion o - ver us!
ev - er Share Thy peace and joy di - vine!

5. Oh, how willingly we'll praise Thee,
   Gentle Shepherd, when Thou then
   Yonder in that glorious city
   Thy whole flock wilt gather in!
   Come then soon, O Lord, we pray Thee;
   Gather us before Thy throne.
   O, how joyfully we'll praise Thee,
   Crowned in triumph, God's own Son!

162. BAPTISM IN CHRIST

1. Streams that from Thy wounds are flow-ing Bless for us this
2. As in the great flood the wa - ter Car - ried No-ah's
3. Eyes of faith the spring are see - ing That from Word to
4. But old Ad - am's sin - ful mem-bers Must be bur - ied

wa - ter bath; With the Word in un - ion grow-ing With the
ark to life, So and thou-sand times yet bet - ter, Flows here
wa - ter flows, How the Christ, from sins us free - ing, Shed His
in the flood, And a new man rise, re - mem-ber, Pure and

pow'r that Je - sus hath. He charged men to teach all na-tions,
full sal - va-tion rife; Takes a - way all sin and doubt-ing,
blood for all our woes. Grace and strength are nev - er-end-ing;
ho - ly in His stead. The first dies in true re-pent-ance

Bring to faith all His cre - a - tions. He who suf - fered
And re - lieves from death and Sa - tan, Gives us joy, trust
Thus, this great sal - va-tion send-ing, Rich - ly for this
This one lives by faith's ac - cept-ance. Sin - ful serv-ice,

272.

for us all,   Saves the   lost ones   from their   fall.
wor-thi-ness, And the   draught of   bless-ed -   ness.
Flood,our Lord His good   Spir - it   hath out-   poured!
sin-ful lust   Are to   me for -   ev - er   lost.

"Bap-tize   them," is   His di -rec-tion,   "In the Fa-ther's
Oh, that   we would   trust Him bet-ter,   Trust the Word of
Sin - ners   freed He   calls us ev - er   New-born chil-dren
If I   with the   Lord am bur-ied,   Must in me His

name and   ac - tion   In the   Son's sad   death full meas-ure,
Grace for - ev-er;   Saved is   ev- - 'ry   true be-liev-er,
and for -   ev -er   Heirs of   life that   knows no sad-ness;
life be   car-ried,   And to   God's glo -   ri - fi - ca-tion

In the   Spir - it's   pow'r and pleas -   ure!"
Judged the doubt - er   and   de - ceiv -   er.
On this   faith   I'll   die   with glad -   ness.
Prove my-self   a   new   cre - a -   tion.

273.

163. THE COVENANT OF GRACE

142, 169, 216, 252.

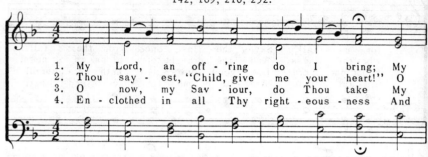

1. My Lord, an off-'ring do I bring; My
2. Thou say-est, "Child, give me your heart!" O
3. O now, my Sav-iour, do Thou take My
4. En-clothed in all Thy right-eous-ness And

heart I give to Thee. I glad-ly give this
what a sweet re-quest! It shows the way that
heart and make it Thine; I'll fol-low Thee, a
in-no-cence I'd be, That I might stand be-

heart of mine, Which Thou dost ask of me.
we must take To life and peace and rest.
serv-ant true, With-in Thy fold di-vine.
fore my God, From sin made pure and free.

5. O, God, unite my heart with Thee
   And with Thy Spirit bright;
   And for the sake of Thine own Son
   Inflame my heart with light!

6. Now grant Thy godly light to me;
   Thy holy love instill!
   May envy, hate, and darkness flee;
   My heart with courage fill!

7. O, give my faith its steadfastness
   In Christ, God's Son, alway,
   That fearless I His name confess,
   Whatever foes may say!

8. Grant that in hope I firm may be,
   Humbly and patiently,
   That when all hath forsaken me
   Thy grace my comfort be.

9. Lord, let my heart Thy temple be
   The while I sojourn here,
   And then, through all eternity,
   Make it Thy dwelling there.

10. I give my heart alone to Thee;
    Use it for Thy design!
    This vain world's I would never be,
    Dear Lord, but wholly Thine.

11. Depart vain world, with all your sin!
    From bondage I am free.
    A humble off'ring do I bring;
    My heart I give to Thee!

164. THE IMAGE OF CHRIST

123, 124, 248, 230.

1. O, Sav-iour, might I thus as Thee, Like-mind-ed, pure, and hum-ble be! With Thee, O Lord, I'll walk a-right, A child and serv-ant in Thy light!
2. My du-ty in Thy life I see; My light and mir-ror shalt Thou be. Our like-ness, Lord, is far from Thine. Thy form and im-age is di-vine!
3. How firm in God didst Thou con-fide, That He with Thee would e'er a-bide. Do share Thy grace that I might be In bonds of faith thus bound to Thee!
4. A-lone out on the moun-tain's height, When round Thee drew the shades of night, Thy pray'rs a-rose to God a-lone Such zeal my heart does wish to own!

5. Thy helping hand and loving heart
To sick and lost didst Thou impart,
And constantly for all didst care;
Thy virtues, Lord, to me do share!

6. Rebuke of man didst Thou endure,
Thus as a lamb so meek and pure;
But Thou couldst glorify the name
Of God with earnest zeal and fame.

7. Thy fearless zeal wilt Thou impart;
With courage do inflame my heart!
Discreetly let me walk with Thee;
Let all my motives holy be.

8. Thy servants who have gone before
With Thee their cross and sorrows bor
On Zion's mount the ransomed band
Rejoicing by the throne they stand.

9. O, Saviour, help, and lead the way
To heaven's gates, this child, I pray.
When sorrows no more burden me,
I'll praise Thee in eternity!

276.

165. CHILDREN'S PRAISE

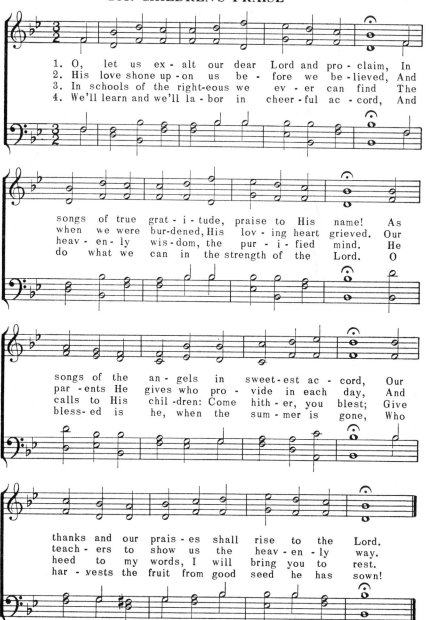

1. O, let us ex-alt our dear Lord and pro-claim, In
2. His love shone up-on us be-fore we be-lieved, And
3. In schools of the right-eous we ev-er can find The
4. We'll learn and we'll la-bor in cheer-ful ac-cord, And

songs of true grat-i-tude, praise to His name! As
when we were bur-dened, His lov-ing heart grieved. Our
heav-en-ly wis-dom, the pur-i-fied mind. He
do what we can in the strength of the Lord. O

songs of the an-gels in sweet-est ac-cord, Our
par-ents He gives who pro-vide in each day, And
calls to His chil-dren: Come hith-er, you blest; Give
bless-ed is he, when the sum-mer is gone, Who

thanks and our prais-es shall rise to the Lord.
teach-ers to show us the heav-en-ly way.
heed to my words, I will bring you to rest.
har-vests the fruit from good seed he has sown!

166. MORNING HYMN

38, 197.

1. O, how love-ly is the morn-ing, When it
2. Let our eyes be raised to heav-en Where the
3. E-ven as the spring-time flow-ers Grow be-
4. This day al-so He will guide us, In our

is be-gun with God; Joy and thanks our
sun is shin-ing bright, And on hill and
neath the sun's warm rays, So the Lord by
work His help pro-vide, And on wis-dom's

hearts a-dorn-ing, As be-hooves a child of God,
dale and mead-ow Is dis-pens-ing life and light;
His own pow-ers Makes us gar-lands for His praise;
ways He'll lead us, Stand-ing ev-er by our side,

Wak-ing aft-er night so fair In the Mak-er's
But far more than sun in space Beams the Sav-iour's
He in-vites most lov-ing-ly: Lit-tle chil-dren,
That on this whole bless-ed day No mis-hap can

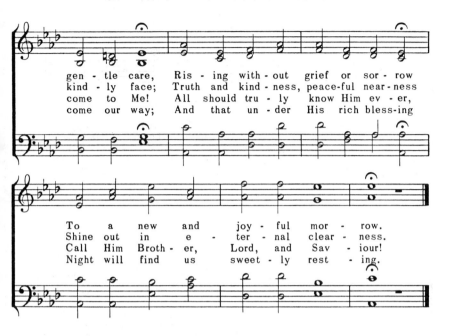

gen - tle care, Ris - ing with - out grief or sor - row
kind - ly face; Truth and kind - ness, peace-ful near - ness
come to Me! All should tru - ly know Him ev - er,
come our way; And that un - der His rich bless-ing

To a new and joy - ful mor - row.
Shine out in e - ter - nal clear - ness.
Call Him Broth - er, Lord, and Sav - iour!
Night will find us sweet - ly rest - ing.

5. Through His grace made sweet and easy,
   We'll His teachings understand,
   When He on the path of duty
   Gently leads us by the hand.
   O, how blest the child that may
   In His grace begin the day,
   Whose desire and wish is wholly
   By His love to be made holy.

6. Come then, Lord of life eternal,
   Step into our midst, we pray;
   Help that we may not be merely
   Hearers of Thy Word today.
   To our teacher, O, be near;
   Bless the children gathered here;
   May we thrive in fullest measure,
   And Thy heart in us find pleasure!

167. JESUS, THE FRIEND OF CHILDREN
96.

1. God, my life's Cre - a - tor, Grant me
2. On those heights up yon - der, Hosts shall
3. Je - sus, friend of chil - dren, Thou who
4. Blest is he who loves Thee; Blest, who

grace and fa - vor Not to live in vain.
stand a - sun - der In bright ra - di - ance;
for the sin - ners Didst on earth ap - pear,
aims sin - cere - ly, God, Thy child to be.

Lord, Thy love so ho - ly, And Thy Spir - it
Those, who in life's morn - ing, Sin - ful pleas - ures
O, how kind and ten - der Was Thy heart to
Such pure in - cli - na - tions, Thy love's in - spi -

low - ly, In my heart shall reign.
scorn - ing, Went to Thee from hence.
ren - der Lov - ing help and cheer!
ra - tions, Give, O Lord, to me,

Thy like - ness Let me pos - sess; With Thy care and
There - fore they Shall ev - er stay With the saints whose
Lord, that we Be - come like Thee In our thought and
That I wear in heav - en fair Thy blest, pure and

Thy di - rec - tion, Bring it to per - fec - tion!
song in - creas - es In Thy praise, Lord Je - sus!
con - ver - sa - tion, Be our em - u - la - tion.
ho - ly like - ness In e - ter - nal bright - ness.

168. TARRY NOT!
6.

1. Flour - ish - ing youth, Thou our hope and our fond ex - pec -
2. Of - fer the live - ly, the cheer- ful and beau - ti - ful
3. Ten - der - ly Je - sus em- brac - es the lambs as His
4. Liv - ing for Je - sus will bring thee to joy ev - er -

ta - tion,   Hark to the voice that is
flow - er,   Of - fer with glad - ness and
treas - ure.   Youth, thou shalt furn - ish the
last - ing,   Dai - ly and hour - ly His

call - ing in kind in - vi - ta - tion!
will - ing - ness thy youth - ful pow - er
Shep - herd His fa - vor - ite pleas - ure.
great and e - ter - nal love tast - ing.

That hand o - bey Which oft has point - ed the
To Christ, thy friend, Who thy soul e'er will de -
Bless - ing and glee Show - ers the Fa - ther on
This shall suf - fice, But on the path - way of

282.

way	To	the	dear	Sav - iour's	sal -	va -	tion!
fend,	Safe	in	His	heav - en - ly		bow -	er.
thee,	Prize	of	His	flock, with - out		meas -	ure.
vice,	Bod - y	and	soul	you'd	be	wast -	ing.

5. Trees of sweet youth filled with holy, devout animation,
   In grace and wisdom expanding through Christ's inspiration,
   With loving care, God will in due time prepare
   For His good work of salvation.

6. Honor and grace with the Lamb and God ever possessing,
   No earthly glory compares with this heavenly blessing.
   Then in your youth Turn to the Saviour in truth,
   Lest your time vainly be passing.

7. If thou wilt seek Him, His angels around thee will hover;
   In their communion great happiness thou shalt discover,
   If thou wilt stay With Him until thy last day,
   Who is thy bridegroom and lover.

8. Think what great honor and glory the Lord then will render
   Him who from childhood and till his last years did surrender
   All to the Lord; Even old age will accord
   Crowns of God's mercy so tender.

9. Surely there follows a happy, contented departure,
   All who the Lamb's reconciling and soul-healing torture
   Long years have known. Yea, in this service alone
   Will I inherit my fortune.

169. A BLESSED MAN

142, 163, 216, 252.

1. It real - ly is not dif - fi - cult A bless - ed
2. Then one is nei - ther slave nor lord But just a
3. We la - bor with a good de - sign, In good and
4. We do not view our la - bor as A task that

man to be; We trust the Lord with good re-
hap - py child, Be - comes more bless - ed as he
bad re - pute, Like as a tree in prop - er
we must do; The Lord in us at all time

sult, And live in Him so free.
gives His life to Him so mild.
time Brings forth its flow'r and fruit.
has Done what He asks to do.

5. One gladly yields to His good care
In everything while here,
Is happy always, everywhere,
As long as God is near.

6. So blessed is a trusting child,
So rich in love and rest;
And if we're thus not satisfied,
We'll nevermore be blest.

170. AT HOME 'TIS WELL!

1. At Home, 'tis well! There shall the pil - grim tar - ry, When tired and worn by sor - row, grief, and strife; In heav'n, when the hard race of earth - ly life Is run, the long-borne load no more he'll car - ry.

2. At Home, 'tis well! With God in close re - la - tion, The soul for - gets the sor - row it has borne, With pains o'er-come on that bright, gold- en morn, Re - joic - es in our God's sub-lime sal - va - tion.

3. At Home, 'tis well! There palms of peace a - bound - ing Are gent - ly cool - ing us, hot from the strife; O'er-come now are all pains of pil - grim life; The cries of fear give way to psalms re - sound - ing.

4. At Home, 'tis well! There God in ad - o - ra - tion A - dorns each vic - tor's brow with wreath of gold. All who be - lieve and hope like those of old Sing praise and thanks in high-est ex - ul - ta - tion.

5. At Home, 'tis well! Then let us hasten thither
Through pain and death on to our homeland shore!
On, boldly on! When this short life is o'er,
New life will bloom for us and never wither.

171. THE CROSS

73.

1. The might - y tree, the cross, is spread - ing
2. With thou - sand fig - ures dark and drear - y,
3. Though far or near if thou wouldst trav - el,
4. O, do not fear the cross' af - flic - tion!

Its arms of suf - f'ring ev - 'ry - where; For
The cross comes nigh with pain and dart; Re -
A cross is ev - er stand - ing nigh; And
The Sav - iour suf - fered on it, too, To

where - so - e'er man's foot is tread - ing, The
proach, con - tempt, and suf - f'rings wear - y Will
thou wilt al - ways draw it near - er If
cause e - ter - nal joy and pleas - ure To

cross is cer - tain to be there.
hold their sword close to thy heart.
thou wilt try to pass it by.
rip - en ev - er - more for you.

5. But if thou wouldst relieve its pressure,
   The figure of the cross then heed.
   'Twill teach thee how to ease thy suff'ring;
   To consolation it will lead.

6. Two beams are in the cross united;
   A short one lies across the long,
   But instantly the cross is lightened
   When short lies parallel to long.

7. This figure then explains the meaning:
   Why often hard our suff'rings press;
   And how relief we may be gaining
   When souls are laden with distress.

8. The longer beam is God's direction;
   Across it lies thy will, perverse.
   Thus brings the cross pain and affliction;
   God's dispensation seems for worse.

9. Resist not then God's regulation,
   Although His hand may press thee hard;
   But conquer thy own will with patience;
   Soon cross and suff'ring will depart.

10. If thus thou'lt overcome thy wishes
    And let God's will prevail in thee,
    Then thou wilt find peace in thy suff'ring;
    And grace thy great reward will be.

11. Then bear thy woes with Jesus gladly,
    And fear the cross of life no more,
    For when thy journey here is ended,
    The cross will open heaven's door!

172. BE TRUE!

1. Be true; be true! The Lord is by thee stand-ing; Joy-ful with Him at last will be the end - ing! Tho' hard the strife and long the con - flict be, Through faith-ful-ness the Lord will hon-ored be!

2. Be true; be true! For God has crowns a - wait-ing, Where - with for - ev - er He'll be com - pen - sat - ing; But on - ly if in pain and in dis-tress, Un - to the death we prove our faith-ful - ness.

3. Be true; be true! If guard we are not keep-ing, Then we are lost, for Sa - tan is not sleep-ing; And if we are not watch-ful at the post, That which we once had won will all be lost.

4. Be true; be true! Those who in all temp - ta - tion Have prov - en true, de - serve our com - men - da - tion. Were there no test, how should it prov - en be, Who weak, who strong, who true or un - true be?

5. O, faithful Lord, Thy love and truth sincerely
Thou dost bestow on us each day so clearly,
So grant that we also each day anew
Become more faithful, loving, kind, and true!

173. HEART'S WISH
116.

1. Ye of my bless-ed pil-grim-age, Dear and be-
2. O, may the small flock be in-creased In grace 'neath
3. May ev-'ry sin-ner com-fort find In pen-i-
4. May each one then in his own place On Him, the

loved com-pan-ions, Who have the pre-cious priv-i-lege, The
His pro-tec-tion, And en-ter in-to heav'n-ly rest, For
tent sub-mis-sion; In love to Him may Je-sus bind All
Rock, be ground-ed; By His good Spir-it, Word, and grace At

Ho-ly Ghost's com-mun-ion, God's bless-ings on you
this is God's di-rec-tion. May all be child-like,
who have found sal-va-tion; With will-ing heart may
all times be sur-round-ed; May all be hal-lowed

I ac-claim, And greet you in the Sav-iour's name!
lov-ing, kind, That we the path to heav-en find!
ev-'ry child Ac-cept His guid-ance sweet and mild.
by God's might; He is our star and shin-ing light.

5. This is the wish from all my heart
For you, my loving comrades;
In our alliance may the Lord
Be felt in blessed nearness.
The power of His cross and blood
Unites us in true brotherhood.

174. THE POWER OF PRAYER

1. Pray, O Church, be sanc-ti-fied With the ho-ly
   oint - ment! Je-sus' Spir-it be ap-plied In thy
   soul's ap-point-ment! Be there-fore, Ev-er-more,
   Pray'r and fer-vent plead-ing From thy lips pro-ceed-ing!

2. Con-se-crate thy of-fer-ing And thy spir-it's
   long-ing Un-to Him, whose suf-fer-ing Draws thee
   to Him strong-ly! Sweet in-cense Be it hence,
   That to God's throne soar-eth, When thy heart im-plor-eth!

3. This as-sem-bly's ar-dent pray'r And its meek pe-
   ti-tion Will up-on God's al-tar there Find due
   rec-og-ni-tion. God ad-vised Je-sus Christ,
   Priest and in-ter-ces-sor, For each true con-fes-sor.

4. God thus hears most gra-cious-ly All the prayers we
   of-fer; And the an-gels glad will be Wor-ship
   there to prof-fer To the Lord, In ac-cord
   With us poor and low-ly, To God, high and ho-ly.

290.

5. All the incense of the saints
Must produce great favor;
On the coals we lay our grains
Unto a sweet savor.
Then it may Melt this day
All our minds together
In love's flame forever!

9. O the strength and might unknown
Of the Christians' praying!
Without this could not be done
All they are essaying;
Thus alone There is won
Vict'ry o'er deceivers,
Triumph for believers!

6. If a single fervent pray'r
Of a soul prevailing
On the tender heart of God
Brings its fruit unfailing,
How much more Is in store,
When whole congregations
Bring their supplications?

10. But this longing must at first
In thy soul be gleaming;
Then from out your pray'rs will burst
Thunder, lightning streaming.
They are sent With intent
That your foes shall tremble,
When God's hosts assemble.

7. When the righteous, there and here,
Great and small invited,
Angels, mankind, all sincere,
All in pray'r united,
It will blend And ascend
To the regions o'er us;
What a mighty chorus!

11. All your prayers that now aspire
To your God in heaven
Should thus be an holy fire
On His altar given.
Worldly fire, False desire,
Should not then be blended
With what hath ascended.

8. Draw in spirit ever nigh;
Pray within your chambers;
Lifting holy hands on high,
Holy keep your members.
Holy be Ev'ry plea
That to God is springing,
Strength and blessing bringing!

12. Pray ye that time's latter end
Quickly may be nearing,
That our Lord may soon descend
For His great appearing.
Come then all, Great and small,
Join the angels' yearning
For our Lord's returning!

13. Prayers from inmost depth of heart
Find the Master's favor,
And the Christian's highest art
Is to please the Saviour.
So should we Watchful be,
Waiting, hoping, longing
For His second coming.

175. THE FAITH OF THE FATHERS

33, 36, 51, 203.

1. Spir - it, by whose op - er - a - tion Faith and
2. Lord, en - due us with Thy bless - ing; That, though
3. Give us A - brah'ms faith un - shak - en That Thy
4. Give us Jo - seph's chaste be - hav - ior When the

ho - li - ness pro - ceed, Source of heav'n - ly
babes we be in grace, Faith and love and
prom - ise must be true, And what God has
world with craft - y wiles Seeks to draw us

con - ver - sa - tion, Strength in weak - ness, help in
zeal pos - ses - sing For Thy house and ho - ly
un - der - tak - en He as - sur - ed - ly will
from the Sav - iour To her - self with frowns or

need; Spir - it, by whose in - spi - ra - tion
place, We may give our dear - est treas - ure,
do; Which not on - ly could un - mov - ed
smiles. Give us grace and strength for shun - ning

292.

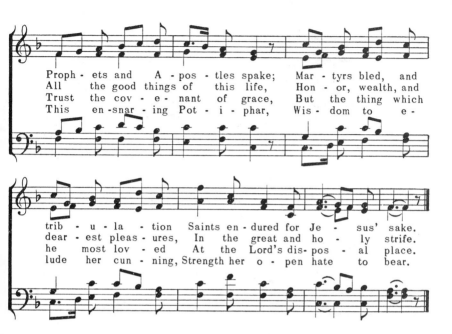

Proph - ets and A - pos - tles spake; Mar - tyrs bled, and
All the good things of this life, Hon - or, wealth, and
Trust the cov - e - nant of grace, But the thing which
This en -snar - ing Pot - i - phar, Wis - dom to e -

trib - u - la - tion Saints en - dured for Je - sus' sake.
dear - est pleas - ures, In the great and ho - ly strife.
he most lov - ed At the Lord's dis- pos - al place.
lude her cun - ning, Strength her o - pen hate to bear.

. Give us David's bold defiance
Of the Lord's and Israel's foes;
And in trouble, the reliance
Which in God, his Rock, he shows;
His right princely disposition,
Friendship, constancy, and truth;
But still more, his deep contrition,
For the errors of his youth.

. Arm us with the stern decision
Of Elijah, in these days
When men, led by superstition,
To idols new altars raise.
Let us shun the mere profession
Common in our days and land,
Witnessing a good profession,
Even if alone we stand.

7. Give us the Apostles' daring
And their bold, undaunted mood,
Threats and fierce reproaches bearing
To proclaim the Saviour's blood;
Let us to the truth bear witness;
Truth alone can make us free;
Nor leave off until its sweetness
All shall taste and know through Thee.

8. Give us Stephen's look collected
And His calm and peaceful mind,
When we meet with unexpected
Trials of the fiercest kind;
In the midst of shouts and crying,
Let us with composure stand;
Open heav'n to us in dying;
Show us Christ at God's right hand.

9. Spirit, by whose operation
Faith and hope and love are giv'n,
Source of holy conversation,
Bearing seed and fruit for heav'n;
Spirit, by whose inspiration
Prophets and Apostles spake,
Visit us with Thy salvation;
Dwell with us for Jesus' sake!

176. THE WORD OF LIFE

33, 51, 161, 198.

1. Word of Life, the foun-tain flow-ing Pure-ly from the throne a-bove, Life and strength to him im-part-ing, Who ac-cepts the Word in love. As a blos-som that is blight-ed From the

2. What were earth to be with-out Thee? But a vale in dark des-pair. Heav'n would have no joys to cheer me, If I could not find Thee there. What were life to live with-out Thee? As a

3. Word of Life, Thou dost en-light-en, And Thy warmth and love we feel. Sin-ners in Thee read their por-tion; Heav-en's joys it does re-veal. Sin-ners by the Word are wak-ened From their

4. Through the Word we fear the Mas-ter, As a judge with right-eous pow'r. Yet we love the Lord, who car-ries Us in pa-tience ev-'ry hour, And we love the God who giv-eth His own

sun's own heat se - vere, Thirst - ing in the
nev - er end - ing night. Death, with - out Thee,
sleep; They stand dis - mayed. Yet the pen - i -
Son, a ran - som true; Sin in Him is

bar - ren val - ley, Stoops to drink 'its wa - ters clear.
would be dark - ness; There would be no dawn - ing light.
tent finds mer - cy; Thus his sor - row is re - paid.
judged for . ev - er, And in Him we live a - new.

5. Full redemption is the promise
Made to him who heeds the Word.
They, who in their hearts retain Thee,
Shall receive the great reward.
In my heart I'll strive to keep Thee,
Word of truth, and strength, and love,
Conq'ring as a sword in battle,
Then I'll wear the crown above.

177. CONFIDENCE

55, 106, 109, 153.

1. I place my - self in Je - sus' hands And there a - bide for ev - er; No griefs, no joys, shall loose the bands, Nor yet our un - ion sev - er! In these dread days When earth de -

2. A Rock and Cas - tle is the Lord; And they shall see and won - der Who build on His al - might - y Word, And there - on deep - ly pon - der. And what He saith In life or

3. And let Him do with me His will, What He will do shall please me; I cleave to Him with strong faith still And hope that He will bless me. He must be blest Who loves Him

4. When things seem at their worst, I will Still joy in His pro - tec - tion, Who loves to bring out good from ill, And grieves in my af - flic - tion. His tri - als sent Are all well

296.

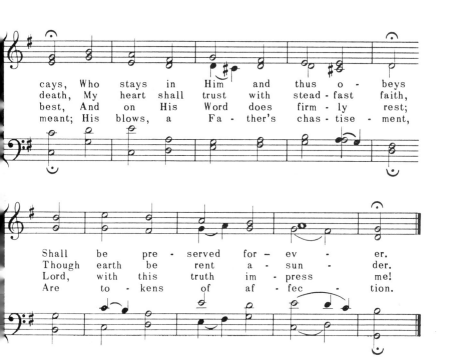

cays, Who stays in Him and thus o - beys
death, My heart shall trust with stead - fast faith,
best, And on His Word does firm - ly rest;
meant; His blows, a Fa - ther's chas - tise - ment,

Shall be pre - served for — ev - er.
Though earth be rent a - sun - der.
Lord, with this truth im - press me!
Are to - kens of af - fec - tion.

5. His pledge in faith will ever stand;
It is His blessed pleasure
That naught me from His mighty hand
Shall separate or sever.
He will not break The Word He spake;
So confidence in Him I take,
And praise Him then forever.

178. LIFE AND FULL ABUNDANCE IN JESUS

50, 83, 154.

1. O, bless-ed Sun, whose splen-dor Dis-pels the
2. A deep and heav'n-ly feel-ing Oft seiz-es
3. To win this pre-cious treas-ure And match-less
4. I know no life di-vid-ed, O Lord of

shades of night; O, Je-sus, my De-fend-er, My
on my breast; Ah, here is balm for heal-ing; Here
pearl I would Give hon-or, wealth, and pleas-ure, Yea,
Life, from Thee; In Thee is life pro-vid-ed For

soul's su-preme de-light; All day I hear re-
on-ly is true rest! Though for-tune should be-
ev-'ry earth-ly good; I glad-ly would sur-
all man-kind and me; I know no death, O

sound-ing A voice with sil-ver tone, Which
reave me Of all that I pos-sess, If
ren-der The dear-est thing which might Ob-
Je-sus, Be-cause I live in Thee; Thy

speaks of grace a - bound - ing Through God's e - ter - nal Son!
Christ His love still leave me, I free - ly give the rest.
scure my Sun's bright splen - dor, And rob me of His light.
death it is which frees us From death e - ter - nal - ly.

5. I fear no tribulation,
   Since, whatsoe'er it be,
   Can make no separation,
   Between my Lord and me;
   If Thou, my God and teacher,
   Vouchsafe to be my own,
   Though poor, I shall be richer
   Than monarch on his throne.

6. If, while on earth I wander,
   My heart is light and blest,
   Ah! what shall I be yonder,
   In perfect peace and rest?
   O, blessed thought! In dying
   We go to meet the Lord,
   Where there shall be no sighing,
   A kingdom our reward.

7. Lord, with this truth impress me
   And write it on my heart,
   To comfort, cheer and bless me,
   That Thou my Saviour art;
   Without Thy love to guide me,
   I should be wholly lost;
   The floods would quickly hide me,
   On life's wide ocean tossed.

8. Thy love it was which sought me;
   Thou wast unsought by me,
   And to the haven brought me,
   Where I would gladly be;
   The things which once distressed me
   My heart no longer move,
   Since this sweet truth impressed me
   That I possess Thy love.

299.

179. FAITHFULNESS IN SMALL THINGS
66, 67, 158.

1. This is the test of true de-vo-tion, To keep and
2. Re-mem-ber, soul, that not the hum-blest O-be-dience
3. If thou the great sins wouldst be shun-ning In fear of
4. For who would whol-ly be the Sav-iour's Will fol-low

hold fast to the Lord; And ev-er-more with-out o-
shall the Lord for-get; Be-cause the most un-self-ish
pun-ish-ment and yet The less-er faults in thee al-
Him in all things here, Will shun the small-est sin and

mis-sion In all things to o-bey His Word. In small and
spir-it In hum-ble serv-ice here is met. In small things
low-ing,'Twould not true hon-es-ty be-get. That would not
e-ven The things that sin-ful do ap-pear, Will seek in

un-im-port-ant mat-ters, Yet to be care-ful
then be-gin thy train-ing; The small-est sin shun
be a true de-vo-tion, Which sac-ri-fi-ces
all things Je-sus' glo-ry, Will strive in all sin-

300.

and sin - cere, Not know - ing - ly to faults con -
and ab - hor; For in o - bey - ing, love is
all to God; 'Twould be to fol - low self - ish
cer - i - ty To be con - formed un - to the

sent - ing, How - ev - er small they may ap - pear.
gain - ing; And loy - al - ty grows more and more.
mo - tives And serve two mas - ters in your thought.
im - age Of Him whose serv - ant he would be.

5. In every deed, at every hour,
   His care it is unto his Lord
   In everything to be found faithful,
   And loyal to His holy Word.
   For Him he suffers every trial,
   Dishonor, sorrow, cross, and woe;
   Enough that he may say sincerely:
   "My loving Lord hath willed it so!"

6. O, heart, for truthfulness in living
   Endeavor, strive, sincerely plead;
   And day by day be more aspiring
   To love and honor Him indeed!
   Not in the lofty, but in humble
   And small things serve Him, be thy aim;
   And diligence will then accomplish
   What slothfulness could not attain.

7. O, do not say, "In greater trials
   Will I to Jesus faithful be!"
   That is what Peter also promised,
   And yet thou dost him weeping see.
   So learn true faithfulness in small things;
   In little conflicts faithful be;
   Or else thou shalt perhaps like Peter
   For faithlessness weep bitterly.

301.

180. FATHER, SON, AND HOLY GHOST

146.

1. O Fa - ther hand, that guides me so se - cure - ly, O
2. O my Re - deem - er, who for me ex - pir - ed And
3. O Ho - ly Spir - it, who with gen - tle prompt - ing Dost

Fa - ther eye, that watch - es o - ver me! O Fa - ther
pur - chased me with His own pre - cious blood! Who par - don
com - fort, chas - ten, and im - pel to prayer! Who per - fect

heart, that hears my pray'r so sure - ly, And
from all sin for me ac - quir - ed, That
peace and ho - ly un - der - stand - ing, Faith,

thinks of me in love and char - i - ty! Con - duct me
now my heart can rest in peace with God! De - liv - er
hope, and love from God to me doth share! O gov - ern

fur - ther on my pil - grim jour - - ney, The nar - row
me from all dis - tress and wor - ry, And from all
me; im - press on me the like - ness Of Je - sus

way that leads to heav'n a - bove; And make me
bond - age ful - ly make me free; In con - flict
and the seal of broth - er - hood. O, fill my

wor - thy of that life e - ter - nal, A -
with the cun - ning ad - ver - sar - y, Be
heart with peace and pray'r - ful si - lence, A

like in sore dis - tress, in peace and love.
Thou the He - ro who gives vic - to - ry.
ho - ly tem - ple of the liv - ing God.

181. UNITY IN LOVE
77, 132.

```
1. O    how   love - ly   'tis   to   be     With   our
2. As   the   oint - ment, pre - cious,  true,  Then   from
3. So   de - light - ful   it    is    here,   When   in
4. As   the   dew   from   Her - mon's  height  Did   de -
```

```
Lord   in    u  -  ni - ty;      And   u  -  nit - ed
Aar - on's   hair  did  flow,    Scent - ing  his  whole
Christ's way  we   ap - pear,    And   in   u  -  ni -
scend  on   Zi - on  bright,     So   flows  grace  and
```

```
voi - ces  raise  Him  to   bring  our  songs  of   praise.
rai - ment  fair,  Fra - grance fill - ing  all  the   air!
ty    do   stand,  All   to   Him   look hand  in  hand.
bless - ing free   On   the  breth - ren's  u  - ni - ty.
```

5. See in faith, and hope and love
   Lies the power from above;
   But one Baptism, faith, and Lord,
   Spirit, head, in one accord.

6. This adorns our brotherhood,
   For God's reign is always good;
   Brethren, look upon your way
   To your Saviour ev'ry day.

7. Love each one in truth sincere,
   To confess, O, do not fear
   God's free grace in Christ, our Lord,
   Who to us gave this reward!

8. Father, Son, and Holy Ghost,
   Three in one, so shall the host
   Of those born of God above
   Be as one in holy love.

9. As the water, spirit, blood,
   All unite in holy flood,
   Unto him who God's advice
   Did accept as good and wise.

10. Also does this bond unite
    Heart and heart in faith and light;
    Many in one body be,
    Many souls in unity.

11. Just one Lord and just one Bride,
    Whose gaze does on Him abide,
    May the Spirit love inspire,
    Calling: "Come, my heart's desire!"

12. Come, O Jesus, come, appear;
    Call Thy bride from far and near;
    Show Thy countenance so bright
    In eternal heaven's light!

182. TO MY REDEEMER

1. As I think of Thee, A gen-tle rap-ture
2. One long train of dark and trou-bled ho-urs
3. Ere I knew Thee and Thy sweet com-pas-sion,
4. Full of youth-ful zeal, I was pur-su-ing

O-ver-whelms the soul that Thou dost love;
Shroud-ed me in youth-ful days gone by;
My un-hap-py heart sought peace in vain;
Noth-ing but de-ceit and van-i-ty;

This is one of those bright pre-cious mo-ments
Since I've felt Thy great, al-might-y pow-ers,
For a thou-sand lusts of e-vil fash-ion
Sham and shad-ow I was ev-er woo-ing,

Grant-ed Thy be-lov-ed from a-bove.
Light and strength flow on me from on high.
Burnt with-in me, yield-ing naught but pain.
And the truth re-mained un-known to me.

306.

5. Filled with false ambition, pride, and cunning,
Wanting meekness, sense of right, and light,
Into error's mazes I was running,
Oft unwilling, slave to sin's dread might.

6. Were I loved and honored, thus I fancied
All this longing would be satisfied;
And these came to me in ample measure,
Yet I felt that vacant, unfilled void.

7. Shepherdless in heathers dry and barren,
As a lost and famished sheep I strayed,
Finding naught to satisfy my hunger,
Naught whereby my thirst could be allayed.

8. O, in misery I would have perished,
Crushed by great affliction and distress,
Had I not by Thee been found and cherished,
Had I not by Thy grace been refreshed.

9. What a wretched life had been my portion;
Torn by doubt, remorse and fear was I,
Till at last my faith in Thee was anchored
And Thou heardst my pleading and my cry!

10. Long a downcast spirit did depress me;
Now Thou cheerest both my heart and mind;
Only peace and happiness possess me
Since my blessed lot in Thee I find.

11. Since those sacred days of heav'nly blessing,
I can conquer over passions strong,
Over discontent and dark depression;
Heav'nly pleasure fills my breast with song.

12. Nor will there be dreary clouds above me
That will overcast my heaven's blue,
If I evermore, O Lord, will love Thee
Without discontent, to Thee be true.

13. Woe unto the world, such love despising,
That such joy in Jesus casts away;
For its value never realizing,
It is led by vanity astray!

14. O, forsake me not, Thou ever faithful,
Though to try me Thou Thy face dost hide;
Till I bear Thy likeness and impression,
Purge me as the gold is purified!

15. When at last these bitter trials are ended,
And I finish this my earthly race,
There within the land of joys unblended,
Dare I hope it? -- I shall see Thy face!

16. Purified in heart, enraptured, Saviour,
With my song I'll praise Thy Name most blest,
That Thou, all earth's anguish past forever,
Hast bestowed on me Thine endless rest!

307.

183. CHRIST THE RESURRECTED

53, 80, 82, 249.

1. Rise, O soul and break the bond-age Of the van-i-
2. Turn your heart to the fair cit-y, To the peace-ful
3. To the Sav-iour's grave now has-ten, Where He lay in
4. Je-sus bore all our trans-gres-sions With Him there up-

ties of life! Jour-ney on-ward to the king-dom;
Zi-on there. Let no world-ly hope de-ceive you;
calm re-pose. Christ, in strength from God the Fa-ther,
on the cross, And for us en-dured the an-guish,

Leave the tur-moil and the strife! In this world and
Has-ten now its joys to share. Let naught lead you
From the grave in tri-umph rose. Thus the path of
As a meek lamb suf-fered loss; There He won for

time we see Naught but end-less van-i-ty.
e'er a-stray, As you walk the heav'n-ly way.
life He made, With His blood your ran-som paid.
me and thee Life and joy e-ter-nal-ly.

5. Death, the first, is now forever
   Conquered and his might laid low,
   For the Hero broke that scepter
   When He to the grave did go.
   Bonds are broken, dungeon's might;
   Liberty is brought to light!

10. As to Christ I cling forever,
    He the Head, I, member true,
    So He will forsake me never
    Whatsoe'er I might pass through.
    He, the First-fruit, goes ahead
    That I may by Him be led.

6. Now the very sting is taken
   That gave second death its power;
   Vanquished is the evil dragon
   That so long did fiercely lower.
   Now the serpent's poison may
   No believer's heart dismay.

11. Adam being dead within me,
    Henceforth live Thou, Lord, in me.
    What Thy sacred death did win me,
    May it bring much fruit to Thee;
    May the Spirit victor be
    And the flesh succumb to Thee.

7. O, the lovely, glorious portal,
   That o'er Jesus' grave I see:
   "Jesus lives!" O words immortal,
   Like a magnet drawing me!
   "Jesus lives!" This, too, I see:
   "Who believes shall live with Me!"

12. Thou of life the Prince and Giver,
    For Thy death I now thank Thee!
    Now my faith is fruitless never;
    And my hope in death shall be
    That in death I trust in Thee,
    I shall not forsaken be!

8. Thought of death does not appall me;
   Jesus is my life and all.
   I am now an heir of glory.
   Though the mortal body fall
   Into dust, again I'll rise
   When He calls me from the skies.

13. O, how will the voice be ringing
    That doth call us from the grave!
    What sound will the trump be bringing,
    Piercing every burial-cave!
    "Come, ye dead," it loudly cries;
    "Nothing hinders ye, arise!"

9. Now with Job I say believing:
   Jesus, my Redeemer, lives!
   New life I will be receiving
   By the power that He gives;
   He, the Strong, will me not leave,
   Till He fin'lly breaks my grave.

14. Thou the dust will then enliven;
    All the bones new life will see;
    A new form I will be given,
    Then I shall immortal be;
    And transfigured by Thy hand,
    In Thy likeness I shall stand.

15. In my Saviour's resurrection
    There is comfort; I am blest.
    In His life my hopes renewing,
    In His love my soul shall rest.
    Everything I have in Thee,
    Life and hope and victory.

184. BEHOLD THE LAMB OF GOD

16.

1. O, slaugh-tered Lamb, by whom the seal was bro - ken,
2. All Sa - tan's host has been by Thee de - feat - ed;
3. Thou pre - cious Lamb, what great things Thou hast prom - ised!
4. Yet more: "And I, when I shall be up - lift - ed

That gave me com - fort and e - ter - nal cheer! My
There - fore I lack not strength when bat-tles rage; My
Words of e - ter - nal truth didst Thou de - clare, "No
A - bove the earth, shall draw all men to Me!" O

faith sends up to yon - der Zi - on's moun - tain, A
free - dom from death's bond has been com - plet - ed; I
wolf shall pluck a sheep out of my bos - om; No
bless - ed word! Let care and pain be lift - ed From

look of long - ing to Thee, Lamb so dear! Thou
know where-to now leads my pil - grim - age. The
foe shall e - ven bend a sin - gle hair!" I
off my heart, as I flee un - to Thee. O,

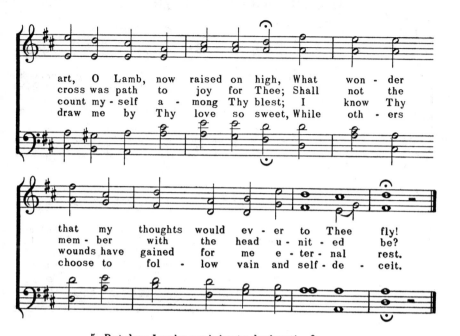

art, O Lamb, now raised on high, What won - der
cross was path to joy for Thee; Shall not the
count my - self a - mong Thy blest; I know Thy
draw me by Thy love so sweet, While oth - ers

that my thoughts would ev - er to Thee fly!
mem - ber with the head u - nit - ed be?
wounds have gained for me e - ter - nal rest.
choose to fol - low vain and self - de - ceit.

5. But dare I make such hasty declaration?
   Perhaps this is too great a claim for me?
   Yea, should I trust my own imagination,
   I would not dare so confident to be.
   But now I cling in faith to Thee;
   And trust that Thou, Almighty One, my strength will be.

6. O precious Lamb, Thou wilt that we be guided
   As Thine own people, by Thy Spirit's call.
   The question thus is easily decided,
   For I am naught; but Thou art all in all.
   O, Truth, grant that I may be true;
   O, Love, love me, that I in love be burning too!

7. My whole salvation then is to Thy credit,
   To Thee alone, O, Son of God and man;
   My ransom is achieved through Thy own merit;
   I take as a free gift the purchased crown.
   So this must then conclusive be,
   That Thou, my slaughtered Lamb, my all in all shall be.

8. O Lamb of God, Who bled for my transgression,
   And for my guilt on Calv'ry's brow hast trod!
   Who could unto such great love give expression?
   Who is like Thee, Thou chosen Lamb of God?
   As often as my pulses beat,
   I lay my life, my blood, my all at Jesus' feet.

185. THE JOURNEY TO ZION

1. Come, chil - dren, let us jour - ney; The eve - ning draw - eth near; Our path is full of dan - ger; The des - ert, dark and drear! En - cour - age now your heart To fu - ture life to wan - der, Grow strong, un - til up

2. We shall not be re - gret - ting We chose this pil - grims way; We know the One, so faith - ful, Who leads us day by day. Be - lieve and serve ye Him, Each one his face di - rect - ing, The nar - row way se -

3. The go - ing out from Ba - bel We nev - er will re - gret, But hope to grow more per - fect, More sep - a - rat - ed yet. Nay, chil - dren, do not fear; De - spise the world's al - lur - ing, Its wrath and hate en -

4. Go up a - gainst your na - ture, And you'll go straight and fine; Those who nurse flesh and crea - ture Will nev - er fall in line. Cre - a - tion count but loss! For - sake all that would bind you; Leave e'er your "Self" be -

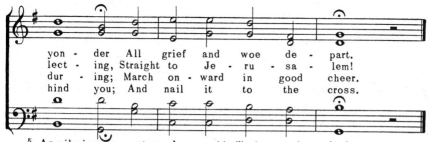

yon - der   All   grief   and   woe   de - part.
lect - ing, Straight to   Je - ru - sa - lem!
dur - ing;   March on - ward in   good cheer.
hind   you;   And   nail   it   to   the   cross.

5. As pilgrims we must wander,
From earthly burdens free;
Else as we journey yonder
Our path would trying be!
He fails who will not heed!
The least can satisfy us,
All things we would deny us
Save what we truly need.

6. Adorn not house nor body,
Embellish but your heart!
We are but weary strangers,
And soon we shall depart.
All fleshly ease deceives;
As pilgrims all resigning,
All worldly lust declining
At home you'll find relief.

7. We must not pause to dally
With child's play by the way!
Our powers we must rally;
Sloth follows on delay.
Pay no attention here.
On then! All ease now spurning,
Away from vain thoughts turning,
For danger's always near!

8. And be the path quite narrow,
So lonesome, steep, and bent,
Though thorns be without number,
And many crosses sent,
Yet there is but one way!
Let us but journey onward;
Attend our Leader homeward,
Through darkness unto day.

9. What may take place about us,
We scarcely hear or see;
May these go on without us;
No idle dreams have we.
Eternal is our goal;
Our dealings are in heaven;
Our life to God is given;
Our very heart and soul.

10. The meek Lamb's disposition
Is here on us impressed;
Our actions give expression
How childlike and how blest;
How quiet, straight and still
The lambs will face the distance,
And go without resistance
Just as their Shepherd will.

11. We journey in seclusion,
Despised and quite unknown,
Unseen mid the confusion
Of this land, not our own;
Yet, if the world pays heed,
It hears our voices ringing,
Songs of the home-land singing,
For which we yearn indeed.

12. Up, then, let naught defy us;
The Father with us goes;
And He Himself stands by us;
Each bitter step He knows.
He will our courage raise;
His looks of grace attend us;
He will refresh, defend us;
Oh, we have blissful days!

13. Then onward, sister, brother;
Let us go hand in hand,
With joy in one another,
In this bewildered land.
Oh, let us childlike be;
Let here no strife divide us!
The angels walk beside us,
God's children, they and we.

14. Should weak ones ever stumble,
The stronger will take hold;
We care and help each other
And plant love in the fold.
In closer union found,
Let each one be the humblest,
But also be the purest,
As pilgrims homeward bound.

15. Come, let us journey gladly!
Day follows after day;
The way grows shorter daily;
The flesh soon proves but clay.
With courage and more love
To be a little truer,
Of earthly matters freer,
And turned to things above!

16. Then journey on reliant;
The goal is well worthwhile.
Of all things be defiant
That hinder or beguile!
Earth, thou art small indeed:
With Christ Himself to guide us,
Eternity shall hide us;
For Christ is all we need!

186. HUMILITY
28, 93, 217.

1. Meek - ness is the no - blest vir - tue, Ev - 'ry
2. Be - hold Je - sus, He was hum - ble; He ex -
3. He who ex - er - cis - es meek - ness Is be -
4. Tru - ly meek-ness great - ly bless - es, And ob -

Chris - tian's hon - or bright; It a - dorns the
alt - ed not Him - self; He was gra - cious,
lov'd by ev - 'ry - one; He who does not
tains the Fa - ther's grace. Who this vir - tue

youth - ful mem - ber And the a - ged with its might.
lov - ing, gen - tle, Asked no hon - or and no wealth;
vaunt his know - ledge God will hon - or in His Son.
here pos - ses - ses, Know-ing her most fit - ting place,

Though it does not stand in fa - vor With those
In Him dwelt no vain am - bi - tion, Nor a
Hum - ble - ness to God is pleas - ing, And to
Will in all his deeds find fa - vor, And his

314.

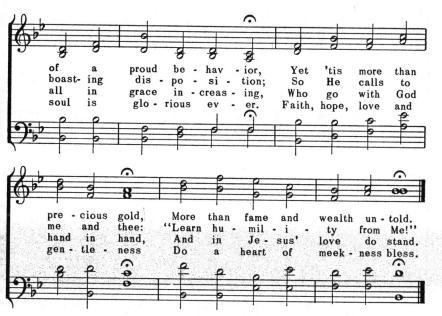

of a proud be - hav - ior, Yet 'tis more than
boast- ing dis - po - si - tion; So He calls to
all in grace in - creas - ing, Who go with God
soul is glo - rious ev - er. Faith, hope, love and

pre - cious gold, More than fame and wealth un - told.
me and thee: "Learn hu - mil - i - ty from Me!"
hand in hand, And in Je - sus' love do stand.
gen - tle - ness Do a heart of meek - ness bless.

5. These good fruits of God, the Spirit,
   That are given to the meek,
   They, through Jesus, may inherit
   Who for them sincerely seek.
   Only where true faith is dwelling
   There true meekness is excelling;
   And thereby is manifest
   Who Christ's Spirit knows the best.

6. So I'll strive to be more humble,
   Evermore be meek and kind;
   Humbleness shall rule my actions,
   Meekness dwell in heart and mind.
   In my manner and my being
   All my neighbors may be seeing
   That it is God's Spirit's might
   Leading me in truth and right.

7. After meekness follows rapture,
   God's good blessing in this time;
   There is at that joyful meeting
   Peace and happiness sublime.
   Then humility in grandeur
   Shall receive the crown of honor;
   What was slighted here below
   Shineth there in heav'nly glow.

187. THE NEW BIRTH OF WATER AND SPIRIT

28, 93, 186, 217.

1. Hark the voice of Je - sus teach- es; All who
2. This new birth must be ac - com- plished Thro' bap-
3. Fur - ther - more the Ho - ly Spir - it As a
4. So by love and con - stant striv - ing Man must

are not born a - gain Out of wa - ter and of
tis - m and God's Word; And if we do not op-
com - fort - er is sent, Pluck-ing out the roots of
serve God's ho - ly name; And the world - ly sin des-

Spir - it Shall be lost. 'Tis clear and plain That to
pose Him, Soon it shall be seen and heard; If His
e - vil, Sow-ing seeds of good in - tent. All our
pis - ing, Let per - fec - tion be his aim; For God's

en - ter heav - en's por - tal And in - her - it
grace we do not ban - ish, How all wick - ed-
mo - tives and de - si - res Are re - newed; and
mer - cy he is grate -ful, And to him all

life	im	-	mor	-	tal,	New	cre	-	a	-	tions	we	must
ness	will		van	-	ish;	For	if		God		pos	- sess	the
He	re	-	qui	-	res	That	our		con	-	duct	shall	be
things	are		hate	-	ful	Which	his		sin	-	ful	heart	had

be,	On	this	earth	from	sin	made	free.
heart,	Sin	and	e	- vil	must	de	- part.
right,	Serv	- ing	God	with	all	our	might.
loved	And	in	for	- mer	times	ap	- proved.

5. Singing, praying, God adoring,
   Fills the new born person's mind;
   From the world to God returning
   Strength and power he will find.
   And in all his operation,
   Showing that regeneration,
   Surely maketh all things new,
   And gives grace God's will to do.

6. Thus there will be manifested
   An entire change of heart,
   Which as will be seen and noticed,
   Holiness of life impart.
   Heart and mind and self renewing
   All the evil thoughts subduing,
   Faith and love will be the theme,
   And God's Spirit rule supreme.

7. O, my God, I bow before Thee:
   Now in me Thy work fulfill!
   By Thy Spirit's hov'ring o'er me
   Sanctify my heart and will.
   Let me not be lost forever,
   But reborn of Thee, O Saviour;
   May I, child-like, Thee adore,
   Learn to love Thee more and more.

8. Lord, let me continue ever
   In this state, so richly blest,
   Until death earth's bonds shall sever,
   And I enter into rest.
   O, let nothing from Thee take me;
   Thou art mine, do not forsake me;
   Then with joy I hence depart,
   E'er to be where Thou, Lord, art!

317.

188. REDEEMING OUR TIME
164, 123, 124, 248.

1. The time flies on and death draws nigh; U-
2. Thou know - est, Lord, the ev - 'ry need Of
3. De - ny us not the truth and light, Thy
4. The right - eous host en - light - en Thou, And

nite us, Lord, with Thee on high! Pre-
them who for Thy mer - cy plead. With
pre - cious gift so clear and bright, The
with Thy bless - ings all en - dow. Thy

pare us now to live with Thee For
help - ing hand Thine aid be - stow To
word of truth to teach us true, And
lit - tle fold do Thou still bless With

ev - er in e - ter - ni - ty!
guide Thy chil - dren here be - low.
nour - ish heart and soul a - new.
stead - fast faith and ho - li - ness.

5. Thy blessings in each house shall reign;
   And may Thy flock increase and gain.
   O, Lord, from Thee all blessings flow
   Which cause good works to thrive and grow!

6. Grant to Thy servants grace and might
   And wisdom, working virtues bright,
   That in this time good seeds they sow
   From which eternal fruits may grow.

7. The treasure of pure love anew
   Preserve among Thy children true!
   Let not their innocence depart,
   But guard and hallow every heart!

8. O, may young men devote in truth
   To Thee the flower of their youth;
   Be maidens' beauty holiness,
   The fear of God their glorious dress!

9. By word and deed is brought to light
   How Thy great name is glorified.
   And pure and clean our life shall be,
   A living witness, Lord, for Thee.

10. O, sanctify our heart and mind,
    That we, Thy chosen ones, may find
    The path from this turmoil on earth
    To God's bright home of peace and mirth!

189. INTERCESSION

39, 40.

1. Je - sus, Thou a - lone canst gov - ern Thy as -
2. Share Thy grace and heav'n - ly bless - ing To Thy
3. Lord, I love Thy chil - dren dear - ly; All who
4. I em - brace, O Lord, Thy serv - ants, Joined to

sem - bly as its sov - 'reign, Bless me then, Thy
mem - bers, thus im - press - ing Each, Lord, with Thy
fol - low Thee sin - cere - ly, They are pre - cious
them in love so fer - vent, Ask - ing, Lord, that

hum - ble child! O, in - fuse in me new
Spir - it's call. Scat - tered o - ver all cre -
to my heart! Thou know'st how my soul re -
from Thy face They re - ceive a thou - sand

mer - it To o - bey Thy Ho - ly Spir - it;
a - tion, And in ev - 'ry clime and na - tion,
joi - ces, Meet - ing those whose hearts and voi - ces
bless - ings; In Thy ways, Thy strength pos - sess - ing,

Strength -	en	me	with	bless -	ings	mild!
Thou	dost	know	them	one	and	all.
Are	with	Thee	in	one	ac -	cord!
Lead	them	in	Thy	light	and	grace.

5. From the world Thine own deliver,
   And let Satan soon forever
   Wholly 'neath their feet be trod!
   By Thy Spirit in them dwelling,
   Earthly lust and nature quelling,
   Be their only joy, O God!

6. Those who sorrow's cross are carrying,
   Strengthen so that without tarrying,
   They to Thee their souls confide.
   Purge them; make them ever purer,
   Yet more humble, and yet surer,
   That in Thee they may abide.

7. Let Thy children, while here stationed,
   After Thine own heart be fashioned,
   Beautiful for piety;
   Quiet, set apart, and lowly,
   Upright, as Thy will most holy,
   And as Thou wouldst have them be!

8. Look upon with special favor,
   Those who ask of me, O Saviour,
   That for them my prayers may rise;
   To Thy mercy I commend them;
   To each one such blessing send them
   As they need; for Thou art wise.

9. Visit in their hour of sadness
   All their hearts; may they find gladness
   When Thy face alone they see.
   Draw, with love's divine attraction,
   All their joy and satisfaction
   Into union close with Thee!

10. On the cross hast Thou, Lord, suffered,
    Full redemption to us offered;
    For our sins didst Thou atone!
    Hold us fast while we are living,
    And here in this desert grieving;
    Leave us nevermore alone!

11. Till above Thy saints shall gather
    In the mansion of the Father,
    Free from every spot and stain.
    Thy eternal throne erected,
    Thy likeness in us reflected,
    Ever with Thee to remain.

190. ADORATION

40, 189.

1. Je - sus Christ, as King e - lect - ed, All things
2. But in Him -- O con - so - la - tion -- Can we
3. Hear the hymn and learn the sto - ry: Christ doth
4. Nor does His dear Church so ho - ly, Have these

are to Him sub - ject - ed. All things God lays
find our full sal - va - tion, The sal - va - tion
lead His own to glo - ry! Grace and peace He
gra - cious bless - ings sole - ly, She has Him as

at His feet! Ev - 'ry tongue shall make con -
in His blood; List! for us His life is
giv - eth thee. Lo, He death and hell de -
Head, who lives! With His blood the Sav - iour

fes - sion That Christ is the Lord ac -
smil - ing And e - ter - nal re - con -
fi - eth: "Death, where is thy sting?" He
bought her, As His heav'n - ly Bride He

322.

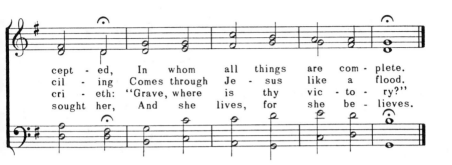

cept - ed, In whom all things are com - plete.
cil - ing Comes through Je - sus like a flood.
cri - eth: "Grave, where is thy vic - to - ry?"
sought her, And she lives, for she be - lieves.

Give your hearts to Him, ye sinners;
Tell, ye ailing, Him your illness;
Bring, ye poor, to Him your need.
Thro' His wounds He heals and cleanses,
Healing ointment He dispenses,
Lasting treasures after death.

Haste then! Shame and care, O, leave it!
Seek ye grace? 'Tis yours; receive it!
Seek ye life? Pray Him who lives!
He, the sinner, justifieth;
Grace to no one He denieth;
Everlasting gain He gives.

Here the ransomed souls shall treasure
All His good in boundless measure,
And praise God in full accord.
Hallowed words! Most precious teaching!
Unto all the world are reaching,
Sweet Evangel of our Lord!

Though the cross of Christ oft presses,
And the saints a while distresses,
Yet their suff'ring soon will end;
Joy will soon displace affliction,
With their Lord in close connection
They with Him to God ascend.

9. Wealth and honor here may fail us;
Pain and sorrow may assail us,
Yet shall scorn and death be gain!
Tho' men threaten, tho' there's danger,
All things are to him a stranger
Who this Treasure would obtain!

10. Heaven's open gate discloses
What for them in grace reposes
All that fondest hopes can bring.
In white robe the Bride's appearing,
Knowing that the time is nearing
When in joy she'll greet the King.

11. Ye, His servants, sing His glory;
All ye righteous, tell His story;
Ye who bear the palms, rejoice.
Sing, all ye redeemed and crowned;
Sing, ye choir where He is throned,
Praise His name with harp and voice!

12. Even I in lowest station,
I will join in exultation,
Though I'm still a pilgrim here.
Jesus Christ as King elected,
All things are to Him subjected,
Honor, love and praise Him there.

191. NOW AND THEN
180.

1. Sing praise to God, all ye who love the Sav-iour;
2. O, love Him, all that are His cov-'nant's chil-dren,
3. O, gra-cious Sav-iour, Thou hast left us du-ly
4. There-fore, ye Christ's dis-ci-ples, all to-geth-er,

Ex-tol His ac-tions; praise His faith-ful-ness!
Who un-to sin, and world and lust have died,
Thy dear ex-am-ple, and we fol-low Thee;
O, con-se-crate your-self to Him a-new!

Sing praise to Him, Who first showed us His fa-vor;
And in His cru-el death, with Him, the Con-qu'ror,
O, now en-fold us with Thy love most tru-ly,
U-nit-ed stand; and let love's flame for-ev-er

His lov-ing kind-ness in your song ex-press!
Are bur-ied by bap-tis-m's bath ap-plied!
That will-ing bear-ers of Thy shame we be!
In-flame your hearts with pas-sions, strong and true,

In love and grace He ev - er greets His chil - dren,
He gave in love His life and blood so pre - cious,
How blest, all this for Thy sake to be shar - ing!
And love in Him a - like His hum - ble chil - dren,

Gives them sal - va - tion and con - tent - ment, grace;
To ran - som us from guilt and sin - ful debt;
Thou dwell'st in us; we fol - low faith - ful - ly.
Whom He has cho - sen as His sa - cred bride!

E - ter - nal - ly will be with them in un - ion;
He raised us up un - to a life of new - ness;
Through cross - es here Thou art Thine own pre - par - ing
He loves us all and names us all His breth - ren;

Be - stows on them all heav - en's bless - ed - ness.
By His great love and grace we here are kept.
For glo - ry there: O, tru - ly blest are we!
We are His peo - ple who in Him a - bide.

325.   (Cont'd)

5. He will us as His people then acknowledge,
   When He appears on that great Judgment day;
   Before His Father He will then confess us;
   His love for us no one can take away!
   O, what a happiness for us is waiting
   When He, our bridegroom, will appear with might
   Us, as His holy bride, with Him uniting
   And dry our tears in that eternal light!

6. With bliss eternal we shall be rewarded:
   The crown of life will then the bride adorn.
   The tears, the pain, the scorn, the gown of mourning
   Shall change to rapture on that joyful morn.
   Fulfilled will be what faith is hoping ever;
   There we will greet the One our heart doth love;
   The stream of life is flowing there forever,
   So clear and crystal for us from above.

7. As King of Glory we shall see our Saviour,
   Before whose face all earth and heaven flee;
   Before whose feet, as humble subjects ever,
   The heavenly host in reverence bows the knee.
   Yea, there at length must every knee be bowing,
   When He appears upon that judgment-morn;
   When He Himself as World-Judge will be showing,
   Of whom the present world but speaks with scorn.

8. O, woe to all who here His Word disdaining
   Now proudly, boldly walk the sinner's way,
   Whose only thought is gold and honor gaining,
   Who think the Christian foolish in his day.
   How the Avenger, then Himself revealing,
   Shall recompense what every one hath done!
   How foolish then shall seem their earthly dealing
   Who here upon the scorner's path have gone.

326.

9. Then shall their laughter all be changed to sorrow,
   When earthly joys their final end shall gain,
   Yea, gnashing teeth shall have an endless morrow
   In late remorse, in torment and in pain.
   Their worm, the evil conscience, never dying,
   An endless fire at the spirit gnaws,
   For worldly sowing brings endless destroying;
   Woe him who not unto the Spirit sows!

10. It shall be well, if we with tears are sowing
    The seed in hope of blest eternity,
    Despising scorn our foes are here bestowing,
    And bearing persecution patiently;
    Eternally will prosper fresh and vernal,
    The seed of faith that we have planted here,
    When we shall harvest 'mid the joys eternal,
    And see the ripened sheaves in glory there.

11. The harvest there will truly our hearts gladden,
    So let us freely sow while here we may;
    And let us bear all crosses that would sadden,
    The Father will reward us in that day.
    There will the joys of heaven be unended;
    The pain of earth will soon forgotten be.
    Here sowing days with signs and cares are blended;
    There we shall reap with joy eternally.

12. Beloved pilgrims, faith's association,
    Keep on in striving for the promised land!
    Be praying, fighting without hesitation,
    For that great harvest day is near at hand!
    Behold the fields; they are soon ripe for harvest;
    The fig tree now is putting forth its leaves.
    Up, gather in! who slothful is in harvest,
    No crown of righteousness from God receives.

192. AWAKE, YE WITNESSES

1. A - wake, ye wit - ness - es! Be burn -
2. Has love's bright flame died out a - mong
3. Thou, Shep - herd, hast each one en - treat -
4. The cross shall be our prep - a - ra -

ing In deep - est love; in - flame al - so our
us? Nay, it shall burn in - tense - ly and with
ed To work and do with dil - i - gence Thy
tion, Our hearts as ho - ly tem - ples to or -

hearts; Let from a - bove de - scend up -
zeal, Shall be the pow'r and in - spi -
will; Ne'er shall Thy love in us be
dain, Lest in e - ter - nal con - dem -

on us The fier - y tongues that with their
ra - tion That brings forth fruit of sweet - ness,
wan - ing, And as it bound the saints, so
na - tion Our soul shall suf - fer tor - ment,

328.

flam - ing darts Rise up and
pure and real; It wafts to
bind us still. It gives us
grief and pain, Sound there - fore

melt to - geth - er, we im - plore, In
us the cool - ing heav'n - ly breeze, Gives
hope where we in fear would groan, Leads
loud and clear Thy Shep - herd's call; In -

fer - vent heat the faith - ful ev - er - more!
us in con - flict vic - to - ry and peace.
us to trust in Thy good help a - lone.
to our hearts its e - cho e'er shall fall.

5. The heaven's gates are standing open,
   And in Thy holy covenant we stand.
   If we but honor, if we trust Thee,
   Thou wilt adorn us with Thy gracious hand,
   Yea, though the earth and heaven pass away,
   Yet in Thy covenant we'll ever stay.

6. We are engaged in mortal combat;
   A coward soon despairs, turns back and flees,
   But he whom Christ gives sword and armor,
   Will persevere and gain eternal peace.
   Then joyfully, O brethren, ever on;
   For after victory we'll wear the crown.

329.

193. CELEBRATING THE SABBATH
232, 235.

1. To Thee, O Lord, be this day ded - i -
2. The heav'n - ly hosts ex - tol Thee with their
3. In vain this world would tempt me with its
4. Let us in meek - ness, Fa - ther, come be -

cat - ed! Let all re - joice who join to - cel - e -
prais - es; Our tongue its voice in hon - or to Thee
pleas - ure; My spir - it in Thy stat - utes finds a -
fore Thee; I know Thou lov - est those who would a -

brate it! Let us with joy be in Thy pres - ence
rais - es. Then be our thanks and all our sup - pli -
treas - ure. The ho - ly word Thy mes - sen - gers are
dore Thee. What Thy flock needs each day of earth - ly

stand - ing, Thy grace de - mand - ing!
ca - tion Thy ex - al - ta - tion.
preach - ing Shall be my teach - ing.
liv - ing, Thou wilt be giv - ing.

5. May we today, through Thy good Spirit learning,
   From ways that please Thee not our steps be turning!
   O let us through Thy Word new pow'rs receiving,
   To Thee be cleaving!

6. This is a day of blessing and rejoicing;
   On gospel pastures Thou Thy flock art leading.
   From fountains clear and living waters flowing,
   Good fruits are growing.

7. This we remember with devout thanksgiving,
   That Thou this day didst break the grave, and living,
   Didst show Thyself to Thy disciples, saddened;
   And their hearts gladdened.

8. Yea, praise be Thine! Grim death hast Thou defeated;
   O Prince of Life, salvation is completed!
   For us, Redeemer, Thou hast been victorious; --
   Thy praise be glorious!

9. Thy fame resound in highest exultation
   Today from this, Thy faithful congregation.
   Praise ye His name, ye saints in earth and heaven
   Forever. Amen!

194. THE CITY OF GOD

59, 60, 233.

1. God has built on firm foun - da - tion His ho - ly
2. Zi - on's gates the Lord is bless - ing; His grace up -
3. Great and ho - ly is the teach - ing His mes - sen -
4. Dry your tears, ye hearts nigh bro - ken, Of Zi - on

cit - y and the na - tions In un - be - lief a -
on them He's dis - pens - ing, And makes their bars and
gers in thee are preach - ing, Such as no oth - er
it shall yet be spo - ken:"Her cit - i - zens in

gainst it stand. Yet it shall en - dure for -
cross - beams fast, Fills its cit - i - zens with
na - tion hears. God's own Word is thy sal -
num - ber grow!" Men shall see with fear and

ev - er, And men shall see with fear and won - der
pleas - ure, Re - wards and bless - es with-out meas - ure
va - tion; He gives His Spir - it's in - spir - a - tion,
won - der How God builds Zi - on; they shall pon - der

Who gov - erns it with might - y hand. The God of
Those who will trust Him to the last. How no - ble
By which all dark - ness dis - ap - pears. We hear from
The grace and strength He doth be - stow. Lift up your

Is - ra - el With - in its gates does dwell;
is His grace! With pa - tience He al - ways
time to time Thy gos - pel's love - ly chime:
souls and hearts; The na - tions' day de - parts.

Hal - le - lu - jah! Re - joice with glee, For blest shall
Bears His chil - dren. O Cit - y rare, So rich and
"Grace e - ter - nal." How sweet the sound That here is
Then His day comes; Zi - on shall rise, And Ju - dah's

be Whose priv - 'lege is to dwell with Thee.
fair, Which God does as His own de - clare!
found, Where crowns of end - less life a - bound!
eyes The One it pierced will rec - og - nize!

5. Mother thou of ev'ry nation,
   That here hath sought and found salvation,
   O Zion, thou shalt truly be.
   What a chorus of rejoicing
   Shall once the saints in thee be voicing!
   The Fount of Life is found in thee.
   In thee the waters well
   That every thirst can still.
   Hallelujah!
   From death's dread cave,
   From dangers grave,
   No one but Zion's God can save!

6. Zion's city, God's creation,
   Thou shalt be mother of the nation
   That finds eternal life in thee!
   Songs of praising and rejoicing
   From thee to heaven will be rising;
   In thee the stream of life shall be!
   From thee the waters burst
   That quench the burning thirst.
   Hallelujah! Save us from death,
   From all distress,
   Thou, Zion's God of righteousness!

333.

195. FAREWELL

1. Live peace - ful - ly! Said Christ, the Lord, Un - to His own e - lect - ed. My breth - ren dear, O heed His Word As those with God con - nect - ed. To you I tell As my fare - well, In con - cord
2. A pain of heart pos - ses - es me, I sigh with deep af - fec - tion. Be - cause the Lord has thus de - creed My so - journ's term - in - a - tion. My deep dis - tress I must con - fess At this our
3. A Chris - tian man - ner ev - er show, As you have been in - struct - ed; On firm foun - da - tion you must grow, On Christ's way be con - duct - ed. My breth - ren, see, This is my plea In part - ing
4. We've lived in peace to - geth - er here, As all can see most clear - ly; We've lived as Chris - tians all can do Whose faith is true; And hence I who would bear The Sav - iour's name sin - cere - ly, E'en

334.

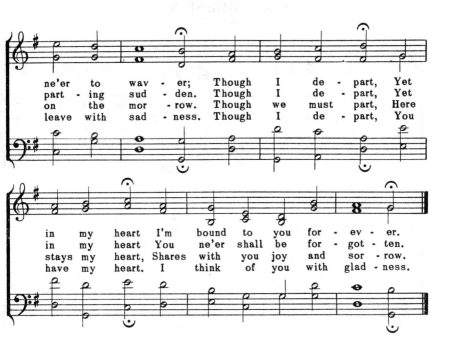

ne'er   to   wav - er; Though I   de - part, Yet
part - ing sud - den. Though I   de - part, Yet
on   the   mor - row. Though we must part, Here
leave with sad - ness. Though I   de - part, You

in my heart I'm bound to you for - ev - er.
in my heart You ne'er shall be for - got - ten.
stays my heart, Shares with you joy and sor - row.
have my heart. I think of you with glad - ness.

. My loving friends, full many a tear
Have I shed for you, weeping;
This has been done in love sincere
While I my watch was keeping.
For night and day My heart did pray:
"God keep you ev'ry hour!"
Though I depart,
You have my heart
That you with love will shower.

. Ye fathers, strive with courage bold,
In sowing and in reaping;
With watchful care attend the fold
That God puts in your keeping.
Then Christ the Lord As your reward
The crown of life will render.
Although we part,
Yet shall my heart
In love to you surrender.

7. Ye children, in submission yield
Due rev'rence to the fathers.
Through love and peace shall be revealed
How good fruits you may gather.
Each heart increase In perfect peace
And joy in Christ the Saviour;
Though now we part,
Yet pleads my heart:
Learn wisdom, truth and favor!

8. Praised be the Lord who gives us strength,
Who leads and gives direction.
My brethren, when you kneel in pray'r,
For me make intercession.
'Twill not be vain; Pray'r as a chain
Binds us in God together,
And when we part,
Unites each heart
In Jesus' name forever.

196. SUBMISSION
96, 167.

1. Nay, I will not sor - row! Who knows if to- mor - row Light will shine for me? He who safe - ly guid - eth, All good things pro - vid - eth, Ne'er will part from me. If in - deed His

2. Nay, I will not mur - mur, But in faith grow firm - er, Though His help de - lays; When my heart is long - ing, When my tears come throng - ing, He'll not hide His face. Im - pa - tience Be -

3. Nay, I'll not be choos - ing, Lest, His help re - fus - ing, I should be de - ceived; My im - per - fect vi - sion, Sees but the be - gin - ning, Not the end a - chieved. My own choice Would

4. In my God con - fid - ing, And in faith a - bid, - ing, Hope shall cheer my heart; Though the storms be blow - ing, God His love is show - ing; Love heals ev - 'ry smart. Ev - 'ry weight Love

hand shall lead, Though on dark way He should
comes of - fence; Tests and tri - als are our
ne'er suf - fice; Though He hides His plans un -
will a - bate; May I but in trib - u -

car - ry, Should I doubt or wor - ry?
train - ing; Let us cease com - plain - ing.
shak - en, God is ne'er mis - tak - en.
la - tion Win His ap - pro - ba - tion.

5. Do I seem forsaken? Is my spirit shaken,
   Knowing not God's will? Yet in all affliction
   I'll accept correction In submission still.
   He'll provide what's good and right;
   All my earthly tribulation
   Serves to my salvation.

6. Oft through bitter conflict, Yet to peaceful concord
   Leads my pilgrim way; He who fought so glorious,
   Over death victorious, He will near me stay;
   Thou, O Lord, O'ercam'st the world,
   So we'll conquer in believing,
   Victory achieving.

197. LOVE TOWARD JESUS
38, 166.

1. Pre - cious Je - sus, Thou my por - tion, Naught on earth so
2. In this life one thing is need - ful, That we may Thy
3. If in tri - als Thou art near me, I shall be by
4. Draw me, as Thou wilt, O Sav - iour; Give to me Thy

dear as Thou! Nev - er can I keep my si - lence;
pleas - ure seek; This shall be my con - stant striv - ing,
Thee con - soled, Though man should seek to de - stroy me,
ho - ly mind! Then my heart shall rest for - ev - er,

Urged by love, to Thee I bow; Love that draws me, Thee to
Thee, Lord, in my heart to keep. He who has Thee in this
Fast to Thee, my God, I'll hold. I have Thee: That will suf-
All my trou-bles left be - hind, For the suf- f'rings of this

own; Love that loves Thee, Lord, a - lone; Love by which, to
life Will not faint in fier -cest strife. He can praise Thee,
fice, For Thy love all need sup -plies, Draw-ing me from
time Meas- ure not the joy sub - lime That in heav - en

338.

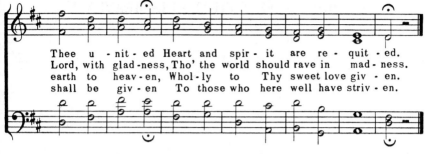

Thee	u - nit - ed	Heart	and	spir - it	are	re -	quit - ed.
Lord, with	glad -ness, Tho'	the	world	should rave in			mad - ness.
earth	to	heav - en,	Whol - ly	to	Thy	sweet love giv -	en.
shall	be	giv - en	To those who	here	well have striv -		en.

5. All this world, its empty pleasures,
These no longer have my love;
They who hold them as their treasures
Void are of the wealth above,
That they who Thine own would be,
Dearest Jesus, find in Thee,
And with those their stand have taken
Who this vain world have forsaken.

6. So my heart is in Thy heaven;
There my spirit too would be,
For this world, by pleasure driven,
But a Babel is to me.
My true homeland is above;
There I'm drawn by bonds of love
Toward Him who love showers on me,
And who giveth Himself for me!

7. Jesus, help me then to conquer
Sinful world and carnal mind;
Let my hope in Thee be grounded
And in Thee its anchor find!
May my heart and soul and mind
With Thee, Jesus, be entwined.
"Forward" as my watchword choosing,
All my trust in Thee reposing.

8. Thou hast been forever faithful;
Jesus, Thou art ever true!
And Thy love is in all sorrow
Sweet, and every morning new,
And at even I find Thee,
Dearest Saviour, still with me;
There I can bring my vexation
To Thee without hesitation.

9. Lord, Thy tender, loving likeness
Deep into my heart impress!
And that I may fail in nothing,
Give me steadfast watchfulness.
O, direct my heart to Thee.
Govern Thou my tongue in me,
That it speak no other story
But Thy praise, renown, and glory.

198. OUR CONVERSATION IS IN HEAVEN
33, 51, 161, 203.

1. As a trav-'ler home re - turn - ing From some
2. All our choice and our en - deav - or Are for
3. Je - sus, like a mag - net, rais - es Our faint
4. Should our en - e -mies as - perse us, Our dear

far and dis - tant land, Thinks of it with bos - om
Him Who gave us love, And our soul would live for-
spir - it to the skies; And we seem in pray'r and
Lord, who loves us so, Bids us bless e'en those who

yearn - ing, Ere his foot has touched the strand,
ev - er For Him Who came from a - bove.
prais - es As on ea - gle's wings to rise.
curse us And to love our great - est foe.

So a - mid the nois - y pleas -ures Of the world
Here a - lone it finds con - tent - ment; Here a - lone
All our life and con - ver - sa - tion Is be - fore
He, who died for our sal - va - tion And on us

340.

the heart oft sighs   For the no - bler, high - er
de - lights to be;   Glad - ly leaves the world's en-
our Sav - iour's face;   All our thoughts and oc - cu-
hath life be - stowed,   Wills that by our con - ver-

treas - ures   Laid up for us in the skies.
chant - ment   For the joy it shares with Thee.
pa - tion   This vain world can - not em - brace.
sa - tion   We should glo - ri - fy our God.

5. Can we have our hearts in heaven
   And yet earthly-minded live?
   Can we, who have been forgiven,
   Not forget and not forgive?
   Can we hate an erring brother,
   Only love when we are loved,
   And not bear with one another,
   By Christ's Holy Spirit moved?

6. Nay, no hater or blasphemer,
   None who slander and defame,
   Can be one with the Redeemer,
   Who was gentle as a lamb.
   Love will cause assimilation
   With the object of our love;
   Love will work a transformation
   And renewal from above.

7. Let me ne'er from Thee be parted,
   Saviour true and full of love!
   That I may live true and holy,
   Send Thy teaching from above!
   Keep me from the world unspotted,
   That I may not only be
   To Thy service here devoted,
   But abide in heav'n with Thee!

341.

199. THANKS AND PRAYER

7.

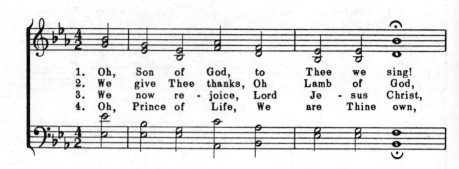

1. Oh, Son of God, to Thee we sing!
2. We give Thee thanks, Oh Lamb of God,
3. We now re-joice, Lord Je-sus Christ,
4. Oh, Prince of Life, We are Thine own,

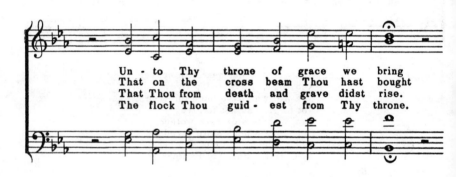

Un-to Thy throne of grace we bring
That on the cross beam Thou hast bought
That Thou from death and grave didst rise.
The flock Thou guid-est from Thy throne.

Our song in cho-rus, full and clear;
For us sal-va-tion, peace and grace
Thou liv-est now, Oh Lord, and we
And we our-selves and all a-ward,

In -	cline	to	us	Thy	heart	and
With	Thee	in	heav	- en's	rest	- ing
Hope	Thou	wilt	take	us	un	- to
For	- ev -	er	un	- to	Thee,	Oh

ear.	To	Thee	we	sing!
place!	We	give	Thee	thanks!
Thee.	We	now	re	- joice!
Lord!	We	are	Thine	own!

5. Draw us to Thee, exalted One!
   Extend Thy hand from heaven's throne,
   That we may follow faithful, true,
   In trials and afflictions, too;
   Draw us to Thee!

6. Abide with us, Immanuel!
   Thou Prince most strong in Israel!
   Our Strength and Fortress be, we pray;
   And lead us safely all the way.
   Abide with us!

343.

200. COMMUNION HYMN

199.

1. O, Spir - it of God's strength and might,
2. O, may we all u - nit - ed stand
3. May we in per - fect love be found
4. Then come in - to our midst to - day;

Cre - ate in us new life and light;
By ho - ly tie and sa - cred band,
When we Thy ta - ble, Lord, sur - round;
Im - part Thy - self to us, we pray.

O, join us all in heart and mind,
As mem - bers of Christ's bod - y here,
Keep soul and bod - y pu - ri - fied;
This cup and loaf are proof and sign

That ac - cess to God's throne we
Led by Thy Spir - it true, sin -
Thy bless - ings, Lord, be mul - ti -
Of this, Thy cov - e - nant di -

find	With - in	Thy	light!
cere,	With one	ac -	cord.
plied	Up - on	this	feast.
vine	In Je -	sus	blood.

5. Anew, Lord, we are bound to Thee
Through Thy blest sacrament, which we
Partook, that joined in heart and hand;
To Zion's realm and holy land
We journey on.

6. Lord, lead us then by Thy strong hand
As pilgrims through this desert land;
We are pursued by many foes;
Deliver us from all our woes,
For we are Thine.

7. To Father, Son, and Spirit praise
For help and guidance on our ways!
Thou givest power from above,
Hast chosen us, through Christ, in love
To be Thine own!

8. Our joyful praise we sing to Thee,
O, Lord of glorious majesty!
Through Jesus Christ to Thee we pray
And bring our thanks to Thee today
Before Thy throne!

201. THE BOUNDLESSNESS OF GOD'S GRACE
202.

1. O, my Lord Je - sus Christ! By grace I
2. O, this re - demp - tion bond, It goes so
3. As Je - sus died for me, And in the
4. The bod - y that be - lieves, Thy Son as

am ap - prised Of gifts es - teemed;
far be - yond My car - nal view.
grave did lie So I the same,
head re - ceives In un - ion strong;

Filled with the Ho - ly Ghost, A - mong Thy
Thy mer - ci - ful na - ture For - ev - er
Im - mersed and bur - ied there, I'm res - ur -
So I, the scorn - ful one, This mem - ber -

cho - sen host,	I may now take my post,
will en - dure,	And Thy word doth as - sure
rect - ed where	I no more death shall share.
ship have won,	Since to the bless - ed Son

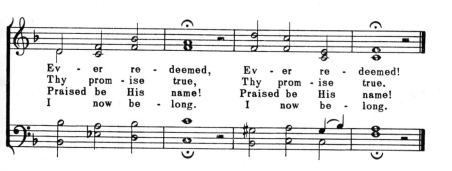

Ev - er re - deemed,	Ev - er re - deemed!
Thy prom - ise true,	Thy prom - ise true.
Praised be His name!	Praised be His name!
I now be - long.	I now be - long.

5. Thy grace so rich and free,
   To me in high degree
   Thou dost unfold;
   Thou only, great and strong,
   Couldst break the dreadful thong,
   And draw from Satan's throng
   :: Into thy fold.::

6. Therefore my voice I'll raise
   In glad and joyous praise
   Now on this shore,
   And then in chorus clear
   I'll sing Thy praises near,
   O Lord, to Thy blest ear
   :: Forevermore. ::

202. CHRIST MY ALL
201.

1. Oh, Thou foun - tain of love, Whose bleed - ing,
2. Oh, Lord who art a - bove, Thou au - thor
3. My Sav - iour's right - eous - ness Is now my
4. He that con - demn - eth me Like - wise shall

dy - ing move e - rased my sin, Im - man - u -
of this love! Thou Lamb of God! With Thy most
glo - rious dress Be - fore my Lord. Thy Spir - it
al - so Thee, Je - sus, de - spise. It is not

el so dear, Thou foun - tain true and clear,
pre - cious blood, That pure and cleans - ing flood,
and Thy blood To me re - demp - tion brought;
me that lives, But my Lord Je - sus gives

Be Thou to my heart near, And flow with - in.
Hast Thou my free - dom bought; Up - on the cross.
In like - ness of my God I serve His word.
Life to him who be - lieves, Oh, God All - wise.

5. Oh, my Immanuel!
   Though Satan would compel
   Us all to die,
   Yet Thou art ever near;
   In conflicts most severe,
   With world and Satan here,
   Thou standest by.

6. Thou art my Light and Pow'r,
   My Joy and Life each hour,
   Redeemer blest!
   While pilgrim here I be,
   I lift mine eyes to Thee,
   My faith's security,
   My soul's true Rest!

7. Faith's language this shall be
   Through all adversity:
   Faithful is God!
   In Christ, His Only Son,
   He dearly loved each one,
   Chose them to be His own,
   Ere man earth trod.

8. Worship and laud and praise
   In strength and clarity,
   O Lord, to Thee!
   Now feeble, verily,
   One day Thy praise shall be
   Unclouded, pure and free,
   Eternally!

203. THOU HAST WORDS OF LIFE

36, 161, 198, 205.

1. Oh, how joy - ful is the ho - ur When we,
2. At Thy feet, O Lord, we lin - ger; Speak to
3. Teach us to es - cape de - struc-tion Through the
4. O - pen, Lord, our un - der - stand-ing, As to

Lord, draw nigh to Thee, And the words of
us in ac - cents clear! Let us hear Thy
pow - er of Thy grace, All of - fense, with
Thy dis - ci - ples there. May our hearts be

life and pow - er From Thy ho - ly lips re - ceive.
word so ten - der Ea - ger - ly with god - ly fear.
Thy in - struc - tion To for - sake and to ef - face.
e'er de - mand-ing Wis - dom's light with Thee to share.

May we not in vain as - sem - ble 'Round Thy
Teach us fol - low Thy ex - am - ple; Teach us
And ac - cord - ing to Thy pleas-ure Think and
Heav'n-ly Light that oft has ban - ished Man - y

350.

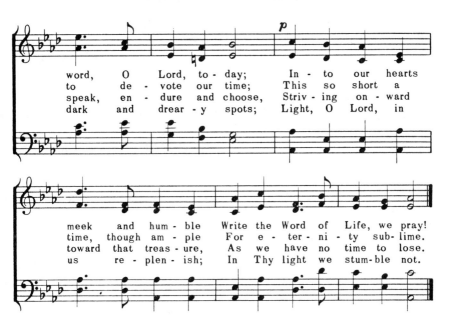

word,   O   Lord, to - day;   In - to   our   hearts
to   de - vote   our   time;   This   so   short a
speak,   en - dure   and choose, Striv - ing   on - ward
dark   and   drear - y   spots;   Light, O   Lord, in

meek   and   hum - ble   Write   the   Word   of   Life,   we   pray!
time,   though am - ple   For   e -   ter - ni - ty   sub- lime.
toward that   treas - ure, As   we   have   no   time   to   lose.
us   re - plen - ish;   In   Thy   light   we   stum- ble   not.

5. And Love's holy fire, we pray Thee,
   Pour into each spotless heart,
   That in joy or in affliction
   Ne'er from Thee we may depart.
   May we never feel encumbered
   With the cross that we must bear,
   Gladly leave in self-denial
   What Thy kingdom cannot share.

6. Let Thy word bring light and gladness,
   Strength and power to our heart;
   May it be the living motive
   Causing each to do his part.
   Help to store in careful keeping
   What this day we may receive;
   Manifest Thy healing power
   In all who Thy word believe.

204. I WILL NOT LEAVE THEE

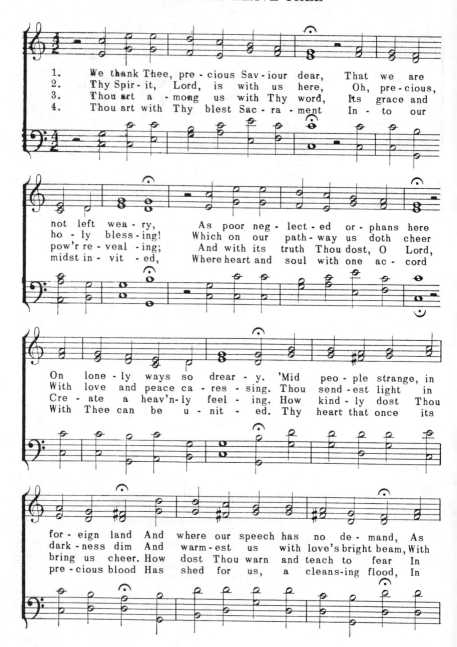

1. We thank Thee, pre - cious Sav - iour dear, That we are
2. Thy Spir - it, Lord, is with us here, Oh, pre - cious,
3. Thou art a - mong us with Thy word, Its grace and
4. Thou art with Thy blest Sac - ra - ment In - to our

not left wea - ry, As poor neg - lect - ed or - phans here
ho - ly bless - ing! Which on our path - way us doth cheer
pow'r re - veal - ing; And with its truth Thou dost, O Lord,
midst in - vit - ed, Where heart and soul with one ac - cord

On lone - ly ways so drear - y. 'Mid peo - ple strange, in
With love and peace ca - res - sing. Thou send - est light in
Cre - ate a heav'n - ly feel - ing. How kind - ly dost Thou
With Thee can be u - nit - ed. Thy heart that once its

for - eign land And where our speech has no de - mand, As
dark - ness dim And warm - est us with love's bright beam, With
bring us cheer. How dost Thou warn and teach to fear In
pre - cious blood Has shed for us, a cleans - ing flood, In

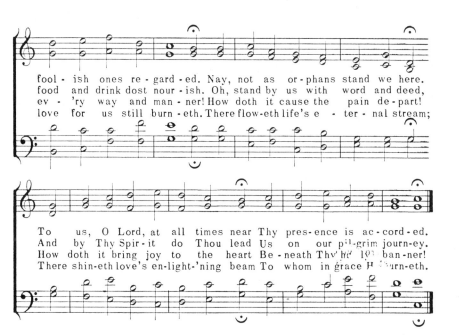

fool - ish ones re - gard - ed. Nay, not as or - phans stand we here.
food and drink dost nour - ish. Oh, stand by us with word and deed,
ev - 'ry way and man - ner! How doth it cause the pain de - part!
love for us still burn - eth. There flow-eth life's e - ter - nal stream;

To us, O Lord, at all times near Thy pres - ence is ac - cord - ed.
And by Thy Spir - it do Thou lead Us on our pil-grim journ-ey.
How doth it bring joy to the heart Be - neath Thy red love ban - ner!
There shin-eth love's en-light-'ning beam To whom in grace He turn-eth.

5.Thou art with us, where two or three
In holy union gather,
And pray in faith, from doubting free,
Unto the heavenly Father.
For Thou Thyself art present, Lord,
Where brethren meet in one accord,
And blessed hours are given,
A foretaste of that heritage,
Beyond our earthly pilgrimage,
Awaiting us in heaven.

6.Thy sacred peace doth rest upon
Our hearts when fears may grieve us;
What, dying, Thou for us hast won
Thou here on earth dost give us.
Though troubles in our path may lie,
And Satan, world, and sin may try
With threats to terrify us;
In Thee our peace shall anchored be
Because we fully trust in Thee,
And Thou wilt well supply us.

7.Thou art with us,--we do not sigh,
Uncertain and forsaken;
We fear not although ills be nigh
Upon the path we've taken;
We dread no cross, tho' dark its night,
No foe's grim wrath or evil might,
Nor even hell's black portal;
For He who is our Lord and King
Beneath the shadow of His wing
Keeps us for life immortal!

8.Although unseen, Thou art with us;
And while we wait in sadness,
The time is brief till we shall pass
Into Thy realm of gladness,
Forevermore to be with Thee,
To view Thy glorious majesty,
And praise Thy name, O Saviour.
Abide with us and be our stay
And guide us safely to the day
We see Thy face forever!

205. ABIDING IN JESUS

52, 161, 198, 203.

1. Dear - est Sav - iour, let me ev - er In Thy serv - ice here a - bide; Ne'er would I from Thee be sev - ered, Walk - ing dai - ly by Thy side. By Thee is my life in - spir - ed: Thou art strength and

2. Could I else - where find such treas - ure As Thou, Lord, with me hast shared, Such rich gifts of grace and pleas - ure Thou - sand - fold for me pre - pared? Could I find a con - sol - a - tion Such as Thou, O

3. Who could find me such a Mas - ter? Who, what Christ hath done, would do, Saved me from sin and dis - as - ter With His pre - cious blood so true? Should not I be His true serv - ant Who His life on

4. Yea with Thee, Lord, I'll con - tin - ue As in pleas - ure, so in grief; And in dai - ly con - se - cra - tion Un - to Thee my life I give. For Thy sum - mons I am read - y, And Thy fi - nal

354.

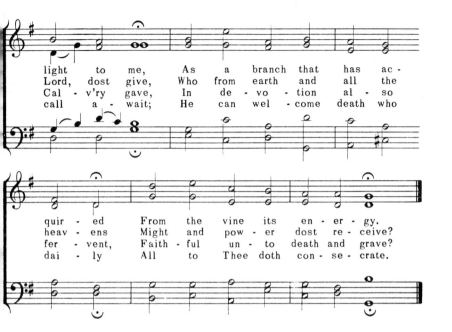

light   to   me,   As   a   branch   that   has   ac -
Lord,   dost   give,   Who   from earth   and   all   the
Cal - v'ry gave,   In   de - vo - tion   al - so
call   a - wait;   He   can   wel - come   death   who

quir - ed   From   the   vine   its   en - er - gy.
heav - ens   Might and   pow - er   dost re - ceive?
fer - vent,   Faith - ful un - to   death and grave?
dai - ly   All   to   Thee doth con - se - crate.

5. Lord, throughout my pilgrim journey,
Let me find Thee by my side;
And when evening shades are falling
Do Thou still with me abide.
And in holy benediction
Lay on me Thy hand of love,
Saying: Son, thy course is finished;
But through faith thou'lt live above!

6. Stay Thou near me when the shadows
Of chill death are drawing nigh,
Like the frosty breath of morning
Ere the dawn in rosy sky.
When the darkness falls around me,
Then illuminate my soul;
As a traveller home returning
May I reach my heav'nly goal.

206. THE FATHER LOVES US

1. Re - joice, the Fa - ther loves us here, In sym - pa - thy re - mem - bers, And all the gifts we need to cheer So gra - cious - ly He ren - ders. What lack we then, Yet fur - ther, when Our Fa - ther
2. Though we may roam the wide world o'er, And have no earth - ly treas - ure, Our Fa -ther's love can give us more Than worlds of wealth can meas - ure. We have no fear Of need while here, For we shall
3. He who for us so much has done To pur - chase our sal - va - tion, Who gave His own be - lov - ed Son For our pro - pi - ti - a - tion, He who be - stows Such love on foes Will He, our
4 Be - fore His throne of grace we may Pre - sent our-selves with bold - ness, Nor fear that He will turn a - way His face from us with cold - ness. He will and can Hear ev - 'ry man Who of - fers

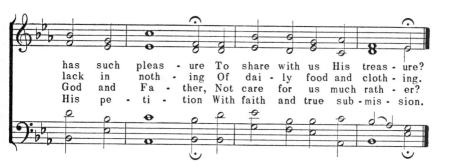

has   such   pleas - ure   To   share with   us   His   treas - ure?
lack   in   noth - ing   Of   dai - ly   food and   cloth - ing.
God   and   Fa - ther,   Not care   for us   much rath - er?
His   pe - ti - tion   With faith and   true sub - mis - sion.

5. In Jesus Christ the Father's heart
   Is open to receive us;
   We fly to Him when inward smart
   And outward troubles grieve us.
   There we may rest
   Secure and blest,
   Exposed no more to dangers,
   To care and sorrow strangers.

6. Think ye the near approach of death
   Can make our hearts feel sadly?
   Ah, no, when "Come" the Father saith,
   We'll travel homeward gladly.
   Far better 'twere
   That we were there!
   "Oh, would that He would call us!"
   We sigh when grief befalls us.

7. He loveth us; that is enough
   To fill our hearts with gladness;
   He loveth us; that is enough
   To banish ev'ry sadness.
   Lord, grant that we
   Love also Thee
   With love true and unceasing,
   Yea, ev'ry day increasing.

207. ASSEMBLY HYMN
215, 222, 234.

1. As-sem-bled con-gre-ga-tion, With thanks and ad-o-ra-tion, Be-fore God's throne ap-pear. With pray'r and sup-pli-ca-tion Each heart shall seek oc-ca-sion To see the light of grace so clear.

2. In si-lence give at-ten-tion, The Lord will cheer and strength-en With His own word and hand. If earn-est-ly we seek Him, And pray'r-ful-ly en-treat Him, He'll not let us as or-phans stand.

3. His word is full of prom-ise; His an-gels He'll ad-mon-ish His serv-ants to at-tend, Who in His grace are shar-ing, And here on earth pre-par-ing For that bright home and hap-py land.

4. Send, Lord, Thy ho-ly teach-ing To us in hum-ble preach-ing, Yet in the Spir-it's pow'r, That we, a new cre-a-tion, In love and true de-vo-tion May bear our bur-den ev-'ry hour.

5. Thy Word alone enlightens,
With light and power brightens
What seems a mystery.
It gives us understanding
In living faith expanding,
Subduing ev'ry enemy.

6. Inspire, O Lord, each servant
With love and ardor fervent
Thy gospel to proclaim;
That, prompted by Thy Spirit,
They work and toil with merit
Unto the glory of Thy name.

7. Thy messengers Thou sendest,
By them to us extendest
The living Bread of heav'n.
That none of us may perish,
Arouse our hearts to cherish
The grace and healing to us given.

8. Give faithful servants ever
Who have but one endeavor,
Thy Gospel to proclaim;
Who heed Thy Spirit holy
And strive and labor solely,
O, Lord, to glorify Thy name.

9. O Father, be the Giver
Of Jesus' powers ever
Unto Thy children here;
Let more and more be given
The inner life from heaven
To all who pray with heart sincere!

10. O, bind together fully
With love's devotion holy
Thy people, dearest Lord,
For whom Thy blood was given
To ransom them for heaven.
O, hallow them and keep them, Lord!

208. PRAISE YE THE LORD

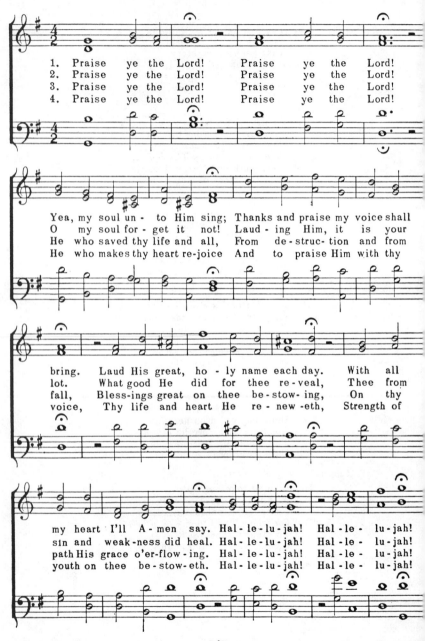

1. Praise ye the Lord! Praise ye the Lord!
Yea, my soul un-to Him sing; Thanks and praise my voice shall bring. Laud His great, ho-ly name each day. With all my heart I'll A-men say. Hal-le-lu-jah! Hal-le-lu-jah!

2. Praise ye the Lord! Praise ye the Lord!
O my soul for-get it not! Laud-ing Him, it is your lot. What good He did for thee re-veal, Thee from sin and weak-ness did heal. Hal-le-lu-jah! Hal-le-lu-jah!

3. Praise ye the Lord! Praise ye the Lord!
He who saved thy life and all, From de-struc-tion and from fall, Bless-ings great on thee be-stow-ing, On thy path His grace o'er-flow-ing. Hal-le-lu-jah! Hal-le-lu-jah!

4. Praise ye the Lord! Praise ye the Lord!
He who makes thy heart re-joice And to praise Him with thy voice, Thy life and heart He re-new-eth, Strength of youth on thee be-stow-eth. Hal-le-lu-jah! Hal-le-lu-jah!

5. Praise thou the Lord! Praise thou the Lord!
   He is truly patient, thus
   With His grace doth comfort us;
   His ways to us He e'er showeth;
   And His light on our path gloweth.
   Hallelujah! Hallelujah!

6. Praise thou the Lord! Praise thou the Lord!
   As a father pity shows
   Toward a child that trouble knows,
   So God doth pity us ever,
   All who fear Him doth deliver.
   Hallelujah! Hallelujah!

7. Praise thou the Lord! Praise thou the Lord!
   Just and faithful is His name,
   And He knoweth well our frame.
   We dust are from the beginning,
   Yet He pardoneth our sinning.
   Hallelujah! Hallelujah!

8. Praise thou the Lord! Praise thou the Lord!
   We are naught without His might.
   He is Source of all true light.
   His loving grace and His favor
   Shall abide with us forever.
   Hallelujah! Hallelujah!

9. Praise ye the Lord! Praise ye the Lord!
   Who His bond of peace here know,
   To His name due honor show!
   To save and lead us to heaven,
   He His Word as rule hath given.
   Hallelujah! Hallelujah!

10. Praise ye the Lord! Praise ye the Lord!
    He the changeless, Holy One,
    Sits upon His heavenly throne
    And dwells in a light most glorious,
    Over all His foes victorious.
    Hallelujah! Hallelujah!

11. Praise ye the Lord! Praise ye the Lord!
    Ye His angels that excel
    And His pow'r and glory tell,
    Ye mighty ones, who so fully
    Do His commandments most holy.
    Hallelujah! Hallelujah!

12. Praise ye the Lord! Praise ye the Lord!
    Ye who His true servants are!
    Preach His Word both near and far,
    Till o'er the world it is ringing!
    O, my soul, His praise be singing!
    Hallelujah! Hallelujah!

209. NOW IT IS DONE

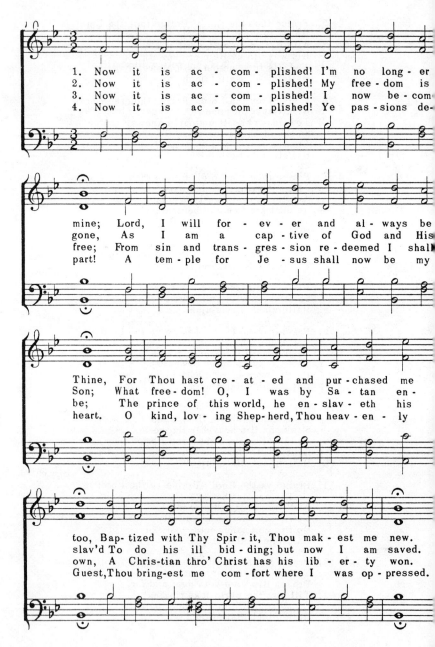

1. Now it is ac - com - plished! I'm no long - er
2. Now it is ac - com - plished! My free - dom is
3. Now it is ac - com - plished! I now be - come
4. Now it is ac - com - plished! Ye pas - sions de-

mine; Lord, I will for - ev - er and al - ways be
gone, As I am a cap - tive of God and His
free; From sin and trans - gres - sion re - deemed I shall
part! A tem - ple for Je - sus shall now be my

Thine, For Thou hast cre - at - ed and pur - chased me
Son; What free - dom! O, I was by Sa - tan en-
be; The prince of this world, he en - slav - eth his
heart. O kind, lov - ing Shep - herd, Thou heav - en - ly

too, Bap - tized with Thy Spir - it, Thou mak - est me new.
slav'd To do his ill bid - ding; but now I am saved.
own, A Chris - tian thro' Christ has his lib - er - ty won.
Guest, Thou bring - est me com - fort where I was op - pressed.

5. Now it is accomplished! My soul He hath healed;
   A portion in heaven to me He hath sealed.
   O, may He direct me through joy and through ill;
   I'll never forsake Him, but follow Him still.

6. Now it is accomplished, O covenant blest!
   His will on my heart and my tongue is impressed;
   To speak or keep silence as He shall command,
   With prayer and with worship before Him to stand.

7. Ah, now it is done! Now I live unto Thee;
   My Light and my Life, oh, abide Thou with me!
   To follow Thee ever shall be my sole aim
   Thro' shade or thro' sunshine, thro' honor or shame.

8. Ah, now it is done! Now I fear not to die,
   For death hath no terrors when Jesus is nigh.
   The body from pain and from labor hath rest;
   The spirit soars up to the home of the blest.

9. Now it is accomplished! Though deep in my soul
   I fear lest in weakness I stray from the goal;
   Yet I will not waver, my Saviour is kind;
   I trust in His mercy; thus courage I find.

10. Now it is accomplished! With heart and with mind
    To thee, my dear Saviour, I now am resigned!
    I'll ever be faithful in life and in death,
    Abiding in Jesus unto my last breath.

210. THE LORD IS YOUR REWARD

2, 3, 4.

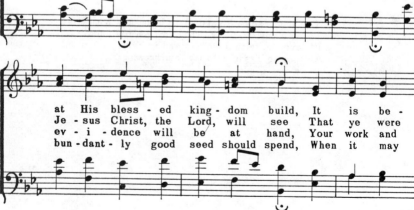

1. Ye shep-herds, Who the Lord do love, And through the
2. Ye mes-sen-gers of peace shall bring The glo-rious
3. Ye guards on Zi-on's walls, pre-pare! For soon your
4. To ev-'ry serv-ant be it told, How he should

Spir-it from a-bove, Pro-claim to men sal-
gos-pel of the King To man in ac-cents
Mas-ter will ap-pear Your full re-ward be-
use with cour-age bold The tal-ent God has

va-tion, How much the Lord to you has willed, Who
truth-ful. How great your blest re-ward shall be When
stow-ing. In joy-ful ranks ye then will stand; The
giv-en. His treas-ure he should well de-fend, A-

at His bless-ed king-dom build, It is be-
Je-sus Christ, the Lord, will see That ye were
ev-i-dence will be at hand, Your work and
bun-dant-ly good seed should spend, When it may

yond ex - pres - sion! There - fore, there - fore,
true and faith - ful! Ev - 'ry broth - er
la - bor show - ing; In great num - bers,
lead to heav - en, Man - y per - sons

Be ye faith - ful! How de - light - ful! God with pleas -
Who such mis - sion And po - si - tion Has been grant -
Souls en - list - ed And as - sist - ed To find fa -
Who re - ceive it And be - lieve it, They'll have glad -

ure Will im - part the crown and treas - ure.
ed, Shall be to the end un - daunt - ed.
vor In the eyes of Christ, the Sav - iour.
ness, And be free from grief and sad - ness.

5. Such servant shall be full of cheer,
His Master's will fulfilling here
With joy and with affection.
His greatest pleasure he will find
In doing good and being kind,
To lead in Christ's direction.
Greatly shall The faithful servants,
Pious virgins, Be regarded
With the bread from heav'n rewarded.

6. Oh, precious Saviour, fill anew
Thy servants who are staunch and true
With light and Holy Spirit,
With joy and with Thy wondrous might,
That in Thy service they delight,
Producing fruits of merit!
Shield Thou, Bless Thou All who labor,
Love their neighbor, And are faithful
With the talent Thou didst render.

7. Hath he that trusted in the Lord,
Here buildeth on His Holy Word,
Not comfort overflowing?
From day to day he brings his need
To Him who giveth all indeed
While perfect peace bestowing.
Who here in faith Sees God truly,
Trusting fully, Him hath taken,
He shall never be forsaken.

8. Though children may have faith within,
And live no more in former sin,
Yet have they need of teaching;
They come into the highest school,
Where Christ, Himself, doth teach, and rule,
And guideth by His preaching.
There His pure love Every hour
Us with power, Animateth,
Faith, love, hope in us createth.

365.

211. THE PROMISED REST

62.

1. God's peo-ple yet shall take pos-ses-sion Of that sweet
2. But on-ly if we have been faith-ful, Have shunned no
3. Ye who are now God's chos-en peo-ple, Look back to
4. There sheaves of joy we shall be bring-ing; The tear-ful

land of rest so bright; Re-joice! From bond-age
cross nor yet con-tempt, So shall we to that
Is-ra-el of old! From their ex-am-ple
sow-ing there will cease. The Fa-ther's man-sion

and op-pres-sion, From serv-ice in this earth-ly
sweet and grate-ful Re-pose and rest in heav'n be
take a teach-ing And cling to God with heart and
shall be ring-ing With songs of praise in end-less

night, Soon Christ will come and will re-lieve you; Your
sent. Then let us watch and pray sin-cere-ly And
soul! With-out com-plaint and lam-en-ta-tion Bear
peace. No pain, nor death, nor trib-u-la-tion When

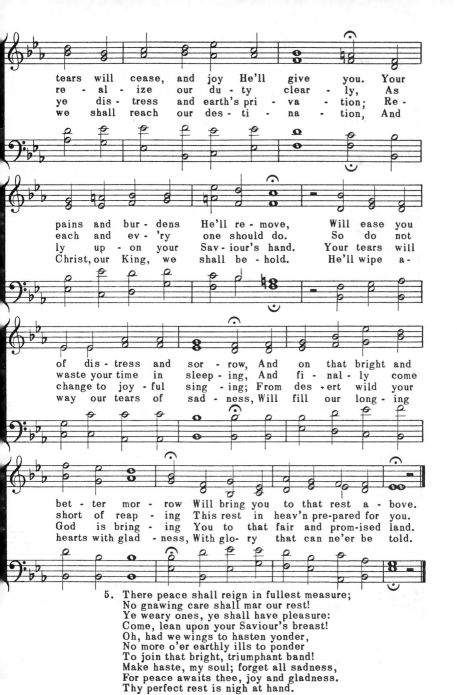

tears will cease, and joy He'll give you. Your
re - al - ize our du - ty clear - ly, As
ye dis - tress and earth's pri - va - tion; Re -
we shall reach our des - ti - na - tion, And

pains and bur - dens He'll re - move, Will ease you
each and ev - 'ry one should do. So do not
ly up - on your Sav - iour's hand. Your tears will
Christ, our King, we shall be - hold. He'll wipe a -

of dis - tress and sor - row, And on that bright and
waste your time in sleep - ing, And fi - nal - ly come
change to joy - ful sing - ing; From des - ert wild your
way our tears of sad - ness, Will fill our long - ing

bet - ter mor - row Will bring you to that rest a - bove.
short of reap - ing This rest in heav'n pre-pared for you.
God is bring - ing You to that fair and prom-ised land.
hearts with glad - ness, With glo - ry that can ne'er be told.

5. There peace shall reign in fullest measure;
No gnawing care shall mar our rest!
Ye weary ones, ye shall have pleasure:
Come, lean upon your Saviour's breast!
Oh, had we wings to hasten yonder,
No more o'er earthly ills to ponder
To join that bright, triumphant band!
Make haste, my soul; forget all sadness,
For peace awaits thee, joy and gladness.
Thy perfect rest is nigh at hand.

212. THE 23rd PSALM

The Lord is my Shep-herd; No want I'll suf-fer; He mak-eth me to lie down in green pas-tures, And lead-eth me by the still wa-ters. He my soul in peace re-stor-eth. He lead-eth me on right-eous path-ways To His name's praise and hon -

or. And though I walk in the vale of dark - ness here,

I need fear no e - vil, For Thou art with

me, For Thou art with me. Thy rod and Thy staff

com - fort me. Thou pre-par-est a ta - ble for me

In the face of my foes. A - noint - est my

head with oil; My cup run-neth o ver.

Sure - ly good-ness and mer - cy Fol-low me

all the days of my life And thus shall I dwell in God's

ho - ly house Now and for - ev - er -

more, In God's ho - ly house ev - er -

more, In God's ho - ly house ev - er - more.

213. PARTING HYMN

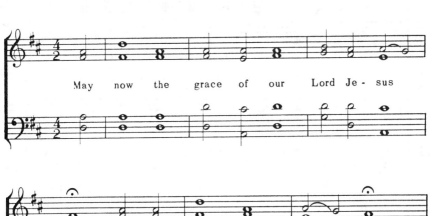

May now the grace of our Lord Je - sus

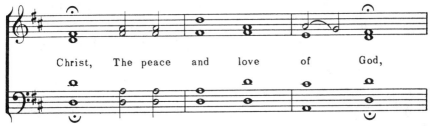

Christ, The peace and love of God,

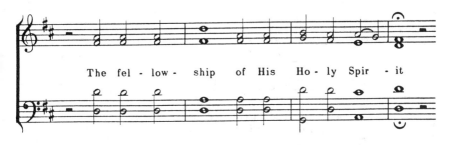

The fel - low - ship of His Ho - ly Spir - it

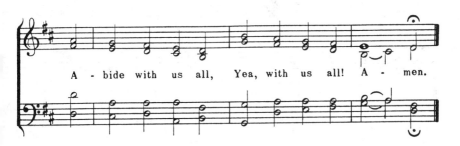

A - bide with us all, Yea, with us all! A - men.

214. BEFORE THE MEETING

15, 33, 36, 51.

1 With your Zi-on's harps now chim-ing, Praise the Lord!
2. They a-bove are ev-er sing-ing An-thems God
3. See them, who their harps sus-pend-ing On the weep-

Let's do our best. Soon will come the time of part-ing;
hath taught to them, And He fail-eth not in teach-ing
ing wil-low tree, Lack-ing zeal, Thy par-don spurn-ing,

We'll be laid in earth to rest. Ex-er-cise your-self in
Us to sing and praise His name. He hath now our hearts in-
They could not re-joice in Thee. But we are in Thee con-

prais-ing The true God, and laud His fame, Tho' our faith at
spir-ed With a true and fer-vent love; Gift-ed us with
fid-ing, Freed from Bab-y-lon and sin; E-ven tho' our

times be wan-ing, We find cour-age in His name.
voice and tal-ents, Thus to praise His name a-bove.
life they threat-en, Thou, O Lord, wilt help us win!

372.

215. PRAYER FOR ACCESS TO GOD'S THRONE

207, 222.

1. Thou great High Priest and teach - er, Give me and
2. An ear to hear Thee glad - ly, An eye that
3. My hands give bless - ed greet - ing. My soul its
4. Oh, friend so kind and truth - ful, Come pour Thy

ev - 'ry crea - ture Much in - cense un - to pray'r,
noth - ing sad - ly Will turn from Thee a - way.
best friend meet - ing, His tem - ple would I be.
Spir - it fruit - ful Up - on each pray'r-ful heart!

True hearts, sin - cere and pi - ous, The light of grace be
My lips be pure and ho - ly, Care - ful my feet and
I feel an ex - ul - ta - tion. Thy Spir - it's an - i -
Each time we come be - fore Thee To wor - ship and im -

nigh us, Of all strange spir - its to be - ware.
whol - ly Pre - pared with Thee to go Thy way.
ma - tion, Which none but God's e - lect can see.
plore Thee, Thy light and grace to us im - part.

373.

216. THE CHILDREN'S SUPPLICATION

142, 163, 169, 252.

1. O Lord, be - hold us gath - ered here,
2. Give us like un - to Ly - di - a
3. O Lord, we pray to us re - veal
4. Lord Je - sus Christ, with us a - bide

As chil - dren 'round a light!
An o - pen heart and ear.
Thy words of grace and might,
In this dark day and time,

We pray Thee, Lord, that Thou come near,
We pray Thee, Lord, O come to us
Which Thou from him dost not con - ceal
Un - til we see the morn - ing light

And guide our hearts a - right.
Through bolt - ed doors ap - pear!
Who seek - eth truth and light.
E - ter - nal - ly sub - lime.

217. ATTENTIVE HEARERS
28, 29, 30, 31.

1. Let us hear and give at-ten-tion, God's own teach-ing to em-brace, For a-gain He mak-eth men-tion Of His cov-e-nant of grace; Words of life and con-so-la-tion Come to us, His con-gre-ga-tion, How thro' Je-sus Christ, His Son, Full re-demp-tion we have won.

2. May our hearts each day be o-pened Un-to Thy good Word, O Lord! Lest our call-ing be neg-lect-ed, Lead us on with one ac-cord! Let Thy Spir-it, we im-plore Thee, Teach us how we may a-dore Thee. Close to Thee let us re-main, Till Thy like-ness we at-tain.

218. PETITION FOR THE LORD'S BLESSINGS

217, 28, 93, 186.

1. Bless-ed, ho-ly is the ho-ur When we, Je-sus, think of Thee, And Thy word in god-ly pow-er Hear and in our hearts re-ceive. So we pray to Thee, im-plor-ing, O-pen Thou our un-der-stand-ing! May we hear, as Ma-ry heard, Sa-cred teach-ings of Thy word.

2. May it reach our hearts, we pray Thee; On good soil may it take root. With Thy heav'n-ly bless-ings nour-ished, May it bring the pleas-ing fruit. May we all in rich-est meas-ure, Lord, to Thy great joy and pleas-ure, As Thy plants of hon-or grow! A-men! Yea, Lord, be it so!

219. GATHERING IN JESUS' NAME

1. Be-hold, O Je-sus, we im-plore Thee, Thy
2. Thy peace shall flow up-on our meet-ing; The

flock as-sem-bled now be-fore Thee, That we may,
kiss of faith shall be our greet-ing, When we are

Lord, Thy bless-ings find! O raise Thy hand in heav'n-ly
gath-ered by Thy side! Should on-ly two or three as-

bless-ing, Thy Spir-it true our hearts pos-sess-ing;
sem-ble In Je-sus' Name, yet meek and hum-ble,

Which makes us hum-ble, meek and kind.
His peace and love in us a-bide.

25, 75, 145, 221.

1. To me is giv - en bound - less mer - cy,
2. And I who naught but wrath did mer - it,
3. To Thee, O God, I must con - fess it,
4. No man shall take this rich pos - ses - sion,

A gift that I did not de - serve;
Shall now in grace with God a - bide!
Thy grace to me Thou didst im - part.
It is my boast and my de - light;

Such won- drous love, It is so mar -v'lous,
He rec - on - ciled my way - ward spir - it,
Be - fore all men I will ex - press it,
My faith in "Mer - cy" finds ex - pres - sion,

That such for me should be re - served.
Through His own blood, and gave me light.
Be - cause I feel it in my heart.
In pray'r I praise its won - drous might.

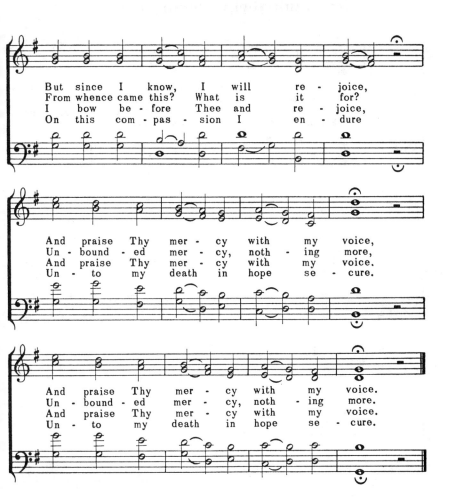

But since I know, I will re - joice,
And praise Thy mer - cy with my voice,
And praise Thy mer - cy with my voice.

From whence came this? What is it for?
Un - bound - ed mer - cy, noth - ing more,
Un - bound - ed mer - cy, noth - ing more.

I bow be - fore Thee and re - joice,
And praise Thy mer - cy with my voice.
And praise Thy mer - cy with my voice.

On this com - pas - sion I en - dure
Un - to my death in hope se - cure.
Un - to my death in hope se - cure.

5. Lord, Thou who art so rich in mercy,
   Take Thy compassion not from me.
   And when death calls, then lead me surely
   Through my dear Saviour's death to Thee.
   Eternally I will rejoice,
   :: And praise Thy mercy with my voice.::

6. Give me, Lord, sympathy and mercy
   With my poor brethren in distress,
   My bitt'rest foe to love and pity.
   Thy love in death Thou didst confess.
   Thy blood for sinners does implore:
   :: Compassion! grace, forevermore.::

221. CHRIST THE FOUNDATION

25, 41, 75, 220.

1. I now have found the firm foun - da - tion Where
2. O depth of love, in which past find - ing My
3. I nev - er will for - get this cry - ing, In
4. Though in the best of all my ac - tions, In

ev - er - more my an - chor grounds! It lay there
sins through Christ's blood dis - ap - pear! This is for
faith I'll trust it all my days; And when o'er
works that are ad - mir'd the most, I must per-

ere the world's cre - a - tion, Where else, but in my
wounds the saf - est bind - ing, There is no con-dem-
all my sins I'm sigh - ing I t'ward my Fa-ther's
ceive great im - per - fec - tions; I sure - ly have no

Sav - iour's wounds? Foun- da - tion which un - mov'd shall
na - tion here; For Je - sus' blood thro' earth and
heart will gaze. For there is al - ways to be
right to boast. Yet this sweet com- fort doth a-

380.

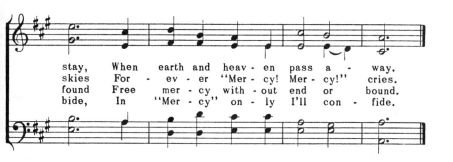

stay,	When	earth and	heav - en	pass	a -	way.
skies	For -	ev - er	"Mer - cy!	Mer -	cy!"	cries.
found	Free	mer - cy	with - out	end	or	bound.
bide,	In	"Mer - cy"	on - ly	I'll	con -	fide.

5. Be it with me as He is willing
   Whose mercy is a boundless sea;
   May He, Himself, my heart be stilling,
   That this may ne'er forgotten be.
   So rests my heart in joy and woe
   On mercy while it beats below.

6. On this foundation I, unshrinking,
   Will stand, while I on earth remain;
   This shall engage my acting, thinking,
   While I the breath of life retain.
   Then I will sing eternally
   Unfathomed Mercy, still of Thee!

222. LOOKING BACK TO THE DAY OF SALVATION

207, 215,

1. O   bliss - ful hour and   ho - ly,   When
2. Ac - cord - ing to   God's   pleas - ure, Christ's
3. Joined   to   His con - gre - ga - tion   In
4. I   was   with Him   re - lat - ed   And

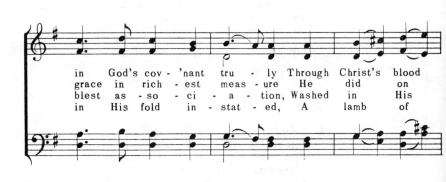

in   God's cov - 'nant   tru - ly Through Christ's blood
grace in   rich - est   meas - ure   He   did   on
blest as - so - ci - a - tion, Washed   in   His
in   His fold   in - stat - ed,   A   lamb   of

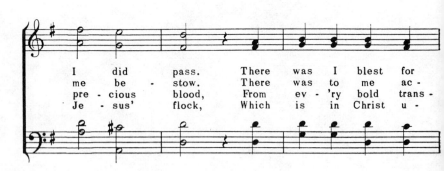

I   did   pass.   There   was   I   blest   for
me   be - stow.   There   was   to   me   ac -
pre - cious   blood,   From   ev - 'ry   bold   trans -
Je - sus'   flock,   Which   is   in   Christ   u -

ev - er, From Sa - tan's realm was sev - ered,
cord - ed The ho - ly gift af - ford - ed,
gres - sion I now find con - so - la - tion;
nit - ed, And through His wounds re - quit - ed;

Then when I took that ho - ly bath.
When Je - sus Christ I learned to know.
How kind and mer - ci - ful is God!
I an - chor now up - on this rock.

223. THE MORNING STAR

2, 3, 4, 210.

1. How bright the morn-ing Star doth shine, A - dorned with
2. Oh treas-ure that no e - qual finds, Oh Son of
3. Pour deep in - to my heart a - new The god - ly
4. But if Thou look on me in love, There straight-way

grace and truth di - vine, So glo-rious in the heav -
God, Thy praise re-minds Us of our Fa - ther's fav -
light and heav'n-ly view, The flame of love's pure fi -
falls from God a -bove A ray of pur - est pleas -

en! Thou ten - der shep - herd, Dav - id's Son, Our
or! Our hearts o'er- flow with fer - vent praise. The
re! Fill me with strength that I may be Thy
ure; Thy Word and Spir - it, flesh and blood Re-

King up - on the heav'n-ly throne, Hast grace and mer - cy
glo - rious gos - pel of Thy grace Gives life and Spir - it's
mem - ber close-ly joined to Thee, Whom all my thoughts de-
fresh my soul with heav'n-ly food; Thou art my hid - den

giv - en! Love - ly, Friend - ly, Fair and glo-rious, All vic - to-
sav - or! Thee, Thee, Will we Hold for - ev - er, For-sake nev-
si - re. T'ward Thee Draws me All my long-ing In me throng-
treas - ure! Now we Pray Thee; Let Thy fav - or, Lov-ing Sav-

rious, Rich in bless - ing, Rule and might o'er all pos-sess- ing!
er, Bread from heav - en, Of the Fa -ther's mer - cy giv - en.
ing, Since I've found Thee, And Thy ten- der love has bound me.
iour, E'er de- light us, And Thy pre- cious Word in - vite us.

5. Lord God, my Father, mighty Shield,
Thou hast Thy love in Christ revealed
Before this world's foundation.
Thy Son is now betrothed to me,
My heart its joy in Him doth see,
And bows in adoration.
What bliss is this! He that liveth,
To me giveth Life forever,
And I praise His Name forever.

6. Lift up the voice and joyful sing,
Let all glad sounds of music ring
In God's high praises blended.
Christ shall be with me all the way,
Today, tomorrow, every day,
Till traveling days are ended.
Sing out, ring out, Triumph glorious,
All victorious, Bow before Him,
King of kings, let all adore Him!

7. O joy to know, that Thou, the Word,
Beginning without end, art Lord,
The First and Last, Eternal!
And Thou at length - O Glorious Grace!
Wilt take me to that holy place,
The home of joys supernal.
Amen, Amen! Come and meet me,
Quickly greet me! With deep yearning,
Lord, I look for Thy returning!

224. OUR SURETY

12, 42, 43, 44.

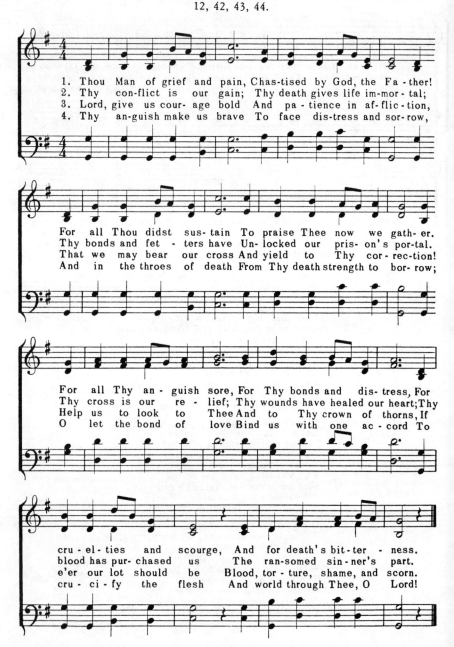

1. Thou Man of grief and pain, Chas-tised by God, the Fa - ther!
2. Thy con-flict is our gain; Thy death gives life im-mor - tal;
3. Lord, give us cour- age bold And pa - tience in af-flic - tion,
4. Thy an-guish make us brave To face dis-tress and sor- row,

For all Thou didst sus- tain To praise Thee now we gath- er.
Thy bonds and fet - ters have Un- locked our pris- on's por-tal.
That we may bear our cross And yield to Thy cor - rec-tion!
And in the throes of death From Thy death strength to bor- row;

For all Thy an - guish sore, For Thy bonds and dis- tress, For
Thy cross is our re - lief; Thy wounds have healed our heart;Thy
Help us to look to Thee And to Thy crown of thorns, If
O let the bond of love Bind us with one ac - cord To

cru - el - ties and scourge, And for death's bit-ter - ness.
blood has pur- chased us The ran-somed sin-ner's part.
e'er our lot should be Blood, tor - ture, shame, and scorn.
cru - ci - fy the flesh And world through Thee, O Lord!

225. CHRIST THE CRUCIFIED AND GLORIFIED

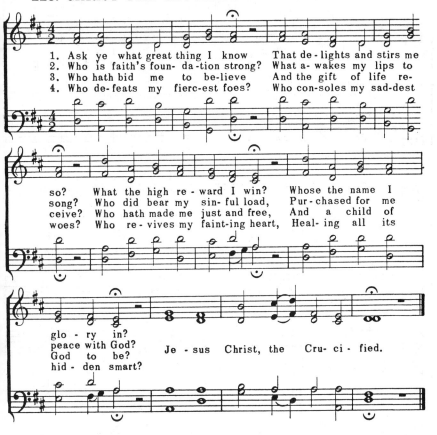

1. Ask ye what great thing I know   That de-lights and stirs me so?   What the high re-ward I win?   Whose the name I glo-ry in?
2. Who is faith's foun-da-tion strong?   What a-wakes my lips to song?   Who did bear my sin-ful load,   Pur-chased for me peace with God?
3. Who hath bid me to be-lieve   And the gift of life re-ceive?   Who hath made me just and free,   And a child of God to be?
4. Who de-feats my fierc-est foes?   Who con-soles my sad-dest woes?   Who re-vives my faint-ing heart,   Heal-ing all its hid-den smart?

Je-sus Christ, the Cru-ci-fied.

5. Who is life in life to me?
Who the death of death will be?
Who will place me on His right
With the countless hosts of light?
Jesus Christ, the Crucified.

6. Who hath loosed the prison door
By His mighty word and pow'r?
Who to life hath wakened me
Ever there with Him to be?
Jesus Christ, our risen Lord.

7. Who hath given strength to me
By His life and victory,
Reconciled me unto God,
Comforts by His staff and rod?
Jesus Christ, exalted Lord.

8. Who directs me from above?
Who is object of my love?
Who rests not till perfect be
All that He hath planned for me?
Jesus Christ, the living One.

9. Now ye know my wisdom clear
And in whom I glory here.
I am His! Who is mine own?
Who gives me of life the crown?
Jesus Christ, the Glorified!

10. This is that great thing I know;
This delights and stirs me so;
Faith in Him who died to save,
Him who triumphed o'er the grave,
Jesus, God of majesty!

387.

226. GOLGOTHA

1. Sit and pause a - while, my spir - it,
2. That your Sav - iour loves you dear - ly,
3. Thus His soul of God for - sak - en,
4. These, the fruits of our trans - gres - sion,

This great mir - a - cle be - hold; See the
He up - on the cross has proved, Where in
Filled with sor - row to its depth, And His
Fell un - to Thee, Sav - iour dear, While this

King of high - est mer - it On the
tor - ments most sev - ere - ly He from
flesh is like - wise shak - en, Tor - tured
wrath - ful con - dem - na - tion We de -

cross, so bare and cold! Out of heav - en
God was far re - moved. In His an - guish
un - to His last breath; All His vi - gor,
served as sin - ners here. These af - flic - tions

God   has   giv - en   His   own   Son   in   love un-   told!
He   must   lan-guish   For   the   sin - ful   men He   loved.
All   His   pow - er   Is   ex -haust - ed   un -to   death.
And   con - vic -tions We   un - worth - y   ones should   bear.

5. Yet Thy suff'ring has defeated
   Satan's pow'r, yea, death and hell;
   Through Thy death Thou hast completed
   Thy dear heav'nly Father's will.
   Thus is given To us even
   Life eternal to fulfill.

6. In humility, dear Saviour,
   Thou for me, I know, hast died;
   Though I was Thy foe, Redeemer,
   Thou for me wast crucified.
   Silence keep I, Humbly weep I!
   Thus through Thee I'm justified!

7. Thou, Lord, hast for me devoted
   Soul and body, life and all;
   So there shall be consecrated
   All I have, both great and small,
   All my efforts and endeavor
   To Thy service and Thy call.

8. Through the power of Thy dying,
   Into Thy death, Lord, draw me;
   Let my body, all my being,
   There be nailéd, Lord, with Thee;
   Calm and gentle May my will be;
   To my love give purity!

227. TO MY REDEEMER

75, 145, 220, 221.

1. Thee will I love, Oh, love e - ter - nal, Thy heart for
2. Thee will I love, my life, my Sav - iour, Who is my
3. A - las! that I so late have known Thee Who art the
4. I wan-dered long in will - ing blind - ness; I sought Thee

me in death did break. Will love Thee out of pur - est
best and tru - est friend; Thee will I love and praise for-
fair-est and the best! Nor soon-er for my own se-
but I found Thee not. For still I shunned Thy beams of

mo - tive Sin-cere-ly, true, though poor and weak. Thee will I
ev - er While light and life to me are lent. Thee will I
lect Thee, Thou high-est God and on - ly rest! I must re-
kind - ness; An earth-ly light filled all my thought. But thro' Thy

love, Oh, light di - vine, So long as ev - er life is mine,
love, Oh, Lamb of God, Whose suf-f'ring my re-demp-tion brought.
pent and sore - ly grieve For this my loath-ness to be - lieve.
love I see Thee now, For Thou in grace to me didst bow.

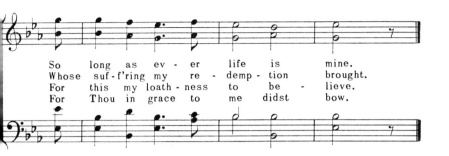

So   long   as   ev - er   life is   mine.
Whose suf-f'ring my   re - demp - tion brought.
For   this   my loath - ness   to   be - lieve.
For   Thou in   grace to   me didst bow.

5. I thank Thee, Jesus, sun from heaven,
   Whose shining beams brought light to me!
   I thank Thee, who hast richly given
   All that could make me glad and free!
   I thank Thee for Thy holy Word,
   :: Which said to me: Be thou restored!::

6. Oh, keep me watchful then, and humble,
   And suffer me no more to stray;
   Uphold me when my feet would stumble,
   Nor let me loiter by the way.
   Fill soul and body with Thy light
   :: Oh, heav'nly radiance strong and bright!::

7. Gush from mine eyes, ye tears most holy;
   Burn in my heart, coals from above!
   Yea, let my soul endeavor solely
   To practice faithfulness and love!
   Yea, let my heart and soul and mind
   :: Still turn to Thee, their rest to find!::

8. Thee will I love, my crown of gladness;
   Thee will I love, my God and Lord,
   Amid the darkest depth of sadness,
   Without a hope of earth's reward.
   And though my flesh and heart decay,
   :: Thee will I love in endless day!::

228. JESUS I WILL NEVER LEAVE

90, 104, 119,

```
1. Je - sus  I   will  nev - er  leave   Who  for  me   Him -
2. Not for earth's vain joy I    crave,   Not  for  heav - en's
3. Je - sus  I   will  nev - er  leave;   Oh,  the  gifts that
4. I   am  His  and  He  is  mine,   Love  has bound  us
```

```
self  has  giv - en;   There-fore un - to  Him  I'll  cleave,
glo - rious pleas - ure;  Je - sus, who  my  soul  did  save,
He   has  giv - en!  Com - fort, rest, and  joy  and  light,
so    sin - cere - ly; Through His wounds and blood di - vine
```

```
Nor  from Him  be  ev - er  driv - en;  Life from  Him  doth
Shall be   my   de - sire and  treas - ure.  He   re - demp-tion
All   are  sent  to   me from  heav - en.  Hope and  life comes
Was  my  ran - som paid  so   dear - ly.  On  Him  I   will
```

light   re - ceive;   Je - sus   I   will   nev - er   leave.
did   a - chieve;   Je - sus   I   will   nev - er   leave.
from   a - bove,   All   be - cause of   Je - sus'   love.
firm - ly   build,   Full   of   hope which shall   not   yield.

5. When the heart would seek the Lord
   To enfold, O blessed hour!
   And how great is the reward:
   Grace and peace to share with power,
   And one glance that for Him yearns,
   With a thousand joys returns.

6. Jesus I shall never leave,
   To His side still firmly clinging,
   Christ leads all who Him receive
   To life's waters ever springing.
   Blest are they who to Him cleave!
   Jesus I will never leave.

229. PRAYER FOR THE TRUE CHRISTIAN LOVE

1, 2, 4, 210.

1. This is my grief and my dis-tress; My fault-i-ness I must con-
2. In jus-tice this shall be my plea: O Je-sus, let my pleas-ure

fess, My love should be more fer-vent. From day to day my want I
be To love Thee more sin-cere-ly, In love and truth to ex-er-

feel That God de-serves a love more real From me, His hum-ble
cise All that is pleas-ing in Thine eyes And Thy word shows so

serv-ant. From Thee, Give me, Of Thy mer-it, In my
clear-ly, Un-til Thy will Shall re-call me, And re-

spir-it, Gent-ly flow-ing, Love and char-i-ty be-stow-ing.
joic-ing, I shall see Thee, Free from ev-'ry trib-u-la-tion.

230. OUR SHEPHERD AND KING

123, 124, 164, 248.

1. All who have learned to know the Lord
2. This is the truth and will re - main,
3. He who this Shep - herd fast does hold,

Be - lieve Him true with one ac - cord; In
For God each prom - ise doth sus - tain; In
Who for the sins of all the world, Him-

those who on His prom - ise build His
trust - ing Him we feel as - sured, Be-
self an of - fer - ing be - came, Has

Word has al - ways been ful - filled.
liev - ing in Je - hov - ah's Word.
made his for - tune in His name.

231. LONGING

29, 30, 31, 32.

1. Not of earth and not of heav-en Is my
2. When my soul and bod-y lan-guish, Doubts and
3. In my weak-ness He's my pow-er; In the
4. What a great and heav'n-ly bless-ing, Lov-ing

thought and my de-sire; I wish that to
fears up-on me press, Yet my heart shall
dark-ness He's my light; And when good deeds
Je-sus Christ a-lone! All the pre-cious

me be giv-en Je-sus Christ, whom I ad-mire.
feel no an-guish, For Christ's love does me re-fresh.
are ac-com-plished, It is on-ly through His might.
gifts pos-sess-ing Which God sends un-to His own.

Be my heart His hab - i - ta - tion, Gift of
He's my joy and con - so - la - tion In my
What good things my heart de - si - res, It in
On - ly through our Lord and Sav - iour Comes each

high - est val - u - a - tion; Je - sus Christ, my
fear and trib - u - la - tion. Je - sus Christ, my
Je - sus Christ ac - qui - res. Oh, the joy that
heav'n - ly gift and fav - or. Je - sus Christ, my

Lord, shall be All and ev - 'ry - thing to me!
Lord, shall be All and ev - 'ry - thing to me!
He shall be All and ev - 'ry - thing to me!
Lord, shall be All and ev - 'ry - thing to me!

232. MAKE ME MORE PERFECT
193, 235.

1. I wish to love my Sav - iour more sin-
2. What shall I do? My Sav - iour, do Thou
3. Thou cam'st to us from Thy throne in the
4. This hast Thou done, Lord, and should I keep

cere - ly, And not to grieve Him,
teach me! Let flames of love and
heav - ens To bear for us our
si - lence? O let Thy love con -

Who loved me so dear - ly; For this would
pure af - fec - tion reach me, That I may
sins and ev - 'ry griev - ance, For us to
strain me to bear wit - ness That Thou, my

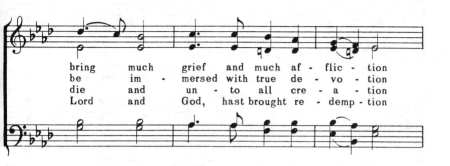

bring　　much　　grief　and　much　af - flic - tion
be　　im - mersed　with　true　de - vo - tion
die　　and　　un - to　all　cre - a - tion
Lord　and　　God,　hast brought re - demp - tion

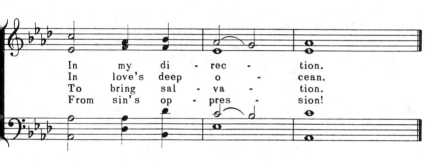

In　　my　　di - rec - tion.
In　　love's　deep　o - cean.
To　　bring　sal - va - tion.
From　sin's　op - pres - sion!

5. Pour deep into my soul from Zion's mountain
   Thy love so pure, a living, flowing fountain,
   That e'er shall flow from my heart, fresh and vernal,
   To life eternal!

6. One day shall faith and hope for us be ended;
   But we shall enter in, by love attended,
   Thy City fair, Jerusalem in glory,
   And there adore Thee.

399.

233. SONG OF PRAISE

59, 60, 194.

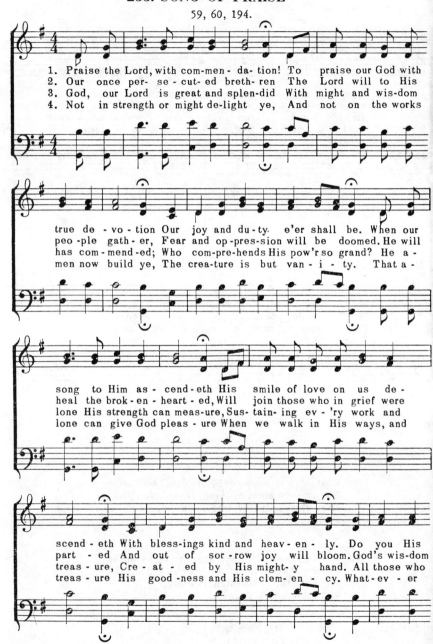

1. Praise the Lord, with com-men-da-tion! To praise our God with
2. Our once per-se-cut-ed breth-ren The Lord will to His
3. God, our Lord is great and splen-did With might and wis-dom
4. Not in strength or might de-light ye, And not on the works

true de-vo-tion Our joy and du-ty. e'er shall be. When our
peo-ple gath-er, Fear and op-pres-sion will be doomed. He will
has com-mend-ed; Who com-pre-hends His pow'r so grand? He a-
men now build ye, The crea-ture is but van-i-ty. That a-

song to Him as-cend-eth His smile of love on us de-
heal the brok-en-heart-ed, Will join those who in grief were
lone His strength can meas-ure, Sus-tain-ing ev-'ry work and
lone can give God pleas-ure When we walk in His ways, and

scend-eth With bless-ings kind and heav-en-ly. Do you His
part-ed And out of sor-row joy will bloom. God's wis-dom
treas-ure, Cre-at-ed by His might-y hand. All those who
treas-ure His good-ness and His clem-en-cy. What-ev-er

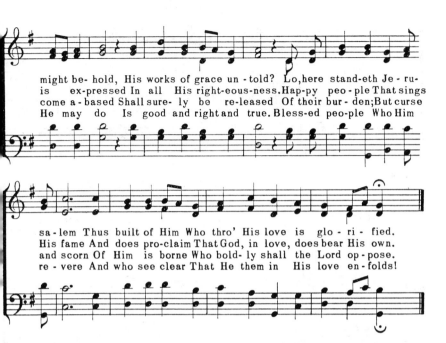

might be- hold, His works of grace un - told? Lo, here stand-eth Je - ru-
is   ex-pressed In all His right-eous-ness. Hap-py peo-ple That sings
come a-based Shall sure- ly be re-leased Of their bur-den; But curse
He may do Is good and right and true. Bless-ed peo-ple Who Him

sa-lem Thus built of Him Who thro' His love is glo - ri - fied.
His fame And does pro-claim That God, in love, does bear His own.
and scorn Of Him is borne Who bold- ly shall the Lord op-pose.
re - vere And who see clear That He them in His love en-folds!

5. Zion, rise! God's praises sing Thou!
   Jerusalem, the proof now bring thou
   That all thy folk are God's by grace.
   He who hath redeemed thee surely,
   And who hath built thy walls securely,
   To children's children thee doth bless.
   He gives thy borders peace,
   And He grants thee increase.
   Blessed people Who Him revere
   And who see clear
   That He them in His love enfolds!

6. His true Word, His testimony,
   God gave to thee, His servant, only;
   O Israel, His love behold!
   Lo, to such exalted station
   He lifted not another nation,
   But let them wander from the fold.
   Thou, Jacob, shalt alone
   The Father's blessing own!
   Hallelujah! O praise the Lord
   With glad accord;
   His service is thy blessedness!

234. THE CHILD'S PRIVILEGE
207, 215,

5. Be Thou my God forever.
   Nothing from Thee can sever;
   I beg: Protect Thou me!
   Confer on me Thy blessings,
   Thy help and love expressing;
   I plead: Oh, Father, help Thou me!

6. As Jacob in his wrestling
   Besought Thee for a blessing,
   Ere he would let Thee part,
   So I embrace Thee ever;
   Thou canst forsake me never,
   For tender is Thy Father-heart!

7. Ye cares, no longer tarry!
   No gentleness you carry,
   For you are stern and hard;
   Go now unto the Father;
   He is my Counselor rather --
   Arise, my soul, unto Thy Lord!

235. THE BLESSEDNESS OF PRAYER
193, 232.

1. How bless-ed to ap - proach un - to the
2. The Lord so glad - ly hears their sup-pli -
3. To pray -- Oh, what a glo - rious oc - cu -
4. Then let us pray in ev - 'ry place and

Fa - ther, Who loves un - to Him - self His
ca - tion And sees their tears of true hu -
pa - tion! What gifts de - rived from hum - ble
sta - tion! Have we no words to tell of

flock to gath - er, To see them on their
mil - i - a - tion. He pours up - on His
ven - er - a - tion! And un - to pray'r the
our e - mo - tion? Our sighs will come be -

knees in rev-'rence bow - ing With hearts o'er-flow - ing.
own, with hands ca - ress - ing, His Fa - ther's bless - ing.
strength from God in heav - en To us is giv - en.
fore His throne of glo - ry To tell our sto - ry.

5. And when our days on earth at last are ended,
The hour of death is near, our strength expended,
Then shall the Spirit through Its holy mission
Make intercession.

403.

236. ALL COME AND THANK THE LORD!
13, 42, 45, 79.

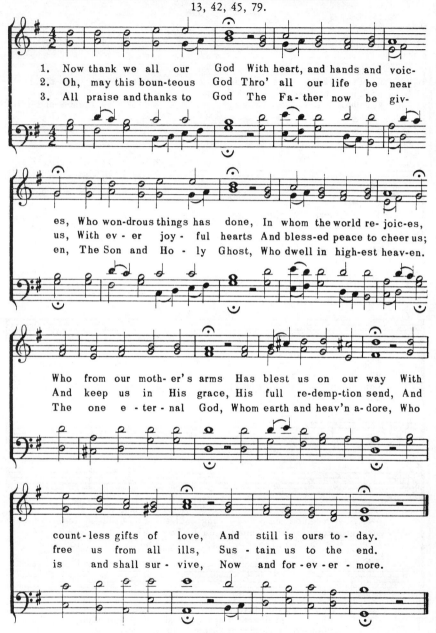

1. Now thank we all our God With heart, and hands and voic-
2. Oh, may this boun-teous God Thro' all our life be near
3. All praise and thanks to God The Fa-ther now be giv-

es, Who won-drous things has done, In whom the world re-joic-es,
us, With ev-er joy-ful hearts And bless-ed peace to cheer us;
en, The Son and Ho-ly Ghost, Who dwell in high-est heav-en.

Who from our moth-er's arms Has blest us on our way With
And keep us in His grace, His full re-demp-tion send, And
The one e-ter-nal God, Whom earth and heav'n a-dore, Who

count-less gifts of love, And still is ours to-day.
free us from all ills, Sus-tain us to the end.
is and shall sur-vive, Now and for-ev-er-more.

237. UNITY

18, 47, 49, 246.

1. Thus u - nit - ed And in con - cord Let us
2. Thus it is our Sav - iour's pleas- ure, As His
3. On - ly He is called a broth - er Whom the
4. With the love of God in - spi - red, There is

walk the path of life; Hand in hand, O
foot - prints plain - ly show. May God's love, our
tie of love does bind; And the love of
joy for us on earth; May the Spir - it,

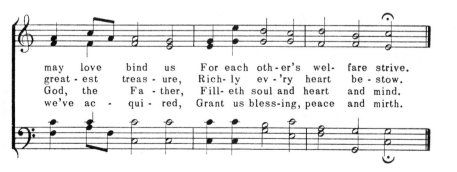

may love bind us For each oth - er's wel- fare strive.
great - est treas - ure, Rich- ly ev - 'ry heart be - stow.
God, the Fa - ther, Fill- eth soul and heart and mind.
we've ac - qui - red, Grant us bless-ing, peace and mirth.

238. DESIRE FOR JESUS

1. Dear - est Sav - iour, draw Thou near, 'Stab - lish my foun - da -
2. Con - cen - trate my scat - tered mind On Thy word, O Sav -
3. From all e - vil make me free, Tru - ly sep - a - rat -
4. Son of Man, Im - man - u - el, As my friend ap - point -

tion, Might - i - ly re - deem - ing me, That with con - se -
iour! For a - part from Thee I find Tor - ment and dis -
ed; True de - vo - tion give Thou me, In Thy peace in -
ed, Fount of love, May heart and soul Be of Thee a -

cra - tion I my zeal May re - veal, Thee in
fav - or. Mor - tal foes Will con - fuse, But in
stat - ed. Child - like, pure, Meek, de - mure, May I
noint - ed! Make my will, Meek and still, And in

love em - brac - ing, Self and all ef - fac - ing.
Thee is giv - en Rest and joy in heav - en.
e'er be - hold Thee, Live and stand be - fore Thee.
all con - di - tions Give me true sub - mis - sion.

5. Mortal creatures stand afar, Cause no interruption!
   Thy word, Jesus, will I hear, Flesh leads to corruption.
   From all woes Give repose, And to give Thee pleasure
   Be my richest treasure.

6. Gather ev'ry fugitive, Make the vain surrender;
   The entangled, true rest give, Make all hard hearts tender;
   Thus my plea E'er shall be: Nothing shall find favor,
   But my Lord and Saviour.

239. COMMUNION WITH GOD

53, 80, 81, 183.

1. Come, my Friend and take me 'sun- der, From all tu - mult
   make me free. Let me sit like Ma - ry yon - der
   In true sol - i - tude with Thee. Sol - i - tude and
   qui -et - ness Leads to ev - er - last - ing rest.

2. Blest is He, who from con- nec- tion With this tur-moil
   here is free; In God's Spir- it seeks per - fec - tion
   With His own a - part to be, Think - ing of such
   works and deeds Which e - ter - nal - ly he seeks.

3. Palms a - long the brook-let flour- ish Thus when we draw
   near to God; Pray'r and truth and love do cher- ish,
   And true wor -ship is our lot. Mark, dis -trac- tion
   ne'er will bring What in sol - i - tude we win.

4. What a lone - ly heart re - ceiv-eth Of the bless-ings
   from a - bove, When it all cre - a - tion leav-eth
   For our true Cre - a - tor's love! Thus will God protect and bless; E'en in suf - f'ring we'll find rest.

5. Thou, O God, in lone seclusion
   Dwelledst in remotest past;
   Blest is he who in communion
   Lives with Thee while ages last.
   In sweet peace let me abide,
   Resting at my Saviour's side.

240. DESIRE FOR JESUS' LIKENESS

1. Qui - et Lamb and Prince of Peace, Thirst for Thee shall
2. May I love Thee faith- ful- ly, Child- like and o -
3. With a gen - tle spir - it bless That is full of
4. Grant that I may here be brave, Lov -ing Thee un -

nev - er cease! Oh be near, Shep - herd dear,
be - dient - ly; May my mind Ev - er find
kind - li - ness, That in me It may be
to the grave, That in pain, Storm and rain,

That my heart be strong, no more to sin or fear!
Fav - or to sub - mit to Thy will, Lord so kind!
The a - dorn - ment, pre - cious, And of worth to Thee.
I may be a lamb and li - on in Thy name.

5. Keep me ever spotless, free,
   And that I may wakeful be,
   Oft to pray, Night and day,
   And to travel faithfully the narrow way.

6. Lamb of God, who overcame,
   Give me grace in Jesus' name,
   That in Thee I may be
   Able, through Thy blood, to win the victory.

7. Lead me then, when I must go
   Through death's valley here below;
   Lord, in death Give me faith,
   And protect and strengthen me in my last breath.

8. When Thou stand'st on Zion's height,
   Grant that I stand at Thy right,
   From pain free, Cleansed in Thee,
   Where Thou wilt, O Lamb, my light and temple be.

408.

241. ENDURE AND BE STILL

1. Why griev-est, my soul, must thou suf-fer great pain? Trust
2. Is thy lot to suf-fer in sick-ness and pain? Let
3. Have thy friends for-sak-en and turned a-gainst thee? De-
4. Must thou bear re-proach and de-ri-sion of men? Con-

in your dear Je-sus, He'll strength-en a-gain. En-dure, and be
noth-ing de-ceive you to mur-mur in pain. En-dure, and be
pend up-on Je-sus, a true friend is He. En-dure, and be
sid-er what God in His Word sai-eth then: En-dure, and be

still, Be-liev-ing it is thy dear Sav-iour's good will.
still, Be-liev-ing it is thy dear Sav-iour's good will.
still, Be-liev-ing it is thy dear Sav-iour's good will.
still, Be-liev-ing it is thy dear Sav-iour's good will.

5. Though shadows of death should encompass thee here,
   The sure hand of God is thy shelter from fear.
   :: Endure, and be still,::
   And say, "Not as I will, but as my God wills."

6. Though fiery temptations come near to thy heart,
   Fly therefore to Jesus, He healeth thy smart.
   :: Endure, and be still,::
   In silence and suff'ring God shows thee His will.

7. When Satan hurls at thee his arrows of fire,
   The strong shield of faith thou must quickly acquire.
   :: Endure, and be still,::
   In silence and suff'ring God shows thee His will.

409.

242. IN THE ANGUISH OF THIS WORLD

121, 137, 138, 139.

1. I'm filled with ap -pre - hen - sion; O Lord, look down on me!
2. I live in tents of Ke - dar; This oft I feel with pain,
3. To dwell a - mong the rest - less, Where peace is so des-pised,
4. My home is up in heav - en; I am a strang-er here.

Time is to me a bur - den; O come, de - liv - er me!
For Sa-tan would con - fuse me; My heart is sore with-in.
Where e - vil spir-its gov - ern, It fills my heart with sighs.
O God, I'll praise Thee ev - er When I am with Thee there!

243. GOD'S LOVE IN AFFLICTION

99, 104, 119, 253.

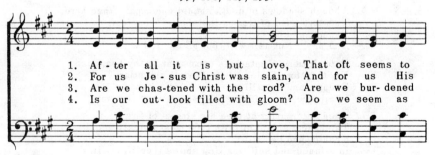

1. Af - ter all it is but love, That oft seems to
2. For us Je - sus Christ was slain, And for us His
3. Are we chas-tened with the rod? Are we bur- dened
4. Is our out- look filled with gloom? Do we seem as

us op - pres - sion; Yea, it is an eas - y yoke,
blood was giv - en; Mur - mur not in earth - ly pain!
with af - flic - tion? Yet we praise the love of God;
if for - sak - en? Yet when to His door we come,

Which He puts in our pos - ses - sion. Bear it
We shall share His joy in heav - en. He to
These are tok - ens of af - fec - tion, For His
Chil - dren al - ways find ad - mis - sion. He whose

with Him pa-tient- ly; Do not mur -mur mourn-ful-ly.
life e - ter- nal leads, Say- ing, "Think not on your needs!"
truth - ful lips are near, Say- ing, "Chil- dren, do not fear!"
word is al- ways true, Says, "I'll o - pen un - to you!"

5. The afflictions of our time
Are not worthy of the glory
Promised in that realm sublime
To the patiently enduring.
See how Jesus as a lamb
Suffered for the sins of man!

6. It was we who caused His death
With our sins and our transgressions,
Yet rejoice while ye have breath;
Jesus bought for us remission;
Reconciled us unto God.
Death and suff'ring pardon brought.

7. Oh, that we might clearly see
What afflictions should accomplish!
Willing in God's ways to be
And obey His Spirit's promptings,
We would soon the fruits behold,
Which afflictions do unfold.

411.

244. THE TIME OF WAITING

1. Wait - ing is to be our earth - ly school - ing
2. Wait - ing was the lot of all God's serv - ants:
3. He Him - self, the crown of all cre - a - tion,
4. See the hus- band - man, his seed now strew - ing

Which here with our first breath takes its start,
Jo - seph, Dav - id, Ab - ra - ham and all
Once in dark - est work- shop was pre - pared;
On the earth - ly field in hope and fear,

Nev - er end - ing till by God's own rul - ing
Who in serv - ice were found true and ferv - ent,
Gloom - y nights pre - ced - ed ex - alt - a - tion;
In God's prom- ise still his trust re - new - ing,

Our faint spir - it shall in peace de - part.
And whom God un - to great deeds did call.
Af - ter suf - f'ring, heav - en's bliss was shared.
Till spring sun - shine makes the sprouts ap - pear.

5. Few fruits ripen from the spring-time sunshine;
   Not till autumn is abundance shown;
   Without waiting we ne'er feel the rapture
   Of a precious, bounteous harvest grown.

6. God oft gave beyond all expectation
   More than heart had wished for to behold;
   Should not this give us new inspiration
   To await what His word has foretold?

7. Ne'er a word of God was uttered vainly,
   Although its fulfillment seemed afar;
   Noble things take time, though promised plainly;
   And the very best we find in God.

8. Battle bravely tow'rd that destination,
   Though the night of waiting now enfold;
   Other brethren bore yet more privation,
   Yet through conflict, vict'ry did behold.

9. Vict'ry shalt thou win through fiery trials
   Pure and in the likeness of thy Lord;
   Worthy to partake of joyful blessings,
   Therefore wait now for that great reward.

10. Waiting, hoping here in darkest silence,
    Leads us to that future happiness;
    Waiting, trusting oft with fear and trembling
    Brings glad tiding of eternal bliss.

245. THE FRUIT OF SORROW
39, 189.

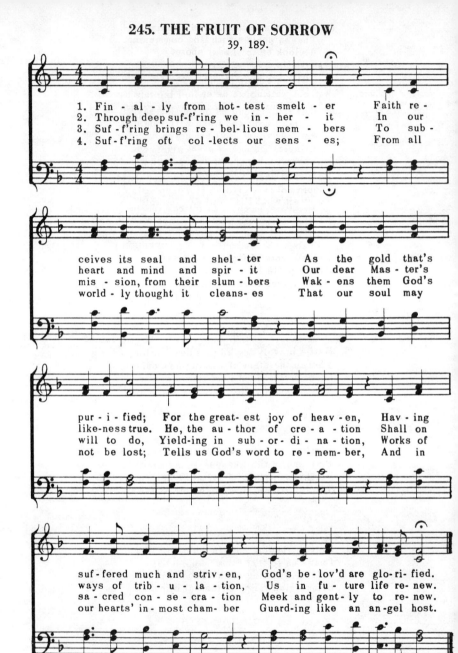

1. Fin - al - ly from hot - test smelt - er Faith re-
2. Through deep suf-f'ring we in - her - it In our
3. Suf - f'ring brings re - bel - lious mem - bers To sub-
4. Suf - f'ring oft col -lects our sens - es; From all

ceives its seal and shel - ter As the gold that's
heart and mind and spir - it Our dear Mas - ter's
mis - sion, from their slum - bers Wak - ens them God's
world - ly thought it cleans- es That our soul may

pur - i - fied; For the great- est joy of heav - en, Hav - ing
like-ness true. He, the au - thor of cre - a - tion Shall on
will to do, Yield-ing in sub - or - di - na - tion, Works of
not be lost; Tells us God's word to re - mem- ber, And in

suf -fered much and striv - en, God's be - lov'd are glo - ri - fied.
ways of trib - u - la - tion, Us in fu - ture life re - new.
sa - cred con - se - cra - tion Meek and gent - ly to re - new.
our hearts' in - most cham- ber Guard-ing like an an - gel host.

414.

5. In our hearts the chords attuning,
   That in psalms with God communing
   We look up to yonder shore.
   With the palms of peace abounding,
   Where the golden harps are sounding,
   Praising God forevermore.

6. Suff'ring speeds us on our journey,
   Hallows soul and flesh with yearning
   For that sleep in silent grave.
   Bringing tidings of great gladness,
   Calling all from death and sadness
   Life eternal to receive.

7. Suff'ring makes our faith more ample,
   Meek and humble, childlike, simple.
   What can e'er with thee compare?
   Here, a heavy load oppressing,
   There a great and heav'nly blessing,
   Which not everyone can share.

8. Brethren, suff'ring is a favor
   Which in various ways the Saviour
   To His own elect has shown.
   Often racked by pain and sighing,
   Often felt the throes of dying,
   When through sleepless nights they groan.

9. Though in health and in enjoyment,
   We to our good Lord's employment,
   Willingly our strength did yield;
   Yet we deem it no privation,
   When through pain and tribulation
   Our faith unto God is sealed.

10. In the depth of sore affliction,
    Our hearts draw in close affection
    To our loving Saviour's heart.
    And for this we cry and tremble:
    May we Thee in death resemble,
    And in Life with Thee take part!

11. When at last our sighs are counted,
    Ev'ry barrier is surmounted,
    And the curtain rends in twain,
    Who is able then to measure,
    What of peace, and joy, and treasure
    In that kingdom we shall gain?

12. Let me then behold in clearness
    Yonder heights, Lord, in Thy nearness.
    When at last my hour shall come,
    When all earthly ties are severed,
    And from death and toil delivered,
    Angel bands shall bear me home!

415.

246. HOLY SIMPLICITY

18, 47, 49, 72.

1. Ho - ly vir - tue, grace- ful won - der, Might of
2. Meek and low - ly, child- like na - ture, Glo - ry
3. God a - lone is its true pleas - ure, Joy and
4. In such sin - cere, child- like be - ings, God re -
5. It has God's sup - port in con - flict, Un - to

God, love, in - no - cence! In Thy face the high are
of hu - mil - i - ty! It a - lone re - stores us
glo - ry of the heart; He gives it a per - fect
veals His might - y arm, And the hum - ble heart - ed
wick - ed - ness is dead; Ne'er be - comes the spoil of

hum - bled, On - ly God's work has de - fense.
ful - ly, And from Ad - am's fall sets free.
treas - ure, And true bliss He will im - part.
choos - es Might - y won - ders to per - form.
Sa - tan, To God's joy - ful rest is led.

6. It has what the Lord has given,
   Grace by grace out of his fill;
   Boasts not of itself, is ever
   Led of God to do His will.

7. It is clearly its own mirror,
   Shuns all false and vain pretense,
   Bears the seal of Jesus' Spirit,
   Journeys on without offense.

8. It us from our "Self" delivers,
   And from all our sinful woe;
   God alone is its selection,
   Therefore God protects it so.

9. Thus in purity it journeys,
   At God's hand, the narrow way;
   And in God here bears in patience,
   Cross and woe from day to day.

10. Hid in God, it lives in gladness,
    Looks to Him in every place;
    Without fear or care or sorrow,
    It beholds His holy face.

11. It entrusts its pilgrim journey
    To God's mighty hand alone --
    Looking toward the glorious ending
    When God will receive His own.

12. It is rich in gifts for others,
    Not too sensitive, or vain;
    Has a heart that shares sincerely
    Every human ill or pain.

13. It seeks neither praise nor greatness;
    Chiding, shame, no hurt impart;
    Thinks no evil; for all goodness
    Has a deeply grateful heart.

14. What is there on earth so precious
    As a child, sincere in love?
    For of such is Jesus' kingdom,
    And eternal joy above.

15. O thou lovely flower of heaven,
    That our Saviour did provide!
    Thou the peace of God enjoyest,
    For which Jesus lived and died.

16. Holy innocence so childlike,
    How my heart here yearns for thee!
    Sun of grace, O purest virtue,
    Jesus, shine Thou forth in me.

17. Son of God, in holy silence
    Us to God Thou didst restore;
    May my will, in true submission,
    Rest in Thee forevermore!

247. DEATH IN JESUS

25, 41, 75, 221.

1. I wish to die in my dear Je-sus, In peace and
2. I wish to die in my dear Je-sus; His griev-ous
3. I wish to die in my dear Je-sus; His wound-ed
4. I wish to die in my dear Je-sus; He holds me

with great joy con-soled, And through His wounds I
wounds make dy-ing joy. All fear of per-ish-
side my ref-uge is. By Him the heav-ens
though all else for-sake, And with His blood He

shall in-her-it The robe of white He will un-fold.
ing now ceas-es; His blood He did to me ap-ply.
I in-her-it; My brok-en heart is turned to bliss.
bought my free-dom. To His en-sign my faith I stake.

In Je-sus I will trust al-way; In Him I live and

pass a-way, In Him I live and pass a-way.

5. I wish to die in my dear Jesus,
   When light and life from me He takes,
   When from my lips the color fadeth,
   And when my heart in death does break.
   In Jesus I will trust alway;
   :: In Him I live and pass away.::

248. AT THE GRAVE OF RIGHTEOUS
123, 124, 164, 230.

1. We lay the bod-y in its tomb Un-til the
2. Of dust the Lord did man cre-ate; "To dust re-
3. The right-eous soul with God doth live, Who hath re-
4. With sor-row, bur-dened was his flesh, But now will

Lord's voice bids him "Come." We sow the seed to
turn!" -- that is his fate. He lies; he sleeps, de-
deemed him from his grief, From all his sin and
God his soul re-fresh. In dark-ened val-ley

rise a-new, And glo-ri-fied, his God to view.
cays, a-wakes When day ar-rives and night for-sakes.
all his woe, Thru Je-sus Christ, who loved him so.
he did go; Now he is free from all his woe.

5. Faithful was he until death's day,
   Now God will wipe his tears away.
   What are the sorrows of this time
   Against God's glory, so sublime?

6. So now, redeemed one, sleep and rest!
   Homeward we turn to do our best,
   That we in joy and trembling be
   Made ready for eternity.

7. Oh Jesus Christ, Thy bitter death
   Shall strengthen us in our last breath!
   Our soul, Lord, we commit to Thee,
   And joyful may our ending be!

249. WHO ARE THEY BEFORE GOD'S THRONE

80, 81, 183.

1. Who are they be - fore God stand-ing Count-less throngs in
2. Loud and clear their hymns are sound-ing:"Praise to Him up-
3. Who are they who in such fav - or Stand be -fore the
4. It were they who came vic - to - rious, Out of life's deep,

heav'n - ly light; Each a gold - en crown is wear - ing,
on the throne! Hail the Sav - iour of His breth-ren,
face of God? Who such great re - ward did mer - it,
trou - bled sea, Bear-ing here the cross in pa -tience,

Shin - ing like the stars so bright? Dressed in white you
Hail the great- est Son of Man!" All the an - gels
For as an - gels is their lot? In what bat - tle,
From all self - ish hon - or free. Robes of hon - or

see them stand, Wav -ing palms in ev - 'ry hand.
prais - es bring; Hal - le - lu - jah! there they sing.
in what war, Did they this great vic - t'ry score?
they pos - sess, Called: The great Lamb's right- eous- ness.

5. It were they who here did struggle
   For the glory of our Lord;
   Satan, world, and death subduing,
   Followed not the sinful horde.
   And in battle they did stand,
   Trusting God's almighty hand.

6. They are branches of that true vine,
   Who to us brought help and grace,
   And they without fear did venture
   Anguish, danger, death to face.
   Now from sorrow and from grief,
   God has granted them relief.

7. It were they in priestly garments,
   Who appeared before their God;
   Ready day and night for service,
   Many sacrifices brought.
   Now in sacred place they stand,
   Happy in the Holy Land.

8. It were they who, overcoming,
   Sacrificed themselves for God;
   In Christ full salvation finding,
   Till they rest beneath the sod;
   They enjoy eternal bliss,
   Crowned with God's own righteousness.

9. As the hart at noontide panteth
   For the brooklet clear and cold,
   So their souls did sigh while watching,
   Living waters to behold.
   Now their thirst is satisfied,
   For they rest at Jesus' side.

10. Now before the throne they're standing,
    Serving God by day and night;
    Casting still their crowns of glory
    Down before the throne of light,
    Where their Mediator stands,
    Guarding them with His own hands.

11. O what word describes the rapture,
    When I with the Holy Band
    And with radiance brightly gleaming,
    Shining like the stars I stand?
    Amen, thanks to Thee above,
    Praise to Thy eternal love!

12. O Lord Jesus, look upon me,
    Heart and hands to Thee I bend;
    Grant that I may soon behold Thee,
    When my pilgrimage will end;
    And by hottest conflicts shared
    By Thee fully be prepared.

250. THE MAJESTY OF GOD

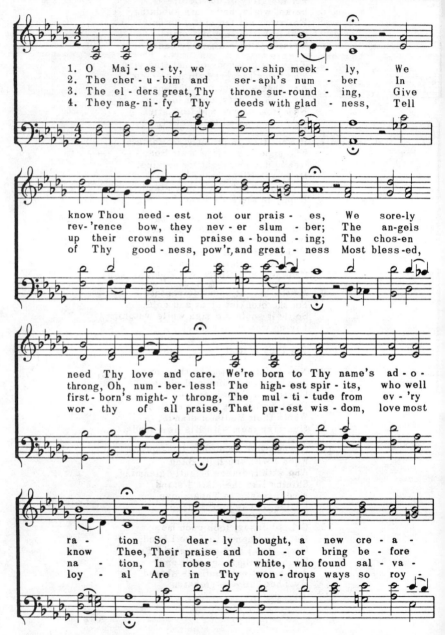

1. O Maj - es - ty, we wor - ship meek - ly, We
2. The cher - u - bim and ser - aph's num - ber In
3. The el - ders great, Thy throne sur - round - ing, Give
4. They mag - ni - fy Thy deeds with glad - ness, Tell

know Thou need - est not our prais - es, We sore - ly
rev - 'rence bow, they nev - er slum - ber; The an - gels
up their crowns in praise a - bound - ing; The chos - en
of Thy good - ness, pow'r, and great - ness Most bless - ed,

need Thy love and care. We're born to Thy name's ad - o -
throng, Oh, num - ber - less! The high - est spir - its, who well
first - born's might - y throng, The mul - ti - tude from ev - 'ry
wor - thy of all praise, That pur - est wis - dom, love most

ra - tion So dear - ly bought, a new cre - a -
know Thee, Their praise and hon - or bring be - fore
na - tion, In robes of white, who found sal - va -
loy - al Are in Thy won - drous ways so roy -

tion, Sal -va -tion, to Thee hon - or bear! In hon - or of Thy
Thee, Thy great-ness and Thy might con-fess. Their bless-ed-ness art
tion, In wor-ship raise their voice and song. Thine is all pow'r and
al, And ev - en more their "A-men" says. Their praise will not suf-

name Is all cre - a - tion's fame. Bless - ed Be-ing! With
Thou, To Thee they hum-bly bow. A - men! A - men! We
might, All wis- dom, praise, and right! A - men! A - men! We
fice; Thy works praise Thee, All-wise! A - men! A - men! We

pray'r-ful hearts to Thee we come, In truth and spir-it be it done.
too are Thine, We so a -gree, Thou, God, our God for-e'er shalt be!
too are Thine, And sing Thy chime, Thou, God, God, art our God, most sublime!
too are Thine, And sing the chime, Thou, God, art our God, most sublime!

. Through Thy good will we see surviving
All Thou hast made, all that is living;
Thy work is marvelous and great!
By all must Thy due praise be given
Of things in earth and sea and heaven:
For these Thy glory all reflect;
All things that move and live
To Thee do praises give:
Amen! Amen! We, too, are Thine, And with them
"Thou, God, alone art King divine!"   (join:

6. Thy friends who here among all nations
Have built their pilgrim habitations
Exalt Thee, O Thou Blessed Good:
They all confess Thee perfect ever,
They call Thee God and only Saviour,
Who hast redeemed them by Thy blood!
Their Portion, Lord, art Thou,
The only Hope they know:
Amen! Amen! We, too, are Thine, And with them
"Thou, God, alone art King divine!"   (join:

7. Thyself in us be glorifying,
And we Thine honor magnifying,
O make our heart Thy Holy Place,
That it with Thy great glory filled,
And by Thy nearness duly stilled,
Be glowing with Thy Godhead's praise!
May heart and mind and soul
Thy goodness, Lord, extol:
Amen! Amen! Hallelujah! Praise God on high!
The Lord is great and good and nigh!

251. JEHOVAH

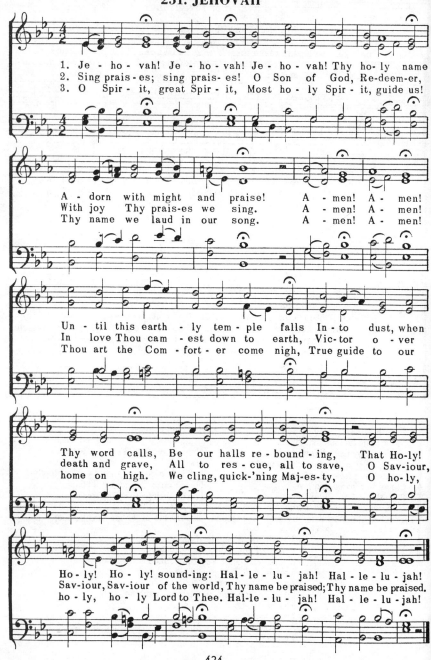

1. Je - ho - vah! Je - ho - vah! Je - ho - vah! Thy ho- ly name
2. Sing prais- es; sing prais- es! O Son of God, Re-deem-er,
3. O Spir - it, great Spir - it, Most ho- ly Spir - it, guide us!

A - dorn with might and praise! A - men! A - men!
With joy Thy prais-es we sing. A - men! A - men!
Thy name we laud in our song. A - men! A - men!

Un - til this earth - ly tem - ple falls In - to dust, when
In love Thou cam - est down to earth, Vic- tor o - ver
Thou art the Com - fort- er come nigh, True guide to our

Thy word calls, Be our halls re - bound - ing, That Ho-ly!
death and grave, All to res - cue, all to save, O Sav-iour,
home on high. We cling, quick-'ning Maj-es-ty, O ho-ly,

Ho- ly! Ho- ly! sound-ing: Hal- le - lu - jah! Hal- le - lu - jah!
Sav-iour, Sav-iour of the world, Thy name be praised; Thy name be praised.
ho- ly, ho- ly Lord to Thee. Hal-le - lu - jah! Hal- le - lu - jah!

252. THE CHRISTIAN'S CROSS

142. 163, 169, 216.

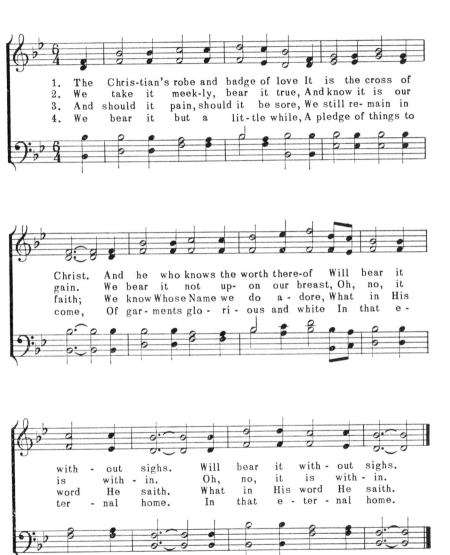

1. The Chris-tian's robe and badge of love It is the cross of
2. We take it meek-ly, bear it true, And know it is our
3. And should it pain, should it be sore, We still re- main in
4. We bear it but a lit-tle while, A pledge of things to

Christ. And he who knows the worth there-of Will bear it
gain. We bear it not up- on our breast, Oh, no, it
faith; We know Whose Name we do a - dore, What in His
come, Of gar - ments glo - ri - ous and white In that e -

with - out sighs. Will bear it with - out sighs.
is with - in. Oh, no, it is with - in.
word He saith. What in His word He saith.
ter - nal home. In that e - ter - nal home.

253. MY LIFETIME DOTH PASS AWAY
99, 104, 119, 120.

1. My life - time doth pass a - way; Hour - ly to the grave I has - ten, And I know each fleet - ing day My al - lot - ted span will les - sen. Think, man, death comes soon or late.

2. Live thou as thy wish will be To have lived when thou ex - pir - est. Treas - ures which have come to thee, Fame and wealth which thou de - sir - est, Will not make thy death more sweet,

3. But a pure and lov - ing heart, Con - science free from con - dem - na - tion Can re - pose and peace im - part, And in death give con - so - la - tion. All who are re - newed in heart

4. And when in thy last dis - tress, Help - less friends a - round thee gath - er, Then this heart of right - eous - ness Yields thee com - fort from the Fa - ther. Judg - ment brings no fear nor fright,

426.

Tar - ry not, it will not wait!
For they are not thine to keep.
Can with joy - ful - ness de - part.
For the Lord is thy de - light.

5. Wouldst thou such a heart attain?
Fear the Lord, His good word keeping!
For the time thou shalt remain
Here on earth is in God's keeping.
Thus thy death thou wilt not fear,
But in welcome hold it dear.

6. Learn by faith to overcome,
Saying, "My Redeemer liveth.
With these eyes I'll see Him come
When eternal life He giveth."
"It is finished," He did call,
Triumphed over death and all.

7. Draw in spirit near the grave;
Watch thy body slowly sinking.
Pray: "O Lord, that I am clay,
Let my thoughts be daily thinking.
Teach me, Father, ev'ry day;
Make me true and wise, I pray."

Topical Index

CHRIST -- HIS RESURRECTION

Christ The Resurrected 60
Jesus Lives! 120
Christ The Resurrected 121
Head And Members 123
Resurrection And Spiritual Life 124
Christ The Resurrected 183

CHRIST -- HIS SUFFERING AND DEATH

The Seven Words Of Jesus On The Cross 89
Behold The Lamb Of God 184
Our Surety 224
Golgotha .226

CHRISTIAN CONSECRATION

On To The Combat 27
The Seven Churches 30
Sowing And Harvest 36
Be Prepared 50
Anticipation 59
The Real Longing For Home 84
Our Pilgrim Way 88
The Heavenly Mind 91
Battle And Victory 99
Faithful Until Death Remain 105
Christ Our Leader 125
The Grace Of God 134
The Pilgrim's Song 136
How Shall It Be? 146
Yearning For Home 147
The Believing Family 160
Be True 172
The Journey To Zion 185
Redeeming Our Time 188
Unity 237

TOPICAL INDEX

CHRISTIAN LOVE AND FELLOWSHIP

Open Wide The Gates 4
The Union In Jesus' Death 11
Who Shall Abide? 32
The Fellowship Of The Saints 33
The New Birth From Above 34
Love 37
All Devoted To One 61
The Magnet 63
Brotherly Love 69
Love And Loving 70
Praise To God In Baptism 71
God's Divine Compassion 74
Faith, Hope, And Love 78
The Union Of Hearts 79
Love Begets Love 80
The Hour Of Prayer 81
Dost Thou Love Me? 117
The City Of God 133
Our Love Shall Not Diminish 137
Faithfulness In Small Things 179
Unity In Love 181
Awake, Ye Witnesses 192
The City Of God 194
Love Toward Jesus 197
The Father Loves Us 206
Assembly Hymn 207
Gathering In Jesus' Name 219
To My Redeemer 227
Prayer For The True Christian Love 229
Make Me More Perfect 232
Unity 237
God's Love In Affliction 243

CHRISTIAN VIRTUES

The Fruits Of The Spirit 62
Humility 186
Holy Simplicity 246

TOPICAL INDEX

CHRISTMAS CAROLS

Christmas Carol 7
Glory To God In The Highest 9

CHRIST OUR SHEPHERD AND FRIEND

The Faithful Shepherd 15
A Lamb Of Jesus 16
Joy In The Saviour 17
Jesus, The Truest Friend 18
The Incomparable 19
Jesus, Our Head 28
The High Priest 55
Pure And Holy Love 72
The Faithful Shepherd, Jesus Christ 116
Arise, For The Light Cometh! 119
Song Of Praise For Redemption 130
The Pilgrim's Song 136
The Lord Is My Shepherd 153
Children's Praise 165
Confidence 177
Life And Full Abundance In Jesus 178
To My Redeemer 182
Love Toward Jesus 197
Christ, My All 202
The Twenty Third Psalm 212
Prayer For Access To God's Throne 215
Our Shepherd And King 230

CHRIST'S SECOND COMING

Lord Jesus, Thou Art King 12
The Coming Of Christ 56

CLOSING HYMNS

Praise And Thanks For God's Blessings 13
The Heart -- God's Sanctuary 129
Jesus Immanuel 138

COMMUNION

Communion Hymn 24
The Lord's Supper 25

TOPICAL INDEX

COMMUNION (Cont'd)

Communion Hymn 26
Communion Hymn 200

CONSOLATION

On To The Combat 27
Comfort In Distress 38
The Best Refuge 46
God's Divine Compassion 74
Give Thanks Unto The Father 75
Happiness Of The Godly 82
The Penitent's Conflict 83
The Lord Will Provide 86
Our Pilgrim Way 88
Trust In God 93
Call To Beginners 98
Battle And Victory 99
The Supreme Sacrifice 100
The Assurance Of True Faith 102
Gratitude For Deliverance 109
Abide With Us 135
Our Happy Lot 145
Why Art Thou Grieved? 151
Self-Sacrifice 159
Jesus, The Friend Of Children 167
Be True 172
Confidence 177
Life And Full Abundance In Jesus 178
To My Redeemer 182
Christ The Resurrected 183
Redeeming Our Time 188
Love Toward Jesus 197
The Promised Rest 211
Attentive Hearers 217
Christ The Crucified And Glorified 225
Jesus I Will Never Leave 228
Longing 231
The Fruit Of Sorrow 245

TOPICAL INDEX

FAITH AND SALVATION

The Incarnation Of Christ 22
The Fruit Of The Spirit 62
One Thing Is Needful 65
Praise To God In Baptism 71
Faith, Hope, And Love 78
Faith's Confidence. 87
The Assurance Of True Faith 102
Living In Faith 139
God Is Still With Me 148
Adoration 190
The Boundlessness Of God's Grace 201
Boundless Mercy 220
Christ, The Foundation 221
Christ. The Crucified And Glorified 225

FUNERAL AND BURIAL

Sowing And Harvest 36
The Best Refuge 46
Anticipation 59
At The Grave Of The Believer 104
Faithful Until Death Remain 105
Jesus Lives! 120
How Shall It Be? 146
Parting Hymn (Verses 1 and 5) 155
At Home 'Tis Well 170
Jesus I Will Never Leave 228
The Fruit Of Sorrow 245
Death In Jesus 247
At The Grave Of The Righteous 248
My Lifetime Doth Pass Away 253

GREETING HYMNS

Heart's Wish 173
Gathering In Jesus' Name 219

MARRIAGE

The Union Of Hearts 79
Our Love Shall Not Diminish 137
The Twenty-Third Psalm 212

TOPICAL INDEX

OPENING HYMNS

Praise Ye The Lord 1
A Christian's Joy And Hope 2
Jesus, Our Head 28
The Magnet 63
Walking With God 68
The Hour Of Prayer 81
Joy On The Sabbath Day 126
The Heart -- God's Sanctuary 129
Receptive Hearers 144
Thou Hast Words Of Life 203
Assembly Hymn 207
Before The Meeting 214
The Children's Supplication 216
Attentive Hearers 217
Petition For The Lord's Blessings 218
Gathering In Jesus' Name 219

PARTING HYMNS

Our Wish In Parting 114
Jesus Immanuel 138
Farewell Song 143
Parting Hymn 155
Farewell 195
Parting Hymn 213

REPENTANCE

The Penitent's Conflict 39
Bethesda, The House Of Grace 42
Repentance 45
Strive Aright 47
Repent Ye! 52
The Sermon On The Mount 54
God's Power Revealed In The Clouds 67
Happiness Of The Godly 82
The Penitent's Conflict 83
Challenge To The Nominal Christian 95
The Way And The Reward 106
Christ In The Flesh 107
The Field And The Fruit 108

TOPICAL INDEX

THANKSGIVING

Praise And Thanks For God's Blessings 13
The Shepherd And His Flock 14
Morning Hymn 48
Evening Hymn 49
Praise To God In Baptism 71
Give Thanks Unto The Father 75
Awake! 154
Look Upon Jesus! 161
Thanks And Prayer 199
I Will Not Leave Thee 204
All Come And Thank The Lord! 236

THE HOLY BAPTISM

The Resurrection From Baptism 8
Before Baptism 10
Buried With Christ 23
The New Birth From Above 34
The Likeness Of The Creation To Baptism 40
The Baptismal Covenant 41
Bethesda, The House Of Grace 42
Baptismal Hymn 43
Baptism In Christ 162
Now It Is Done! 209
Looking Back To The Day Of Salvation 222

THE LORD'S DAY

Joy On The Sabbath Day 126
Celebrating The Sabbath 193

THE NEW BIRTH

The New Birth From Above 34
The New Birth Of Water And Spirit 187
Now It Is Done! 209

THE WORD OF GOD

The Gospel Of Truth 3
The Magnet 63
The Gospel 97
The Pilgrim's Song 136

THE WORD OF GOD (Cont'd)

Obedience To The Word 142
The Word Of Life 176
Petition For The Lord's Blessings 218

TRIALS AND TEMPTATION

The School Of The Cross 66
The Lord Will Provide 86
In Time Of Persecution 96
Cast Thy Burden On The Lord 150
Why Art Thou Grieved? 151
As Pants The Hart 157
The Cross 171
The Child's Privilege 234
In The Anguish Of This World 242
The Time Of Waiting 244
The Christian's Cross 252

Alphabetical Index
(Titles in capital letters, first lines
in regular type)

A BLESSED MAN 169
A Christian now baptized 43
A CHRISTIAN'S JOY AND HOPE 2
A LAMB OF JESUS 16
Abide with us, Lord Jesus 135
ABIDING IN JESUS 205
ADORATION 190
After all it is but love 243
ALL DEVOTED TO ONE 61
ALL COME AND THANK THE LORD 236
All who have learned to know the Lord 230
ANTICIPATION 59
APPEAL TO THE SAVIOUR 6
APPROACH TO THE THRONE OF GOD 132
ARISE FOR THE LIGHT COMETH! 119
Arise, my song to Christ the King 8
As a hart for water panteth 157
As a trav'ler home returning 198
As I think of Thee, a gentle rapture 182
Ask ye what great thing I know 225
AS PANTS THE HART 157
Assembled congregation 207
ASSEMBLY HYMN 207
At home 'tis well 170
AT THE GRAVE OF THE BELIEVER 104
AT THE GRAVE OF THE RIGHTEOUS 248
ATTENTIVE HEARERS 217
Awake, my heart, and honor 154
Awake, thou soul's first inspiration 111
Awake, ye witnesses, be burning 192

BAPTISMAL HYMN 43
BAPTISM AND COMMUNION 128
BAPTISM IN CHRIST 162
Baptized into Thy name most holy 41

ALPHABETICAL INDEX

BATTLE AND VICTORY 99
BEFORE BAPTISM 10
BEFORE THE MEETING 214
Behold, O Jesus, we implore Thee 219
BEHOLD THE LAMB OF GOD 184
Be not thou discouraged 98
Be our journey and our way 88
BE PREPARED 50
BETHESDA, THE HOUSE OF GRACE 42
Be true, be true, the Lord is by thee 172
Blessed he, who does not follow 82
Blessed, holy, is the hour 218
BLEST ETERNITY 103
BOUNDLESS MERCY 220
Bow Thine ear, gentle Jesus 152
Brethren, be ye not affrighted 38
BROTHERLY LOVE 69
BROTHERLY LOVE · . . . . · 76
BURIED WITH CHRIST · 23

Call and cry, ye watchmen boldly 112
CALL TO BEGINNERS 98
CAST THY BURDEN ON THE LORD 150
CELEBRATING THE SABBATH 193
CHALLENGE TO THE NOMINAL CHRISTIAN . . 95
Cheer up, ye host of righteous 50
CHILDREN'S PRAISE 165
Christian's life in God is hidden 59
CHRIST IN THE FLESH 107
CHRISTMAS CAROL 7
CHRIST MY ALL 202
CHRIST OUR LEADER 125
CHRIST OUR PREDECESSOR 57
CHRIST THE CRUCIFIED AND GLORIFIED . . . 225
CHRIST THE FOUNDATION 221
CHRIST THE RESURRECTED · . . . . · 60
CHRIST THE RESURRECTED 121
CHRIST THE RESURRECTED 183
Christ! Thou my life and my hope 6

Come, children, join in singing 136
Come, children, let us journey 185
Come, come, sweet rest 147
Come, draw near of ev'ry nation 54
Come, follow me, the Saviour spake 57
Come, my friend, and take me sunder 239
Come now, ye great, before Jehovah 67
Come within, come within 24
COMFORT IN DISTRESS 38
COMMUNION HYMN 24
COMMUNION HYMN 26
COMMUNION HYMN 200
COMMUNION WITH GOD 239
CONFIDENCE 177
Consider, man, that heart of thine 108

Dearest Saviour, draw Thou near 238
Dearest Saviour, let me ever 205
Dear Father, now behold us 85
DEATH IN JESUS 247
DESIRE FOR JESUS 238
DESIRE FOR JESUS' LIKENESS 240
Don't you see on heav'nly pastures 15
Dost thou love me, the Saviour said 117
Draw us to Thee, O Lord, may we 125

ENCOURAGEMENT TO FAITH'S BATTLE 51
ENDURE AND BE STILL 241
Enter ye love's kingdom 69
ENTREATY FOR GOD'S BLESSINGS 140
EVENING HYMN 49
EXALTATION 131

Faith and hope and love adorn 78
FAITHFULNESS IN SMALL THINGS 179
Faithful Saviour, we draw near 144
Faithful until death remain 105
FAITH'S CONFIDENCE 87
FAREWELL 195

ALPHABETICAL INDEX

FAREWELL SONG 143
FATHER, SON AND HOLY GHOST 180
Finally from hottest smelter 245
Flourishing youth, thou our hope 168
FOLLOWING JESUS 64
FOLLOW ME 90
Follow me, the Saviour calleth 95
Forever be praised 141
Forsake this world of vanity 107
FORWARD! 92
Forward struggle, e'er contending 39

GATHERING IN JESUS' NAME 219
GIVE THANKS UNTO THE FATHER 75
Glory be to God in heaven 34
Glory to God in the highest 9
God has built on firm foundation 194
God is ever present 68
GOD IS STILL WITH ME 148
God, my hope and consolation 93
God, my life's Creator 167
God of unlimited compassion 75
GOD'S DIVINE COMPASSION 74
GOD'S EXALTATION 101
GOD'S GLORY MAGNIFIED BY HIS WORKS . . . 118
GOD'S LOVE IN AFFLICTION 243
God's people yet shall take possession 211
GOD'S POWER REVEALED IN THE CLOUDS . . . 67
God, the Father of our Saviour 31
God with us, we need not fear 100
GOLGOTHA 226
GRATITUDE FOR DELIVERANCE 109
Great and priestly Mediator 29

HAPPINESS OF THE GODLY 82
Hark, and earnestly be heeding 30
Hark, the voice of Jesus teaches 187
Haste and seek your soul's salvation 52
HEAD AND MEMBERS 123

HEART'S WISH 173
Heart with heart in love united 33
Heavenward, e'er heavenward 91
Holy love, bright flame from heaven 72
Holy One! Holy One! Glorious Immanuel 23
Holy One! Holy One! Holy God of Sabaoth 22
HOLY SIMPLICITY 246
Holy virtue, graceful wonder 246
How blessed, to approach unto the Father 235
How bright the morning star doth shine 223
How shall it be, when we at last returning 146
HUMILITY .186

I and my house, we are prepared 160
I live 'mid my affections 84
I now have found the firm foundation 221
I place myself in Jesus' hands 177
I rev'rence love's great pow'r unending 74
I WILL NOT LEAVE THEE 204
I wish to die in my dear Jesus 247
I wish to love my Saviour more sincerely 232
If God within these evil days 109
I'm a lamb of Jesus' flock 17
I'm filled with apprehension 242
In earth's anguish here I will not murmur 90
In sorrow and pain 46
INTERCESSION 189
IN THE ANGUISH OF THIS WORLD 242
IN TIME OF PERSECUTION 96
Is there any pleasure 149
It is here, the precious moment 81
It really is not difficult 169

Jehovah is the Shepherd true 153
Jehovah! Jehovah! 251
Jesus, bosom-friend so gentle 28
Jesus Christ as king elected 190
Jesus come, O come to me 77
JESUS IMMANUEL 138

ALPHABETICAL INDEX

Jesus in the night of His betrayal 26
Jesus I will never leave 228
Jesus lives! I live with Him 120
Jesus, mighty Liberator 35
JESUS OUR HEAD 28
JESUS OUR PRIEST AND KING 31
JESUS THE FRIEND OF CHILDREN 167
JESUS, THE TRUEST FRIEND 18
Jesus, Thou alone can'st govern 189
JOY IN THE SAVIOUR 17
JOY ON THE SABBATH DAY 126
Joyful songs of praise we bring 71

Labor on! labor on! 20
Let every gate be opened wide 4
Let us hear and give attention 217
Let your whole life be an off'ring 159
LIFE AND FULL ABUNDANCE IN JESUS 178
Life has become so gloomy 83
Little flock, in haste assemble 51
Live peacefully, said Christ the Lord 195
LIVING IN FAITH 139
LONGING 231
LOOKING BACK TO THE DAY OF SALVATION . 222
LOOK UPON JESUS! 161
Lord God, we honor Thee 13
Lord Jesus, honor, thanks and praise 14
Lord Jesus, praise to Thee ascend 55
Lord Jesus, Thou art King 12
Lord, Thou Creator, glorious is Thy kingdom . . . 118
Lord, who liveth in Thy dwelling? 32
LOVE 37
LOVE AND LOVING 70
LOVE BEGETS LOVE 80
Love of all gifts is the greatest 37
LOVE TOWARD JESUS 197
Love, who fashioned me, the likeness 80

MAKE ME MORE PERFECT 232

May grace be with us ever 134
May now the grace of our Lord Jesus 213
Meekness is the noblest virtue 186
MORNING HYMN 48
MORNING HYMN 166
Mortal shell, so now thou art 104
My faith gives joy and sweetest rest 102
My lifetime doth pass away 253
My Lord, an off'ring do I bring 163

Nay, I will not sorrow 196
Noah's ark long drifted 148
Not of earth and not of heaven 231
NOW AND THEN 191
Now another day is ended 49
Now it is accomplished 209
NOW IT IS DONE! 209
Now thank we all our God 236

OBEDIENCE TO THE WORD 142
O blessed sun, whose splendor 178
O Father-hand, that guides me so securely 180
O God be praised, who reigns above 128
O hallelujah, sing God's praise 1
O hallelujah to our King 2
O how joyful are Thy members 161
O how lovely is the morning 166
O how lovely 'tis to be 181
O how welcome is the Sabbath 126
O Jerusalem, the golden 53
O let us exalt our dear Lord and proclaim 165
O Lord, behold us gathered here 216
O Lord, my light 110
O Lord of hosts, how pleasant is 129
O Majesty, we bow before Thee 250
O my Lord Jesus Christ 201
O Saviour, might I thus as Thee 164
O slaughtered Lamb, by whom 184
O Spirit of God's strength and might 200

ALPHABETICAL INDEX

O teach me, Lord, instead of grieving 66
O that Thy ardent flames were kindled 73
O the fount of truth and grace 70
O Thou Holy One, great and merciful 130
O Thou Holy One, great and merciful Lord of . . . 131
O Thou who in the grave didst lay 124
O willingly endure 156
O word of joy, eternity 103
Oh blissful hour and holy 222
Oh how joyful is the hour 203
Oh, I rejoice to praise Thee singing 158
Oh Jesus, look upon 45
Oh my God, my heart desireth greatly 10
Oh Son of God, to Thee we sing 199
Oh Thou fountain of love 202
Oh, what is more delightful 139
Once again a night has vanished 48
One flock and a shepherd dear 119
ONE FOR ALL · · · · · · · · · · · · · · · · · · 44
One there is, to whom we're cleaving 61
One thing's needful 65
ON TO THE COMBAT 27
Onward! strive to reach the goal 92
OPEN WIDE THE GATES 4
OUR BLESSED PORTION 149
OUR CONVERSATION IS IN HEAVEN 198
Our great God, we praise Thee now 101
OUR HAPPY LOT 145
Our lot is found in pleasant places 145
Our love shall not diminish 137
OUR PILGRIM WAY 88
OUR SHEPHERD AND KING 230
Our song of praise to God ascend 7
OUR SURETY 224
OUR WISH IN PARTING 114
Out onto Calv'ry's hill 89

PARTING HYMN 155
PARTING HYMN 213

ALPHABETICAL INDEX

PASSIONATE LONGING 53
PETITION FOR THE LORD'S BLESSINGS 218
PRAISE AND CONSECRATION 141
PRAISE AND THANKS FOR GOD'S BLESSINGS . . 13
Praise the Lord with commendation 233
PRAISE TO GOD IN BAPTISM 71
Praise to Jesus, who has risen 60
PRAISE YE THE LORD 1
Praise ye the Lord, He is King over all 5
Praise ye the Lord! Praise ye the Lord 208
PRAYER FOR ACCESS TO GOD'S THRONE . . .215
PRAYER FOR THE TRUE CHRISTIAN LOVE . . 229
Pray, O church, be sanctified 174
Precious Jesus, Thou my portion 197
Prove ye, prove ye ev'ry spirit 127
PURE AND HOLY LOVE 72
Put on the armor of the Lord and Saviour 115

Quiet Lamb and prince of peace 240

RECEPTIVE HEARERS 144
REDEEMING OUR TIME 188
Rejoice, the Father loves us here 206
REPENTANCE 45
REPENT YE! 52
RESURRECTION AND SPIRITUAL LIFE 124
Rise, oh Christian generation 27
Rise, O soul, and break the bondage 183

SELF-SACRIFICE 159
Should I restrain the Spirit's course 113
Sing praise to God, all ye who love the Saviour . . 191
Sit and pause awhile, my spirit 226
SONG OF PRAISE 233
SONG OF PRAISE FOR REDEMPTION 130
SOWING AND HARVEST 36
Spirit, by whose operation 175
Spirit of true love and strength 140
Steep and thorny is the way 99

ALPHABETICAL INDEX

Streams that from Thy wounds are flowing 162
Strive aright when God in mercy 47
SUBMISSION 196
SUPPLICATION 122

TARRY NOT! 168
Tearful sowing brings glad harvest 36
THANKS AND PRAYER 199
THE ARMOR OF GOD 115
THE ASSURANCE OF TRUE FAITH · · · · · · 102
THE BAPTISMAL COVENANT 41
THE BEST REFUGE 46
THE BELIEVING FAMILY 160
THE BLESSEDNESS OF PRAYER 235
THE BOUNDLESSNESS OF GOD'S GRACE . . . 201
THE CALL FOR LABORERS · · · · · · · · 111
THE CHILDREN'S PRAYER 152
THE CHILDREN'S SUPPLICATION 216
THE CHILD'S PRIVILEGE · · · · · · · · · · 234
The Christian's robe and badge of love 252
THE CHRISTIAN'S CROSS · · · · · · · · · · 252
THE CITY OF GOD 133
THE CITY OF GOD 194
THE COMING OF CHRIST 56
THE COVENANT OF GRACE 163
THE CROSS 171
THE FAITHFUL SHEPHERD 15
THE FAITHFUL SHEPHERD JESUS CHRIST · · · 116
THE FAITH OF THE FATHERS 175
THE FATHER LOVES US 206
THE FELLOWSHIP OF THE SAINTS 33
THE FIELD AND THE FRUIT 108
THE FLAME OF JESUS' LOVE 73
THE FRUIT OF SORROW 245
THE FRUIT OF THE SPIRIT 62
The God who ruleth nations 234
THE GOSPEL 97
THE GOSPEL OF TRUTH 3
THE GRACE OF GOD 134

ALPHABETICAL INDEX

THE HEART --GOD'S SANCTUARY 129
THE HEAVENLY MIND 91
The heavens with God's praise resound 3
THE HIGH PRIEST 55
THE HOUR OF PRAYER 81
THE IMAGE OF CHRIST 164
THE INCARNATION OF CHRIST 22
THE INCOMPARABLE 19
THE INNER LIFE OF A CHRISTIAN 58
The innermost life of the true Christian shineth . . 58
THE JOURNEY TO ZION 185
The light and strength of faith, Lord, give me . . . 62
THE LIKENESS OF THE CREATION TO BAPTISM 40
The Lord again has given 138
The Lord, He is my Shepherd true 116
The Lord Himself did bear 44
THE LORD IS MY SHEPHERD 153
The Lord is my Shepherd 212
THE LORD IS YOUR REWARD 210
THE LORD IS MY LIGHT AND SALVATION . . . 110
THE LORD'S PRAYER 85
THE LORD'S SUPPER 25
The Lord will come, and He is near 56
THE LORD WILL PROVIDE 86
THE MAGNET 63
THE MEDIATOR 29
THE MAJESTY OF GOD 250
The mighty tree, the cross, is spreading 171
THE MINISTERS OF THE GOSPEL 113
THE MORNING STAR 223
THE NEW BIRTH FROM ABOVE 34
THE NEW BIRTH OF WATER AND SPIRIT 187
THE PENITENT'S CONFLICT 39
THE PENITENT'S CONFLICT 83
THE PILGRIM'S SONG 136
THE POWER OF PRAYER 174
THE PRAISE OF GOD 5
THE PROMISED REST 211
THE REAL LONGING FOR HOME 84

ALPHABETICAL INDEX

THE RESURRECTION FROM BAPTISM 8
THE RULER OF ZION 158
THE SCHOOL OF THE CROSS 66
THE SEVEN CHURCHES 30
THE SEVEN WORDS OF JESUS ON THE CROSS . 89
THE SERMON ON THE MOUNT 54
THE SHEPHERD AND HIS FLOCK 14
THE SHIP OF FAITH 94
THE SPIRITUAL CONFLICT 35
THE SUPREME SACRIFICE 100
The time flies on and death draws nigh 188
THE TIME OF WAITING 244
THE TWENTY THIRD PSALM 212
THE UNION IN JESUS' DEATH 11
THE UNION OF HEARTS 79
THE WATCHMEN'S CALL 112
THE WAY AND THE REWARD 106
THE WORD OF LIFE 176
Thee will I love, oh love eternal 227
Thine is the light 122
This is my grief and my distress 229
This is the test of true devotion 179
THOU HAST WORDS OF LIFE 203
Thou great high priest and teacher 215
Thou man of grief and pain 224
Though great dangers oft surround us 94
Though their foes may try them 96
Though troubles assail, and dangers affright 86
Thus united and in concord 237
Thy Word, O Lord, draws us together 63
Thy Word, O Lord, forever is 142
To me is given boundless mercy 220
TO MY REDEEMER 182
TO MY REDEEMER 227
To Thee, O Lord, be this day dedicated 193
To Thee, Saviour, we draw near 132
TO THOSE IN CONFLICT 21
Triumph, O thou city fair 133
TRUST IN GOD 93
Two ways, O Man, are there for thee 106

ALPHABETICAL INDEX

UNITY 237
UNITY IN LOVE 181
Up and strive, up and strive 21

Waiting is to be our earthly schooling 244
WALKING WITH GOD 68
We lay the body in the tomb 248
We'll now depart, ye faithful friends 143
We praise Thee, Lord, with pow'r to save 123
We tarry in this blest and tranquil union 114
We thank Thee, precious Saviour, dear 204
We welcome now the Hero 121
We, who in God's name are here assembled 11
We worship Thee with tears of gladness 25
What glorious state, to be a lamb of Jesus 16
When God did create the planets 40
When pure and upright hearts 79
Wherever, Lord, true love is waning 76
While fear hints, "There's something God will deny." . 87
Who are they before God standing 249
WHO ARE THEY BEFORE GOD'S THRONE? . . .249
Who is He that cares and watches 18
Who is Lord, like Thee sweet repose for me 19
WHO SHALL ABIDE? 32
WHY ART THOU GRIEVED? 151
Why grievest, my soul, must thou suffer great pain? 241
Why should sorrow ever grieve me 151
Why should ye all be weeping 155
Why wilt thou thus for the morrow 150
WILLINGLY ENDURE 156
With all our hearts, O Lord, we praise Thee 64
Within that wondrous pool 42
With your Zion's harps now chiming 214
Word of life, the fountain flowing 176
Word which God has spoken 97

YEARNING FOR HOME 147
Ye of my blessed pilgrimage 173
Ye, shepherds, who the Lord do love 210